Public Library Organization and Structure

Public Library Organization and Structure

by
T.D. Webb

McFarland & Company, Inc., Publishers
Jefferson, North Carolina, and London

British Library Cataloguing-in-Publication data available

Library of Congress Cataloguing-in-Publication Data

Webb, Terry.
   Public library organization and structure / by T.D. Webb.
     p. cm.
   Bibliography: p. 233.
   Includes index.
   ISBN 0-89950-395-0 (lib. bdg.; 50# acid-free natural paper) ⊚
   1. Public libraries — Administration. 2. Public libraries —
Aims and objectives. 3. Public librarians — Professional ethics.
4. Public librarians — Job descriptions. I. Title.
Z678.W4   1989
027.4 — dc19
                                        88-31484
                                         CIP

Manufactured in the United States of America.

McFarland & Company, Inc., Publishers
   Box 611, Jefferson, North Carolina 28640

Contents

Preface

This book is part of a continuing project to analyze the public library and its role in modern society. The primary source materials were collected as part of an earlier study on public library reorganization (T.D. Webb, *Reorganization in the Public Library,* Phoenix AZ: Oryx, 1985). Inasmuch as library organizations are constantly changing, the charts, job descriptions, and other documentation collected here are not intended necessarily to be current. Instead, they are like snapshots of libraries at particular moments along different paths of transformation and change, collected at about the same time from libraries across the country.

Nevertheless, the charts and other documents will show that despite the organizational changes of any one library and the differences in organizational arrangements across libraries in general, some characteristics remain the same. These are the "structures" of the public library. Here can be found the elemental components of the public library and the logic of public librarianship. These structures also contain the social meanings of the public library as an institution, which are manifest in the expectations held for it by its users and its staff.

Not all the materials collected during research for this book are included. Space limitations required selectivity, especially among job descriptions. It is hoped that the selections made will portray the typical features of the public library while providing also a sample of the varieties of forms these features may assume in the practice of public librarianship.

The goal of this book is to clarify the structures of the public library in order to better understand its place in our society. Portions of the text have appeared in different formats in "Reference Service as a Guide in Public Library Organization" in *Reference Service Review* (Fall 1987) and "Diversity and Divergence in Public Library Reorganization: Implications for the Profession" in *Library Administration & Management* (March 1987).

Introduction: Modern Society and the Formal Organization

So integral is the formal organization to the modern era that ours has been deemed "the organizational society,"[1] and we have cornered an entirely new creature who inhabits it — the Organization Man.[2] Although earlier societies certainly utilized formal organizations, in some instances on a massive scale, the quantitative difference between the numbers of organizations present in our society as compared with any other is so immense as to constitute a qualitative difference. Sociologists inform us that organizations may reinforce certain types of attitudes and values, and appear to contribute to the formation of an identifiable set of personality traits among those who work in them. In a monumental study of attitudinal changes in individuals of six modernizing nations, Inkeles and Smith found that participation in formal organizations figures prominently in the development of a syndrome of individual modernity.[3] Organizations, they argue, are like schools of modernity in which individuals learn to be rational and pragmatic through processes of modeling, reward and punishment, generalization, and exemplification. Emerging from this sequence are individuals whom Inkeles and Smith describe as "instrumental activists" who are knowledgeable, innovative, rational, and highly practical. Thus, according to Inkeles and Smith, instrumental activists may be an unwitting by-product of formal organizations.

The Formal Organization: Definitions

According to Wright, "An organization is a contrived open system of coordinated activities by two or more participants to achieve a com-

1

mon goal or goals."[4] He further delineates the goal-oriented aspect of organization by saying, "A formal organization arises when a task, because of its size or complexity, requries the efforts of more than one person."[5] Also, he says an organization "is formed to accommodate intense interaction, of extended duration, requiring higher degrees of structure, through which joint responsibilities for goal attainment can be exercised."[6]

Etzioni's definition of the organization is quite complex:

> Organizations are social units (or human groupings) deliberately constructed and reconstructed to seek specific goals. . . . Organizations are characterized by: (1) divisions of labor, power, and communication responsibilities, divisions which are not random or traditionally patterned, but deliberately planned to enhance the realization of specific goals; (2) the presence of one or more power centers which control the concerted efforts of the organization and direct them toward its goals; these power centers also must review continuously the organization's performance and repattern its structure, where necessary, to increase its efficiency; (3) substitution of personnel, i.e., unsatisfactory persons can be removed and others assigned to their tasks. The organization can also recombine its personnel through transfer and promotion.[7]

Hall is briefer:

> An organization is a collectivity with relatively identifiable boundary, a normative order, authority ranks, communications systems, and membership coordinating systems; this collectivity exists on a relatively continuous basis in an environment and engages in activities that are usually related to a goal or a set of goals.[8]

In what Galbraith calls "the most famous definition of an organization,"[9] Chester Barnard says it is "a system of consciously coordinated activities or forces of two or more persons."[10] Later Barnard expands on this definition:

> An organization is a system of cooperative human activities the functions of which are (1) the creation, (2) the transformation, and (3) the exchange of utilities. It is able to accomplish these functions by creating a cooperative system, of which the organization is both a nucleus and a subsidiary system, which has also as components physical systems, personal systems (individuals and collections of individuals), and social systems (other organizations).[11]

To Galbraith, the most important aspect of the organization is coordination, or cooperation:

> It means that the participating individuals are persuaded to set aside their individual purposes or goals and pursue those of the organization. All having done so, all work to the common goals. They are coordinated. Motivation is the means or inducements by which individuals are led to abandon their own goals and, with greater or lesser vigor, to pursue those of the organization.[12]

All of the definitions given above imply a fundamental concern: To what extent do individuals actually "abandon their own goals to pursue those of the organization"?

The study of the relationship between the activities performed in an organization and the individuals who perform them has given rise to the many divergent schools of organization and management theory. Emphasis on the activities and goals of the organization, as opposed to its persons, has been the primary concern of the so-called scientific or classical school of organization theory. This school of thought holds that the formal organization is the most rational, logical, and efficient form of social grouping because it is directed by rational goals devoid of extraneous or conflicting objectives. It follows that workers, being themselves rational, as well as materialistic, can be induced to labor toward those goals through a system of rewards based on their constructive output. The workers do not entirely abandon their personal goals, which are supposedly materialistic, but instead the organization, while attaining its goals, can satisfy the materialistic needs of its members.

Conversely, emphasis on the persons or personal systems within the organization introduces the fact that organizations are more than formal goals, departmental configurations, and rational activities. Workers may not always labor diligently toward the goals of the organization simply because those goals are rational or because the organization offers its members material rewards. There are other, more personal variables to be considered in the case of each worker. This does not necessarily mean that workers are subject to fits of irrationality or emotional instability, although at times this may well be the case. It means instead that rationality pulls in many directions at once. Workers have their own goals, needs, and agendas that perhaps cannot be satisfied by rational organizational goals or even material gain.

The human relations school of organization and management

theory began as a reaction to the stark rationalism and the rigid self-assurance of the classical approach. This school of thought has been primarily concerned with the interpersonal relations, the private goals, and the other personal systems of an organization's employees. These aspects of the "informal organization," it was argued, were just as important to the efficiency of the formal organization as its stated goals. In fact, according to the human relations school, if these personal systems were inadequately addressed by management, the organization would fall short of maximum efficiency.

The human relations approach has proven to be not so much a contradiction of the classical approach as a refinement in its perception of the intricate relationships between individuals and the organization to which they belong. Workers are not, after all, motivated solely by materialistic aims or rational organizational goals. Other variables can become incentives or hindrances to worker performance. These variables may include esteem, peer pressure, and even membership in an alternate organization such as a profession or professional association, as is the case with librarians. Both schools of thought — the classical and the human relations — share the idea that worker needs and organizational goals can be made compatible, and that rationality is the guarantor of that compatibility. But by focusing on the individuals within the organization, the human relations school uncovered many levels of rationality and worker needs in addition to the materialistic, and gave organizational theory a more complete view of the complexity of human organization.

More recent schools of thought and other refinements to organizational theory have given us an even wider view of the problem of the individual within the organization. These refinements include conflict theory, structuralism, and comparative analysis. But these subsequent developments themselves stem from the people-program dichotomy. These two aspects are like the two axes of a mathematical grid on which we could plot the types of relationships that can exist between the organization and its workers for any given establishment.

Rationalism

Each of the definitions given above speaks to the deliberateness with which the formal organization is created. According to Etzioni, "tribes, classes, ethnic groups, friendship groups, and families are excluded" from consideration as formal organizations because the extent to which these other social units are consciously planned, deliberately structured and restructured, with a membership which is routinely changed, is much less than in the case of those social units we are calling organizations. Hence organizations are much more in control of their nature and destiny than any other social grouping.[13]

Rationalism has become the singular method of our entire society, and the prevalence of the formal organization is only an aspect of our larger reliance on reason. Again Etzioni:

Modern society has placed a high moral value on rationality, effectiveness, and efficiency. Modern civilization depends largely on organizations as the most rational and efficient form of social grouping known.[14]

This has caused a great deal of concern in some contemporary thinkers. Ellul, for instance, disparages "the totality of methods rationally arrived at and having absolute efficiency . . . in every field of human endeavor."[15] The blend of rationality, efficiency, and method of which modern industrialization, mechanization, and organization are the major embodiments, Ellul fears, will finally dehumanize man through a pathological concern for technique instead of product, efficiency instead of values. The concern solely with rationalism threatens the brand of spontaneous behavior that has characterized human freedom, according to Ellul.

Whyte likewise warns that

in our attention to making organization work, we have come close to deifying it. We are describing its defects as virtues and denying that there is—or should be—a conflict between the individual and organization. This denial is bad for the organization. It is worse for the individual. What it does, in soothing him, is rob him of the intellectual armor he so badly needs. For the more power organization has over him, the more he needs to recognize the area where he must exert himself against it.[16]

Speaking of modern anxiety, Barzun observes,

What we discover as the cause of our pain when we examine the burden of modernity is the imposition of one intellectual purpose upon all experience. To analyze, abstract, and objectify is the carrying out of a single, imperialistic mode of thought.[17]

He argues that the machine-like logic of rationalism "must somehow be hushed, tamed, fenced off from the person at certain times and places."[18]

Sociology has risen above the alarmist views of Ellul, Whyte, Barzun, and others. Nevertheless, beneath their alarm lies a mutual recognition of the spread of rationalism, a mentality that can be as intellectually constraining as medieval scholasticism. Since the Romantic reaction against industrialization, many have seen the rise of rationalism as a serious threat to humanity.

The global spread of rationalism and its harbinger, the formal organization, is beyond the scope of the present discussion. Indeed, this introduction has ranged quite far in an attempt to suggest the vastness of the subject of the formal organization in modern society.

The formal organization, be it that of a library, an army, a church, or a factory, is more than a rational enterprise, or a mere means of attaining goals beyond the reach of sole individuals, or a vehicle to produce certain goods. It is a social school, an inculcator of attitudes and dispositions. And it is an arena to which individuals bring their predispositions and concerns, which influence their performance within the organization. The formal organization is the summation of modern philosophical and social conflicts and a symbol system that communicates values to its participants. In this, the formal organization serves a role in our era analogous to that of the Gothic cathedral in the Middle Ages.

Underlying the vast subject, however, are two fundamantal concepts that will be considered in the following chapters: (1) the formal organization is inherently rationalistic in its methods of dividing labor, and (2) a potential conflict exists between the goals of the organization and the individuals in that organization who are charged with pursuing those goals.

With this disclaimer, then, this book does not pretend to treat the subject of organization theory, or even the narrower area of library organization, to the fullest desirable degree. It will not attempt to resolve the problem of individual satisfaction within the collective organization. Rather, the book will demonstrate how the rationale of the public library organization and the search for personal satisfactions among its staff establish a pair of structures that together help explain the purpose and meaning of the public library in modern society.

A second purpose of the book is to provide a collection of documents to assist library managers who wish to investigate alternative organizational arrangements for their libraries. Organizational refinement and even complete reorganization is one method of adapting to lower operating budgets, decreasing staffs, networking, automation, and other influences for change in the public library.[19] Yet published examples of actual library organizational charts and job descriptions are virtually nonexistent. The empirical approach of the present study has resulted in the collection of documents which, though used here primarily for analysis, may themselves be a valuable resource for library administrators.

I
The Public Library
as a Formal Organization

If, at any time, we find that our current organizational structure does not provide the service delivery we want our citizens to receive and which they have indicated they want, we do not hesitate to modify the structure. After all, the structure is only a hatrack for service to citizens. — Lillian M. Bradshaw, former Director of Libraries, Dallas Public Library (from a letter to the author, 5 August 1982).

Bradshaw's statement may well be the most concise and provocative definition of public library organization ever conceived. Her "hatrack" approach to librarianship emphasizes the flexibility of the public library organization and the diversity of services that a library is able to provide.

This has become a popular position among library administrators who are experimenting with new services, new media, and new information storage technologies. One reason for exploiting the flexibility of the public library is to broaden its political base. According to Getz, public library users are typically from the middle and upper classes with higher-than-average income and education levels.[1] This somewhat narrow patronage, says Getz, tends to isolate the library from other agencies within the larger local government structure. It lessens the library's chances for political success as well as its bargaining power in the local government structure. Getz demonstrates his point by citing the arbitrariness with which local government budget makers often cut library funds, exhibiting virtually no regard to actual library effectiveness or usage patterns.

The whole notion of outreach in all its varieties is an example of the flexibility, with potential politically advantageous results, of the public library. Every library actually serves several "publics," each with its characteristic problems and needs. According to Drucker:

8

Every service institution, and libraries are probably very typical, has a fair number of publics. Each of these publics not only makes different demands on it, but each looks at the institution and sees something entirely different. As a matter of fact, the one thing that can be said with absolute certainty about service institutions is that their publics do not have the same image of them as do the people who toil within them.[2]

The library can target its services toward one or another of these publics, broadening its influence in the community. Because the public library is an acquirer of knowledge, its collected subjects are like veins that can be mined and refined into major public service projects and special programs. Each such program demonstrates the flexibility of the public library to which Bradshaw refers.

As with most analogies, however, the simplicity of Bradshaw's comment belies the complexity of the issues it brings to mind, and suggests contradictions because it does not conform to the reality of library organization. The converse of public library flexibility is an issue that is notably absent in Bradshaw's remarks. The public library, after all, has a number of historically proven characteristics and services that make it recognizable as an institution to its users and contribute to its continued existence.

Martin has argued that traditional services such as reference, collection development, and referral are like a safety zone from which libraries can maintain their place even in a changing society by continued emphasis on those areas that libraries have demonstrated they can deliver efficiently and effectively. He advises

a return to and concentration upon some of the traditional services that the library has shown it can deliver – activities that have not disappeared but have faded, as the library took on more and more in a misguided effort to be everything to everybody. A thinning of performance has occurred all along the line under the banner of "giving the people what they want."[3]

Furthermore, a library is an articulation of the professional philosophy and ethics of librarianship, a philosophy built on a commitment to service and free information for all people. Arguing that this philosophy pervades the provision of library services, Buckland states the following:

Libraries have no monopoly on assisting in these matters, but, because they are in the business of providing access to recorded knowledge and because they ordinarily do so at no financial charge, libraries do have an opportunity to play a distinctive role in the distribution of benefits in society. How effective this role is and in which direction the distribution is going will depend in large part on the location, nature, and extent of the service being provided — in other words, on the allocation of resources.[4]

Thus each library articulates the philosophy of librarianship differently, and that articulation changes somewhat over time based on the needs of the users, the condition of the institution's resources, and the talents and personalities involved. Nevertheless, change in libraries has been within the limits of that professional philosophy. If it were otherwise, the institution would cease to be a library.

Accompanying this philosophy is the simple assumption that persons trained as librarians can best be relied on to provide library service. At present, we find this assumption being implicitly challenged in many libraries by the introduction of more nonlibrarians and even nonprofessionals into crucial decision-making levels of the library, and by a reliance on the tastes of the public as the sole guide for the design and delivery of library services. Perhaps more than any other feature, this equivocation in the role of the librarian indicates the amount of stress being placed on libraries and prefigures the degree of change which may soon alter the course of librarianship.

The question becomes, then, how does the work of librarianship influence the organizational hierarchy of the library? This chapter will discuss the main principles by which public libraries are organized, and illustrate them with organizational charts from public libraries around the country. This will help establish the nature of public library organization empirically, using an inductive approach. The degree to which library organization is and is not a "hatrack" should become evident through an examination of the relative flexibility and inflexibility portrayed in the charts.

Chapter 2 will then discuss the actual work of librarianship, and Chapter 3 will attempt to correlate the prevailing organizational arrangement of the public library with the practice of librarianship in an effort to describe the social function of the public library.

Libraries and Management Theory

The development of library organization has been influenced by a succession of management philosophies during the last fifty years. Like other enterprises during this period, libraries became efficiency-conscious, and began the serious practice of management. Libraries that formerly were concerned mainly with collection management and relatively little with overall organization theories became caught up in the scientific management approach to organization during the 1930s and 1940s, which was the period that saw the emergence of very large governmental and industrial organizations.[5]

The major influences of scientific management on librarianship were (1) the introduction of standards by which to evaluate library collections, operations, and performance; (2) strict definition and codification of work within departments and differentiation of professional and clerical tasks; and (3) separation of organizational planning from operational functions.[6]

The human relations approach to management and its attendant study of informal processes within an organization, which began in part as a reaction against scientific management theories, had significant impact on librarians. This impact was partly due to the fact that professionals, be they librarians, physicians, attorneys, or otherwise, resist organizational formalities that may conflict with professional values or training. Experts such as these expect to participate in the management of their organizations. One result of the human relations thought in libraries was an increased allowance for greater participation by non-administrative librarians in the decision-making and planning processes of the library.[7]

A later school of organizational thought, the systems approach, is currently having an impact on library organization and management. This approach studies the kinds of systemic relationships that must be addressed if the formal organization is to operate effectively. These relationships include the internal systems of the organization as well as the position of the organization in its social environment.[8] The ALA's replacement of library standards with a planning document, the introduction of community analyses into the planning process, and the emphasis on establishing goals and objectives that are specific to the institution reflect the influence of the systems approach on library management and organization.

Departmentation

Organizational division of labor, or departmentation, is not as arbitrary as it sometimes seems. In the first place, organizational arrangement is related to management philosophies, such as those just mentioned, in the way departments are established within the organization and labor divided among them. For instance, a manager devoted to the scientific approach to management would probably restrict decision-making to the administrative departments, while one who adopts the systems approach would likely be more inclined to participative management. Also, it is assumed that an optimum efficiency can be achieved by establishing a balance between the method selected by which to divide and supervise labor and the consequent levels of skill of the organization's members. Reorganization and redepartmentation in search of greater efficiency have become common in public libraries recently.[9] Furthermore, some enterprises require specific types of distinguishing departments that are not present in other organizations and which define the nature of the organizations in which they appear. This is very much the case with libraries, as will be seen below.

Stueart and Eastlick identify five primary methods of departmentalizing libraries.[10] Three of them are borrowed from industry: function, territory, and customer. The other two are more or less peculiar to libraries: subject and form of resource. When these several methods of departmentation are compared with those described by Metcalf in 1939,[11] it is apparent that organizational arrangements of libraries have remained largely unchanged for at least the last fifty years, the same period which has seen the greatest growth in the size and number of large libraries requiring complex organization.

Of course, the nature and functioning of the departments organized according to these methods and the relationships between departments within the library have changed considerably in this time. For example, the automation department and the pervasiveness of its influence on existing departments are new to public libraries. Yet automation is not unlike other functional departments that have been common in libraries for some time. Similarly, modern outreach services, however specialized the group targeted for these services may be, are actually a clientele departmentation.

Other departmental types, such as audio-visual services, public relations, regionalization, and microcomputing services, are only contemporary versions of the departmentation methods that have become standard for the public library. Thus the stability of these departmentations reveals a great deal about the underlying structure of the public library as a social institution, as later discussion will show.

Functional Departmentation

This method of departmentation involves division of labor according to the different functions performed in the organization. Charts A–F (pp. 25–44) were chosen to illustrate departmentation by function in six large public libraries. They indicate that upper levels of the public library, as is the case with most organizations, tend to be organized according to function, as in Library A. Here the primary departmentations below the director are datamation, buildings and grounds, public services, finance, personnel, and information services. Lower levels are organized in some cases according to territory (branches), format (audio-visual), and clientele (visually handicapped).

The primary departmentation in the present organizational structure of Library B, although generally organized by function, also uses format (audio-visual) and clientele (young people's). The proposed organization of Library B, however, shifts these alternate departmentation methods to lower levels of the organization and reserves the primary level for functional departmentation.

Library C handles primary departmentation much as do the previous examples, but Library D employs a two-part functional division of labor between public and non-public services. The 1982 chart for Library D shows some organizational change at a lower level of departmentation, but the major two-part primary division remains.

Library E is comparable to D in its division of functions between the assistant and the associate director, although the departments are not named as public and nonpublic, respectively, and although one of the two major divisions reports to the head of the other major department.

The charts from Library F are especially informative because they include not only the organization arrangement, but also the staffing patterns for each department along with a brief narrative description of the function each department performs. A few organizational changes appear between the 1979 and the 1981 charts, such as the realignment of the children's services and public information departments to a secondary level and the addition of the automation department to the primary level. Yet for the most part the organization has not changed greatly between the two sets of charts. The functions have not changed, and the departments that perform them remain basically the same.

Two functional departmentations are present in each of the libraries represented so far, and appear in one form or another in all libraries, public or otherwise. These functions are cataloging and circulation. They are so elemental to library organization that their significance as distinguishing features of librarianship and library organization go unnoticed. Together, these two functions illuminate major purposes of the library and the expectations its users have for it. Consequently, the cataloging and circulation functions relate to the social meanings of the public library as it is perceived by its users and by librarians.

The charts for Library F describe the function of its catalog section: "Catalog, classify, and prepare materials for use; maintain shelf lists; maintain card catalogs." The simplicity of this statement does not minimize its implication of all-inclusiveness. That is, the processes of cataloging and classification, because of their expansive codification and descriptiveness, imply that the library has provision to hold all knowledge, even that which may not yet have been discovered, and that knowledge is retrievable once it is consigned to its proper relative position in the collection. This is an enormously imposing presupposition that cannot fail to have an impact on users of the library.

The function of the circulation department, according to Library F, is to "Maintain registration, circulation, and delinquent records; circulate books and other materials at Central Library." A circulating collection distinguishes a library from all other institutions. Unlike the commodities of a business enterprise, which flow unidirectionally from supplier to consumer, a library's books are part of a circulating inventory that cycles continually between the library and its users and back again. Each item in the collection, therefore, must be meticulously described, identified, and labeled by the library in a manner seldom necessary in the business world. Each book in the collection is then placed in a designated position relative to every other book in the collection both on the shelf and in the library's operational files so that it may be more easily retrieved by either party—library or patron—from the temporary possession of the other.

A circulating inventory is perhaps the most distinguishing feature of the public library as an enterprise. It is a feature stipulated, in unspoken terms perhaps, but mandated nonetheless, by the philosophy of librarianship, and has come to be expected by the public. As such it represents an assumed meaning of the public library as a social institution. The public library is perceived as a provider of free information, information that potentially is unlimited and retrievable. Because of their importance in understanding the nature of the public library, the functions of cataloging and circulation will be discussed more fully in Chapter 3.

Departmentation by Territory

Geographical departmentation usually occurs when an organization wishes to extend its services by establishing facilities to provide them at some distance from the main service site while retaining control of these facilities. Territorial departmentation, while distributing the organization's services more widely, also involves a certain degree of replication of resources. This is difficult among organizations, like libraries, which are suffering from dwindling resources. Services at the extension sites are usually limited. Regional centers are occasionally established to supplement the extension services somewhat, but they still do not provide the full range of services available at the main service facility.

Curtailment of services at extension facilities and regionalization to minimize costly duplication of resources are strategies that library systems often use in geographical departmentation in order to control costs. Along with changes in subject department rearrangements, geographical redepartmentations are the strategies that offer the most immediate results in full library reorganization projects.[12]

Libraries G–J (pp. 45–52) illustrate some examples of geographical departmentation. Libraries G and H use the common organizational division between a central library facility and extension, or branch, facilities. Library H uses a regionalization scheme for further departmentalizing its branches according to territory, while Library G does not. Library I is different in that there is no central facility. The entire library system consists of branches organized by regions. Library J again uses the standard departmentation between a central facility and the branches, but the branches are then organized not so much by region as by type of facility — regional, branch, or neighborhood libraries.

Departmentation by Clientele

Like Library F, Library K (pp. 53–56) has a descriptive narration and staffing pattern to accompany each department shown on its organization chart. The charts for Library K include three departments organized according to clientele — children's, shut-ins and retirees, and the municipal reference library. The description for children's service includes advising on and selecting material for children. This department is clearly organized according to its service group. The service to shut-ins and retirees includes providing small institutional collections at community agencies and hospitals, and the municipal reference library serves local government officials. Although these last two services are performed in designated facilities, they are still specialized services whose purpose is to serve a well-defined clientele.

Subject Departmentation

Libraries L–N (pp. 57–62), along with most of the others mentioned so far, use subject departmentation. Not only is this form of division of labor unique to libraries, it is virtually universal among them. According to Stueart and Eastlick, "Large public libraries and academic libraries use this method extensively today. It provides more in-depth service and reader guidance, and it requries a high degree of subject knowledge on the part of the staff."[13] Furthermore, as the examples show, the subjects involved are rather uniform, although the manner of grouping the subjects into larger departments varies widely.

In its most proper form, subject departmentation includes employment of subject specialists to develop the subject collections and provide subject reference service. Wilkinson sees a conflict between the bureaucratic momentum of the library as a formal organization and the ability of the librarian subject specialist as a professional to provide information services based on "individual subject-specialization and a freedom to make judgments based upon that specialization."[14] He argues convincingly that librarians

> must choose between either offering services based upon independent, accountable judgments that arise from individual expertise and a body of specialized, expanding knowledge, or offering ingress to institutionally generated and controlled collections.[15]

This issue is especially pertinent in light of the increasing popularity of generalism, which is the converse of any type of subject or even age-level specialization by librarians. The goal of generalism is to concentrate on that portion of a library's services addressing a group that is often the most active users of the public library — the avid readers.[16] The question becomes, is that inflation of services to readers at the expense of other user types? The popular reader requires a different sort of staff and collection from a user whose goal is self-education, reference, or research. According to Wilkinson's reasoning, generalism may be damaging to the librarian's professionalism.

The subject of professionalism and its role in the library organization, the conflict between the library as a formal organization and the librarian as an individual professional, and the resolution of this conflict in the set of social functions and symbols the public library has come to embody will be discussed at greater length in the following chapters.

Departmentation by Form of Resource

Perhaps the most common format departmentation involves audio-visual materials and microforms, although rare book rooms and the like could also be considered a similar type of departmentation. Several such departments organized by form of resource appear in the library charts mentioned above.

The communication department of Library O (pp. 63–64) includes a printing division, which is not uncommon among large libraries, and also a video studio, which is rather uncommon. Both instances are additional examples of departmentation by resource format. Departmentation by form of resource has often been linked to the development of nonprint information technologies. The rapid appearance of so many new technologies of this sort may result in a greater incidence of departmentation by form of resource.

"Mixing"

The distinction between the different types of departmentation are not always strictly observed within any single library or even within any single department. According to Stueart and Eastlick,

> Only in the most specialized library would a single one of these organizational methods be used; a library usually uses several of the methods. A large public library generally has a circulation department (function), subject departments (combining several functions), branch libraries (territory), children's services (clientele) ... documents collection (form), etc.[17]

The practice of "mixing" departmentation methods is common in most formal organizations. Etzioni observes:

> In reality, organizations are made up of a combination of various layers that differ in their degree of specialization. The tendency is often for the lower layers to be organized according to area and/or clientele principles, and the higher ones by purpose and/or process. But even this statement should be viewed only as a probability statement which says that effective organizations are likely to be this way, rather than saying that they always or even usually are ... [and] in actuality organizations often combine work units whose organizational principles are only partially compatible. We will see that it is not only possible to find contradictory principles operating simultaneously in the same organization, but that such "mix" provides the most effective organization.[18]

Libraries mix departmentation methods as commonly as any other type of enterprise. Libraries P and Q (pp. 65–70), for instance, provide examples of mixing in their central library facilities. Library P mixes subject departments (e.g. art and music) with a clientele department (children's), functional units (e.g. shelving, lending), and format departments (rare books, films). At its central facility, Library Q also mixes clientele (children's), subjects (e.g. history, social sciences), format (audio-visual), and function (e.g. circulation). Generally speaking, mixing of departmentation methods is more common at the higher levels of an organization, as illustrated by Library R (pp. 71–72). In this library, due to the nature of its primary departmentation, the next organizational level mixes extensively, especially in the public services department.

Organizational Change

As demonstrated by several of the examples already given, organizational change in libraries is a frequent occurrence, especially in this period of shrinking budgets. Libraries S–V (pp. 73–89) provide further examples. In the case of Libraries S and T, the organizational changes cover a substantial period of time.

In Library S we see the transformation of a library with an unwieldy span of control for the assistant director and a few branches in 1957 into a functionally departmentalized institution with four times as many branches in 1984. The charts show the appearance in 1968 of a branch chief and a central chief, and their disappearance in 1979 and 1981, respectively. In 1968, operations were divided functionally between associate directors of public and technical services. The branches move from direct access to the assistant director in 1957, to the branch chief, and then to the associate director in 1979. Regionalization comes in 1977, but is gone by 1979. And all the while, the number of branches increases.

The major change in the organization of Library T is the formation of a technical services department functionally separate from its formerly geographical assignment to the central library department, and the appearance and disappearance of an assistant chief of community libraries. Likewise, the 1982 chart from Library U shows the removal of the neighborhood libraries administrator position, and increased regionalization among the branches. Library V, in contrast, shows more stability. Changes in this library are limited to the creation of the government documents and directory services and the transfer of responsibility of the stacks function in central services, and the creation of the automation department in technical services.

Here the hatrack flexibility of the public library becomes apparent. Yet these charts also demonstrate that beneath the flexibility lies a set of functions that remain constant and that are crucial to providing services users have come to expect; these functions form the basis of the librarian's professional philosophy.

Conclusions

As the organizational charts show, the public library is a formal organization, fashioned in the pyramid hierarchical style, rationally organized according to a complex division of labor. Its organizational arrangement includes a number of departmentations that are intended to enable the classification and circulation of recorded knowledge, in keeping with the philosophy of professional librarianship. The rationalism of the library as a formal organization is implied in its methods of dividing labor and also in its resources. Knowledge is recorded according to logical principles that will allow its ready retrieval. The subject departmentation of the library in itself is a patterned categorization designed to facilitate logical retrieval of knowledge. Thus on two levels, the operational-organizational and the ideational, the library embodies rationalism for its users as well as its employees.

The organizational charts here presented demonstrate the uniformities that lie under the diversity of public library organizational arrangements and the assortment of services the public library offers. Reviewing methods of departmentation, we find that public libraries consistently use several methods of dividing labor that are unique to the library as an institution. These departments—circulation, cataloging and classification, and subject departmentation—exist as a result of the expectations held for the library by both the public and the professional staff: namely, as a repository of free, unlimited, organized information.

Thus the library organization itself communicates these expectations. As such, the library becomes a system of symbols communicating messages about knowledge, its availability, its internal relations and rationality, and its applicability to reality. Classification and cataloging imply that there is a predetermined place in the library for all knowledge, even that yet to be discovered. Subject departmentation breaks that knowledge into categories that approximate and, therefore, reinforce the users' perceptions of the world around them. The circulation function represents the ready availability of the knowledge through the library.

In effect, library functions and the organizational arrangement associated with them may be read almost like words on a page. Because a library's services have become more or less standardized over the years, and because the library fills a recognized need as the public's information provider, users and nonusers alike intuitively see the library as a symbol of learning, regardless of their individual attitudes toward learning. In fact, nonusers, because they do not experience the occasional but inevitable failure of the library to provide information they might wish to have, probably feel its symbolism more keenly than regular library users.

Formal organizations, however, have an operational aspect that may be quite apart from the symbolic. Through its operational functions, an organization seeks to perpetuate itself. The operational may even interfere with the symbolic. This operational conflict is the momentum that Wilkinson speaks of in terms of institutionally generated control, and that he says may conflict with any professional philosophies that may also be present in the organization. Buckland states that

> anyone interested in library services whether as a provider or as a user would be well advised to examine what sort of philosophy is implied by the actual allocation of resources and how coherently and consistently the prevailing philosophy is effected in practice. In other words, what are the actual goals of the organization.[19]

There is a definite relation between the library's organizational arrangement or, in Buckland's terms, the allocation of resources, and the professional philosophy the library seeks to serve. Chapter 2 will explore the professional philosophy of librarianship and its relationship to the library's organization.

Organizational Charts

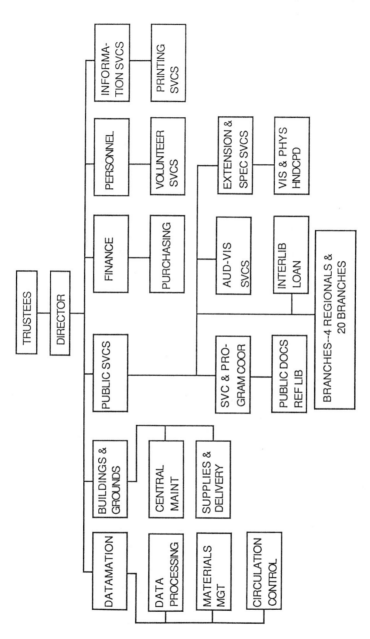

Library A.

26

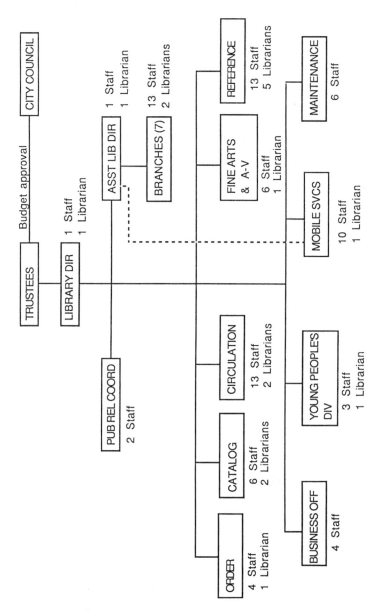

Library B, present.

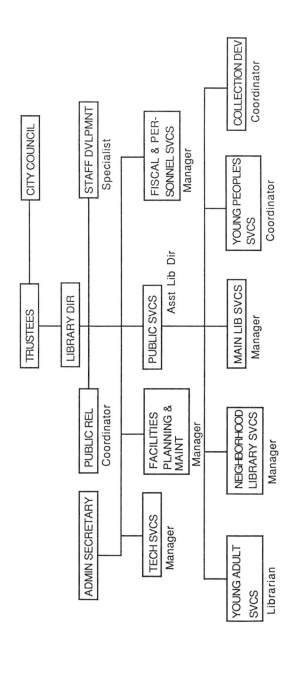

Library B, proposed.

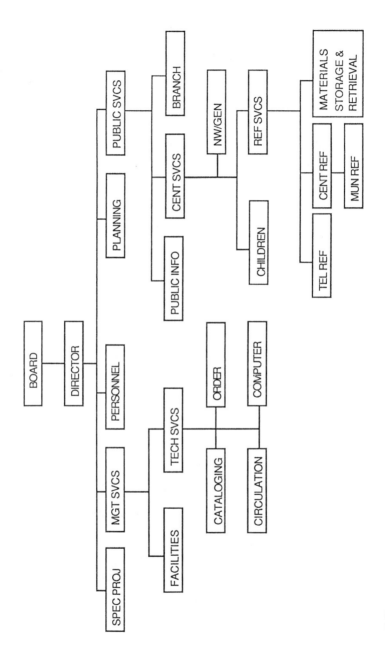

Library C.

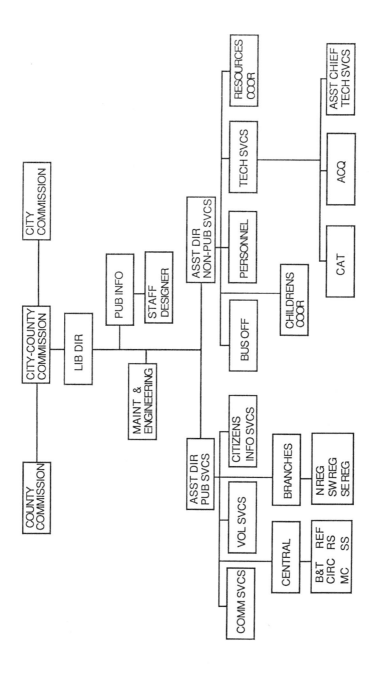

Library D, 1979.

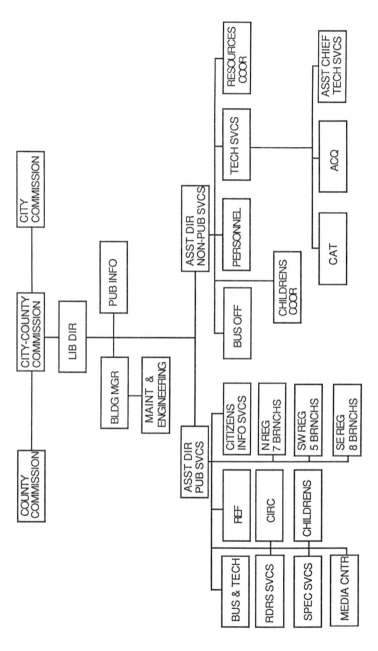

Library D, 1982.

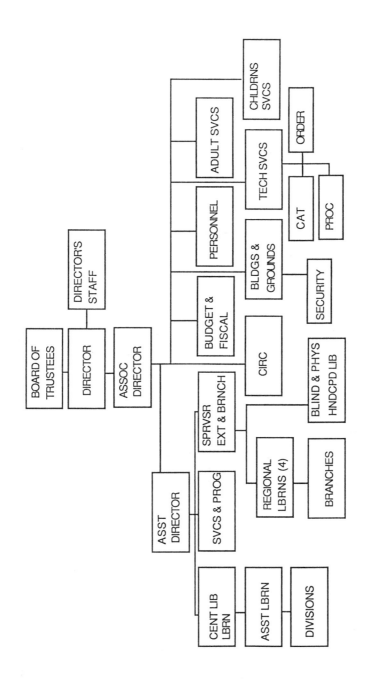

Library E.

32

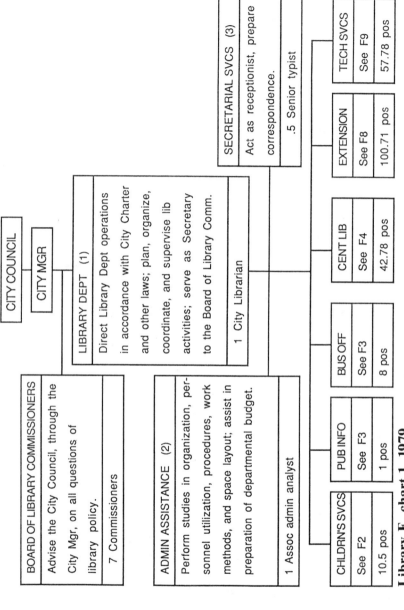

Library F, chart 1, 1979.

CITY COUNCIL

CITY MGR

BOARD OF LIBRARY COMMISSIONERS

Advise the City Council, through the City Mgr, on all questions of library policy.

7 Commissioners

LIBRARY DEPT (1)

Direct Library Dept operations in accordance with City Charter and other laws; plan, organize, coordinate, and supervise lib activities; serve as Secretary to the Board of Library Comm.

1 City Librarian

ADMIN ASSISTANCE (2)

Perform studies in organization, personnel utilization, procedures, work methods, and space layout; assist in preparation of departmental budget.

1 Assoc admin analyst

SECRETARIAL SVCS (3)

Act as receptionist, prepare correspondence.

.5 Senior typist

CHLDRN'S SVCS	PUB INFO	BUS OFF	CENT LIB	EXTENSION	TECH SVCS
See F2	See F3	See F3	See F4	See F8	See F9
10.5 pos	1 pos	8 pos	42.78 pos	100.71 pos	57.78 pos

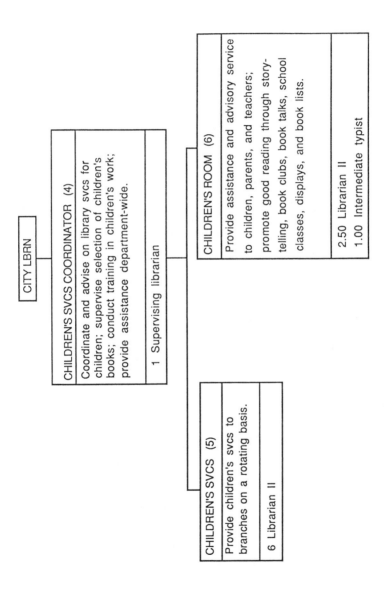

CITY LBRN

CHILDREN'S SVCS COORDINATOR (4)

Coordinate and advise on library svcs for children; supervise selection of children's books; conduct training in children's work; provide assistance department-wide.

1 Supervising librarian

CHILDREN'S SVCS (5)

Provide children's svcs to branches on a rotating basis.

6 Librarian II

CHILDREN'S ROOM (6)

Provide assistance and advisory service to children, parents, and teachers; promote good reading through story-telling, book clubs, book talks, school classes, displays, and book lists.

2.50 Librarian II
1.00 Intermediate typist

Library F, chart 2, 1979.

34

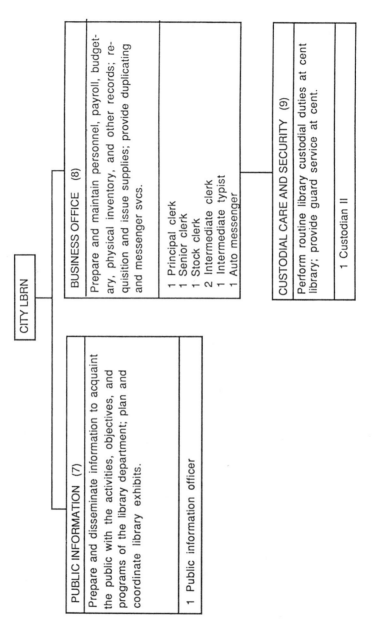

PUBLIC INFORMATION (7)

Prepare and disseminate information to acquaint the public with the activities, objectives, and programs of the library department; plan and coordinate library exhibits.

1 Public information officer

CITY LBRN

BUSINESS OFFICE (8)

Prepare and maintain personnel, payroll, budgetary, physical inventory, and other records; requisition and issue supplies; provide duplicating and messenger svcs.

1 Principal clerk
1 Senior clerk
1 Stock clerk
2 Intermediate clerk
1 Intermediate typist
1 Auto messenger

CUSTODIAL CARE AND SECURITY (9)

Perform routine library custodial duties at cent library; provide guard service at cent.

1 Custodian II

Library F, chart 3, 1979.

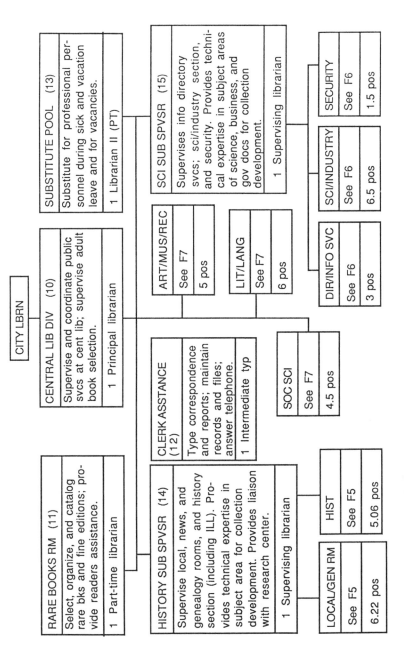

Library F, chart 4, 1979.

36

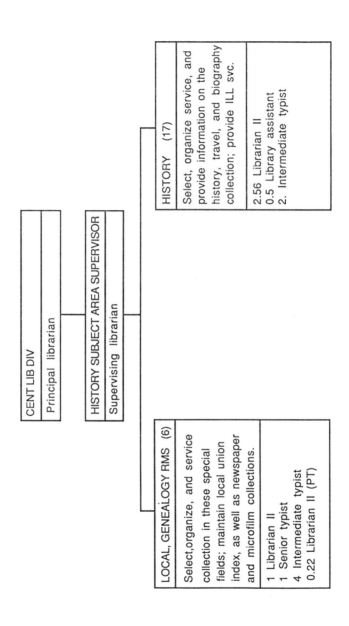

Library F, chart 5, 1979.

CENT LIB DIV
Principal librarian

HISTORY SUBJECT AREA SUPERVISOR
Supervising librarian

LOCAL, GENEALOGY RMS (6)

Select,organize, and service collection in these special fields; maintain local union index, as well as newspaper and microfilm collections.

1 Librarian II
1 Senior typist
4 Intermediate typist
0.22 Librarian II (PT)

HISTORY (17)

Select, organize service, and provide information on the history, travel, and biography collection; provide ILL svc.

2.56 Librarian II
0.5 Library assistant
2. Intermediate typist

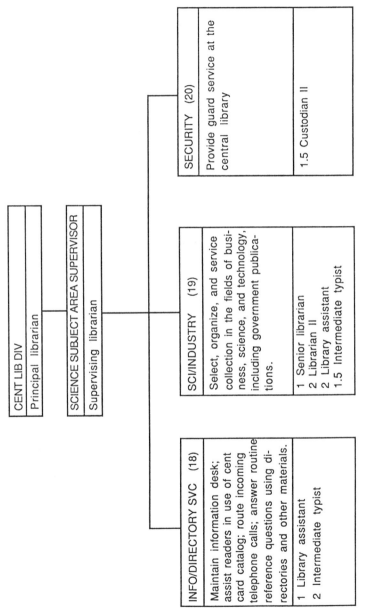

CENT LIB DIV
Principal librarian

SCIENCE SUBJECT AREA SUPERVISOR
Supervising librarian

INFO/DIRECTORY SVC   (18)
Maintain information desk; assist readers in use of cent card catalog; route incoming telephone calls; answer routine reference questions using directories and other materials.

1 Library assistant
2 Intermediate typist

SCI/INDUSTRY   (19)
Select, organize, and service collection in the fields of business, science, and technology, including government publications.

1 Senior librarian
2 Librarian II
2 Library assistant
1.5 Intermediate typist

SECURITY   (20)
Provide guard service at the central library

1.5 Custodian II

Library F, chart 6, 1979.

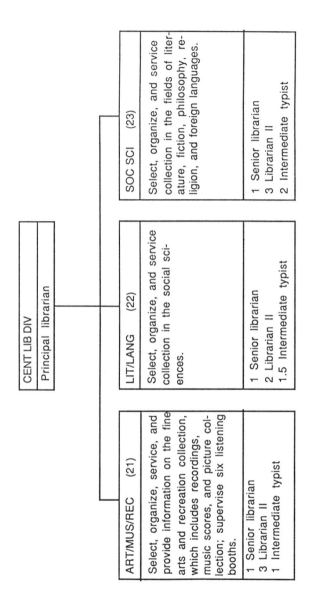

Library F, chart 7, 1979.

CENT LIB DIV

Principal librarian

ART/MUS/REC (21)

Select, organize, service, and provide information on the fine arts and recreation collection, which includes recordings, music scores, and picture collection; supervise six listening booths.

1 Senior librarian
3 Librarian II
1 Intermediate typist

LIT/LANG (22)

Select, organize, and service collection in the social sciences.

1 Senior librarian
2 Librarian II
1.5 Intermediate typist

SOC SCI (23)

Select, organize, and service collection in the fields of literature, fiction, philosophy, religion, and foreign languages.

1 Senior librarian
3 Librarian II
2 Intermediate typist

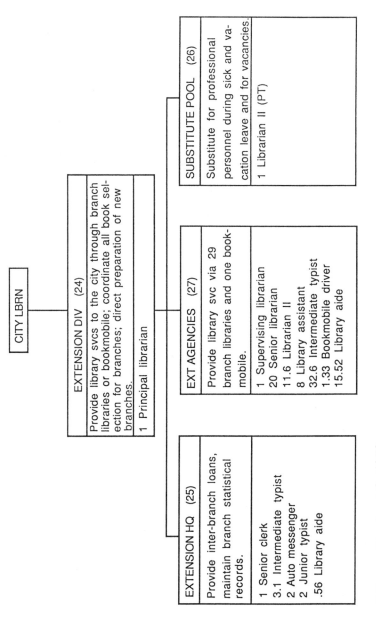

Library F, chart 8, 1979.

CITY LBRN

EXTENSION DIV (24)

Provide library svcs to the city through branch libraries or bookmobile; coordinate all book selection for branches; direct preparation of new branches.

1 Principal librarian

EXTENSION HQ (25)

Provide inter-branch loans, maintain branch statistical records.

1 Senior clerk
3.1 Intermediate typist
2 Auto messenger
2 Junior typist
.56 Library aide

EXT AGENCIES (27)

Provide library svc via 29 branch libraries and one book-mobile.

1 Supervising librarian
20 Senior librarian
11.6 Librarian II
8 Library assistant
32.6 Intermediate typist
1.33 Bookmobile driver
15.52 Library aide

SUBSTITUTE POOL (26)

Substitute for professional personnel during sick and vacation leave and for vacancies.

1 Librarian II (PT)

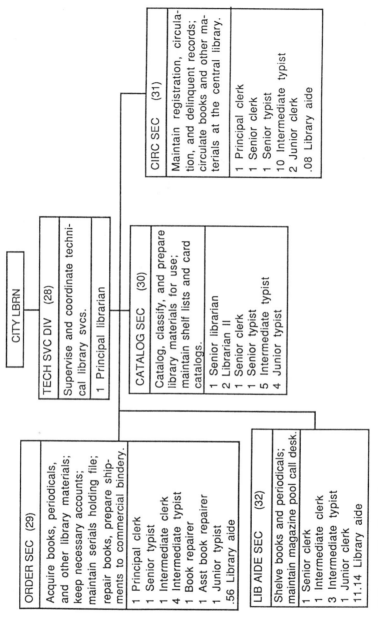

CITY LBRN

TECH SVC DIV (28)

Supervise and coordinate technical library svcs.

1 Principal librarian

ORDER SEC (29)

Acquire books, periodicals, and other library materials; keep necessary accounts; maintain serials holding file; repair books, prepare shipments to commercial bindery.

1 Principal clerk
1 Senior typist
1 Intermediate clerk
4 Intermediate typist
1 Book repairer
1 Asst book repairer
1 Junior typist
.56 Library aide

CATALOG SEC (30)

Catalog, classify, and prepare library materials for use; maintain shelf lists and card catalogs.

1 Senior librarian
2 Librarian II
1 Senior clerk
1 Senior typist
5 Intermediate typist
4 Junior typist

CIRC SEC (31)

Maintain registration, circulation, and delinquent records; circulate books and other materials at the central library.

1 Principal clerk
1 Senior clerk
1 Senior typist
10 Intermediate typist
2 Junior clerk
.08 Library aide

LIB AIDE SEC (32)

Shelve books and periodicals; maintain magazine pool call desk.

1 Senior clerk
1 Intermediate clerk
3 Intermediate typist
1 Junior clerk
11.14 Library aide

Library F, chart 9, 1979.

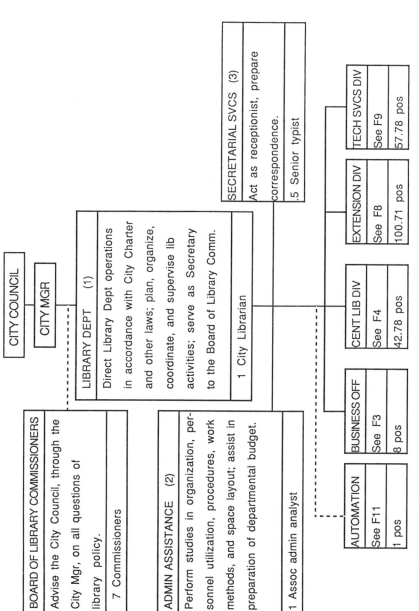

CITY COUNCIL

CITY MGR

BOARD OF LIBRARY COMMISSIONERS

Advise the City Council, through the City Mgr, on all questions of library policy.

7 Commissioners

LIBRARY DEPT   (1)

Direct Library Dept operations in accordance with City Charter and other laws; plan, organize, coordinate, and supervise lib activities; serve as Secretary to the Board of Library Comm.

1 City Librarian

ADMIN ASSISTANCE   (2)

Perform studies in organization, personnel utilization, procedures, work methods, and space layout; assist in preparation of departmental budget.

1 Assoc admin analyst

SECRETARIAL SVCS   (3)

Act as receptionist, prepare correspondence.

.5 Senior typist

AUTOMATION

See F11

1 pos

BUSINESS OFF

See F3

8 pos

CENT LIB DIV

See F4

42.78 pos

EXTENSION DIV

See F8

100.71 pos

TECH SVCS DIV

See F9

57.78 pos

Library F, chart 10, 1981.

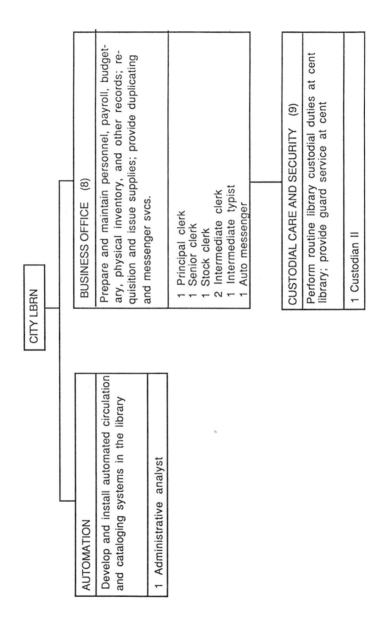

CITY LBRN

AUTOMATION

Develop and install automated circulation and cataloging systems in the library

1 Administrative analyst

BUSINESS OFFICE (8)

Prepare and maintain personnel, payroll, budgetary, physical inventory, and other records; requisition and issue supplies; provide duplicating and messenger svcs.

1 Principal clerk
1 Senior clerk
1 Stock clerk
2 Intermediate clerk
1 Intermediate typist
1 Auto messenger

CUSTODIAL CARE AND SECURITY (9)

Perform routine library custodial duties at cent library; provide guard service at cent

1 Custodian II

Library F, chart 11, 1981.

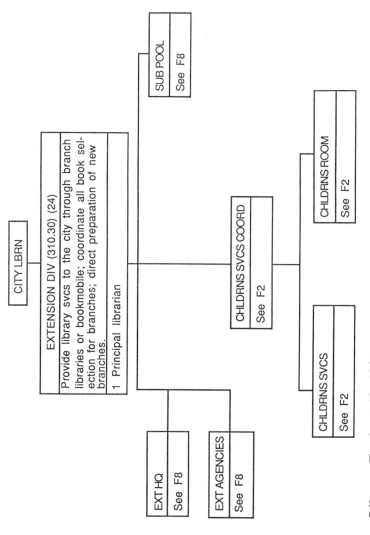

Library F, chart 12, 1981.

44

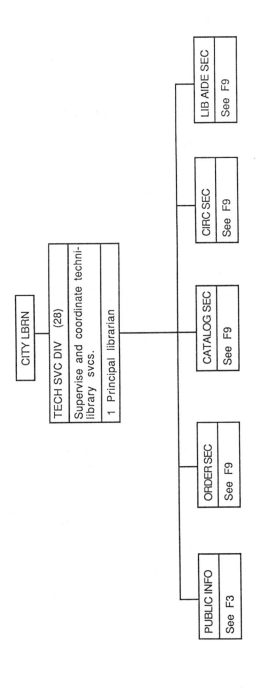

Library F, chart 13, 1981.

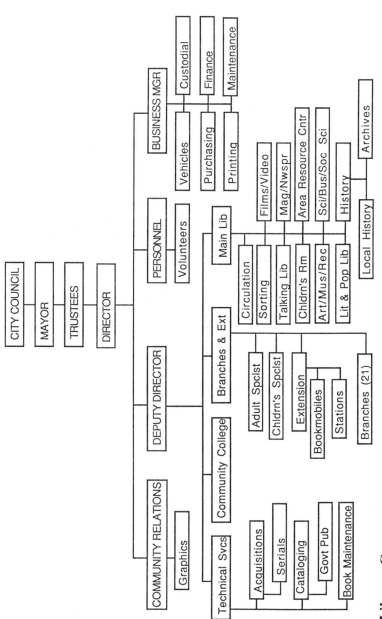

Library G.

46

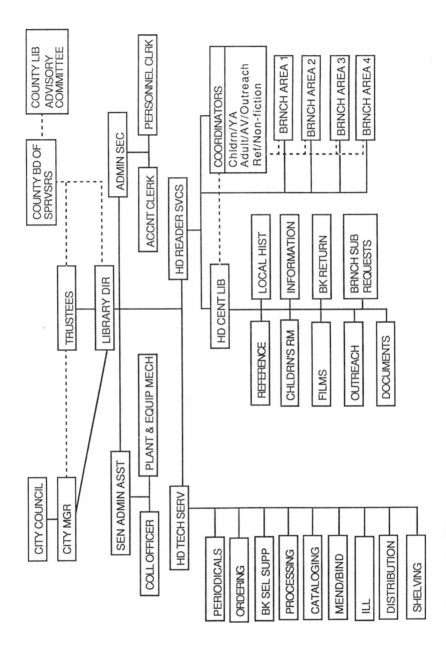

Library H, 1981.

47

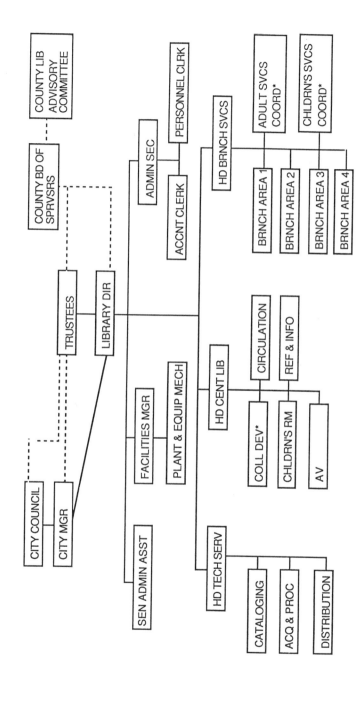

*These positions are advisory to entire library in their areas of specialization.

Library H, 1982.

48

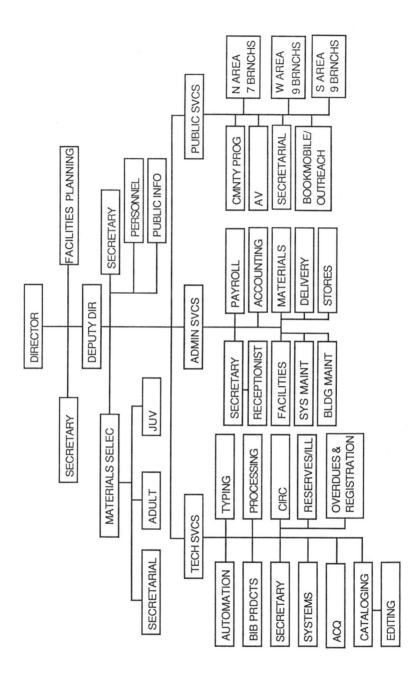

Library I.

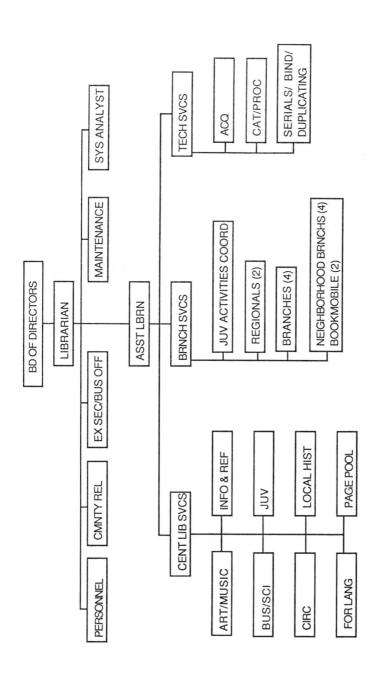

Library J, 1978.

50

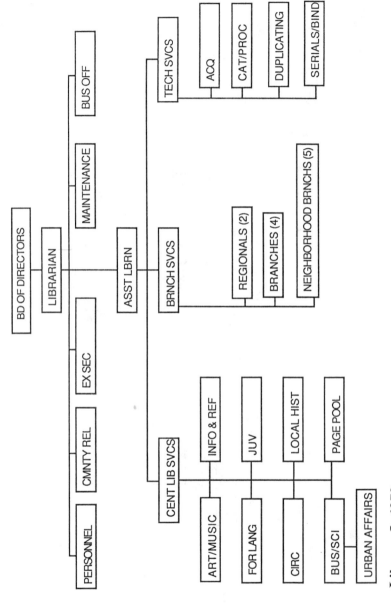

Library J, 1979.

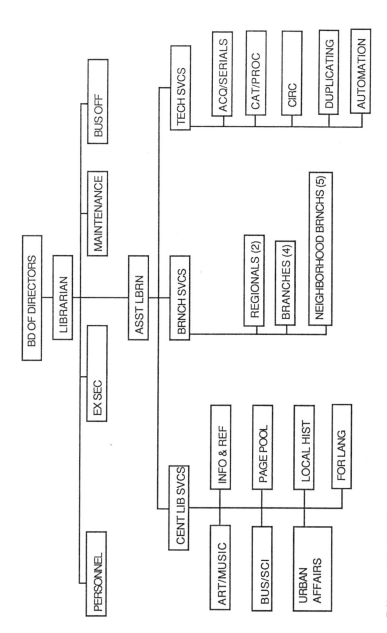

Library J, 1981.

52

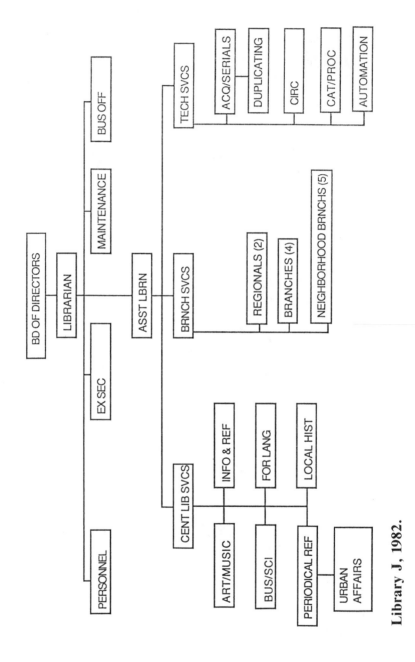

Library J, 1982.

1. LIBRARY COMMISSION
Determining operating policies for the Library Commission.
6 Member; 1 Ex-Officio Member (President, Bd of Ed)

2. ADMINISTRATION
Carrying out the policies and decisions of the commission; acting in the advisory capacity of a professional expert in recommending programs and policies of the Commission; determining and administering internal policies for selection and development of library collections, programs and other services, as well as personnel and operating procedures.
Appointed: 1 Library Director; 1 Library Deputy Director
Classified: 1 Departmental Executive Secretary IV

3. PERSONNEL OFFICE
Directing and coordinating personnel activities; establishing qualifications for positions; developing classifications and pay plans; recruiting, testing, and interviewing applicants; recommending appointments, promotions, transfers and separations; conducting in-service training programs and counseling individual staff members; handling payroll operations; representing Library Commission in labor matters with employee unions; making policy recommendations on above to Director.
Appointed: 1 Library Associate Director of Personnel
Classified: 1 Personnel Officer II; 1 Principal Clerk; 4 Senior Personnel and Payrol Clerk

4. SUPPORT SERVICES
Planning and directing the support services of the Library including managing financial activities; preparing annual budget; purchasing library information materials, supplies and equipment; maintaining inventory records; providing building security and maintenance; maintaining computer processing programs for control circulation; making policy recommendations in above areas to the Director.
Appointed: 1 Library Associate Director of Support Services

5. PUBLIC SERVICES
Providing the public services of the Library.
(See Chart K2)
Appointed: 1
Classified: 56

6. BUSINESS OFFICE
Maintaining financial records; collecting revenue and paying bills; compiling statistical data and preparing statistical reports.
Classified: 1 Senior Accountant; 3 Senior Clerk; 1 Clerk

7. TECHNICAL SVCS
Coordinating and directing all acquisitions, cataloging, bindery, data processing and collection development activities.
Classified: 1 Coord of Major Lib Activity Grade II

8. ORIGINAL CATALOG
Classifying and cataloging material orignal to the OCLC system.
Classified: 1 Chief of Lib Dept; 7 Lib II

COPY CATALOG
Completing cataloging and classification found in OCLC; preparing and maintaining public, departmental and branch card catalogs and shelf lists.
Classified: 1 Chief of Lib Dept; 1 Lib III; 1 Lib II; 4 Senior Copy Catalog clerk 8 Copy Catalog Clerk

9. DATA PROCESSING
Processing IBM cards used to control circulation of books; processing film for photo clerk; writing and maintaining data processing programs.
Classified: 1 Intermediate Data Processing Programmer; 2 Data Processing Equipment operator

10. BINDERY
Binding and repairing books, periodicals and other special materials.
Classified: 1 Bookbinder Super; 1 Bookbinder; 2 Bookbinder Asst
Note: major portion of book and periodical bindery is performed under contract

11. ACQUISITIONS
Making recommendations to the Director concerning general book selection policies; checking the output of all sources of publications in both the U.S. and foreign countries; and directing the buying and receiving of all books, periodicals and pamphlets.
Classified: 1 Chief of Lib Dept; 2 Lib III; 1 Lib II; 3 Senior Clerk; 6 Clerk

12. PROCESSING
Physically processing all monographs and serials and providing cards as needed for branch libraries.
Classified: 1 Principal Clerk; 4 Clerk

13. PURCHASING AND STORES
Making studies of the market for, and purchasing supplies and equipment; keeping cost records; receiving, inspecting, storing and dispersing supplies; certifying as to quality and quantity of supplies received; and preparing packages for shipment.
Classified: 1 Senior Purchases Agent; 1 Senior Clerk; 1 Storekeeper; 1 Clerk

14. GRANTS AND RESEARCH
Searching for and preparing reports for special grants; compiling statistical information and other reports as required.
Classified: 1 Coord of Major Lib Activity

15. BLDG MAINT AND SECURITY
Supervising the maintenance, repair, cleaning, custodial activities and grounds maintenance of the Library Commission.
Classified: 1 Super of Blgds and Mechanical Maint; 1 Senior Clerk; 1 Lib Maint Super

16. CUSTODIAL GROUNDS MAINT AND SECURITY SVCS
Guarding main library bldg, inspecting parcels and books at exits; cleaning main library; engaging in landscaping and grounds maintenance activities at the main library.
Classified: 1 Lib Maint Super; 1 Bldg Custody and Sec Super III; 3 Supervising Bldg Atndt Grade I; 2 Bldg Atndt A; 1 Lib Matron; 7 Lib Guard; 1 Park Maint Frmn; 1 Park Maint Helper; 1 Bookmobile Oper/ Mechanic

17. TRADES
Providing plumbing, electrical, plastering, steam-fitting and other repair and maint svcs to the main library and the branch libraries; repairing and altering wooden parts of bldgs; fabricating and repairing wooden articles, painting interiors and exteriors of bldgs.
Classified: 1 Crpntr Sub-Frmn; 2 Finish Crpntr; 1 Pntr Sub-Frmn; 2 Finish Pntr; 1 Master Plumber; 1 Steamfitter; 1 Elect Worker-Gen; 1 Bldg Refrigerator Equip Operator-1st Class; 3 Bldg Mechanic

18. SHIPPING&MAILING
Receiving, delivering, and mailing books; processing outgoing mail; providing inter-library and inter-branch shipping and trucking service.
Classified: 1 Senior Storekeeper; 1 Asst Storekeeper; 1 Clerk; 2 Delivery-Driver

Library K, chart 1.

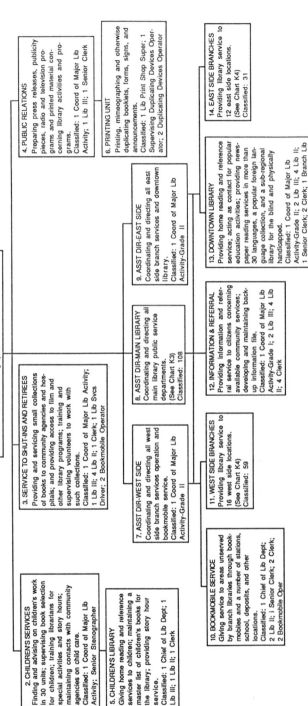

1. PUBLIC SERVICES

Planning and directing the public services offered by the library including home reading service and research; selecting; organizing and preserving collections required for information, study, research and recreational reading; organizing adult education activities; supplementing programs of other educational organizations; preparing bibliographies and indexes; planning and directing publicity programs; registering borrowers and lending books and other materials; providing information concerning available community services; and making policy recommendations in the above fields to the Director.
Appointed: 1 Library Associate Director of Public Service
Classified: 1 Senior Stenographer

2. CHILDREN'S SERVICES
Finding and advising on children's work in 30 units; supervising book selection for children; training librarians for special activities and story hours; maintaining contacts with community agencies on child care.
Classified: 1 Coord of Major Lib
Activity: Senior Stenographer

3. SERVICE TO SHUT-INS AND RETIREES
Providing and servicing small collections of books to community agencies and hospitals; and providing access to film and other library programs; training and supervising volunteers to work with such collections.
Classified: 1 Coord of Major Lib Activity; 1 Lib III; 4 Lib II; 1 Clerk; 1 Lib Svcs Driver; 2 Bookmobile Operator

4. PUBLIC RELATIONS
Preparing press releases, publicity pieces, radio and television programs and printed material concerning library activities and programs.
Classified: 1 Coord of Major Lib
Activity; 1 Lib III; 1 Senior Clerk

5. CHILDREN'S LIBRARY
Giving home reading and reference services to children; maintaining a master list of children's books for the the library; providing story hour service.
Classified: 1 Chief of Lib Dept; 1 Lib III; 1 Lib II; 1 Clerk

6. PRINTING UNIT
Printing, mimeographing and otherwise duplicating booklets, forms, signs, and announcements.
Classified: 1 Lib Print Shop Super; 1 Supervising Duplicating Devices Operator; 2 Duplicating Devices Operator

7. ASST DIR-WEST SIDE
Coordinating and directing all west side branch services operation and bookmobile service.
Classified: 1 Coord of Major Lib
Activity-Grade II

8. ASST DIR-MAIN LIBRARY
Coordinating and directing all main library public service departments.
(See Chart K3)
Classified: 108

9. ASST DIR-EAST SIDE
Coordinating and directing all east side branch services and downtown library.
Classified: 1 Coord of Major Lib
Activity-Grade II

10. BOOKMOBILE SERVICE
Giving service to areas unserved by branch libraries through bookmobiles and a number of stations, school, deposits, and other locations.
Classified: 1 Chief of Lib Dept; 2 Lib II; 1 Senior Clerk; 2 Clerk; 2 Bookmobile Oper

11. WEST SIDE BRANCHES
Providing library service to 16 west side locations.
(See Chart K4)
Classified: 59

12. INFORMATION & REFERRAL
Providing information and referral service to citizens concerning available community services; developing and maintaining back-up Information file.
Classified: 1 Coord of Major Lib
Activity-Grade I; 2 Lib III; 4 Lib II; 4 Clerk

13. DOWNTOWN LIBRARY
Providing home reading and reference service; acting as contact for popular education activities; providing newspaper reading services in more than 30 languages, a popular foreign language collection, and a sub-regional library for the blind and physically handicapped.
Classified: 1 Coord of Major Lib
Activity-Grade II; 2 Lib III; 4 Lib II; 1 Senior Clerk; 2 Clerk; 1 Branch Lib Janitor

14. EAST SIDE BRANCHES
Providing library service to 12 east side locations.
(See Chart K4)
Classified: 31

Library K, chart 2.

55

1. MAIN LIBRARY AND REFERENCE SERVICES
Planning and directing the reference and research services of the main library; selecting and preserving the permanent collections required for information, study and research (including books, periodicals, newspapers, government documents, maps, pictures and other related materials); organizing and maintaining information, clipping and pamphlet files; providing reference and research aid to readers in the use of books, catalogs, bibliographic tools and other sources within the library; providing information to inquiries in person, by telephone and by mail; preparing bibliographies and indexes; planning and coordinating publicity programs.
Classified: 1 Coord of Major Lib Activity-Grade II

2. FINE ARTS DEPT
Providing reference and circulation service in the field of the fine arts; maintaining extensive picture files.
Classified: 1 Chief of Lib Dept; 1 Lib III; 2 Lib II; 1 Clerk

3. HISTORY & TRAVEL DEPT
Providing reference and circulation service in the fields of history and travel; maintaining a large map collection.
Classified: 1 Chief of Lib Dept; 2 Lib III; 1 Lib II; 2 Clerk

4. MUNICIPAL REFERENCE LIBRARY (City-County Building)
Providing reference service and materials in the field of municipal and county administration to governmental departments; serving as official depository for city documents and reports.
Classified: 1 Chief of Lib Dept; 1 Lib III; 2 Clerk

5. FILM DEPT
Lending 16mm films and video cassettes; giving advisory service to individuals concerned with the use of films in programs; aiding special groups with preview showings on definite subjects; planning programs which use films for the library.
Classified: 1 Chief of Lib Dept; 1 Lib III; 1 Lib II; 2 Clerk; 1 Lib AV Tech.

6. GIFTS & RARE BKS DIV
Organizing and guiding the rare book acquisition and display work; performing research necessary to determine the value of rarities considered for purchase and those presented as gifts; receiving, distributing and acknowledging gifts.
Classified: 1 Chief of Lib Dept; 1 Senior Clerk

7. LANG & LIT DEPT
Providing reference and circulation services in the fields of English, foreign languages and literature.
Classified: 1 Chief of Lib Dept; 1 Lib III; 2 Lib II; 1 Clerk

8. MUSIC AND PERFORMING ARTS DEPT
Providing reference and circulation service in the fields of music, drama, and the entertainment arts including music, scores, anthems and phonograph records.
Classified: 1 Chief of Lib Dept; 2 Lib III; 2 Lib II; 2 Clerk

9. HISTORICAL COLLECTION DEPT
Providing reference and research service and a special research collection of books, manuscripts, maps, photographs and other information covering the history of the area; developing and servicing the genealogical collection; preserving printed and manuscript material relating to the local community.
Classified: 1 Chief of Lib Dept; 4 Lib III; 3 Lib III; 1 Senior Clerk; 1 Stenographer; 1 Clerk

10. GEN INFO DEPT
Providing a general reference service in the national and trade bibliographies, biographies and those subject fields not covered by a special department; providing reference service in the field of public documents; maintaining bound periodicals and newspapers.
Classified: 1 Chief of Lib Dept; 1 Lib III; 5 Lib II; 2 Clerk

11. PHIL, REL, & ED DEPT
Providing reference and circulation service in the fields of philosophy, religion and education; maintaining vocational guidance and college catalog files.
Classified: 1 Chief of Lib Dept; 1 Lib III; 2 Lib II, 2 Clerk

12. SOCIOLOGY & ECON DEPT
Providing reference and circulation services in the fields of the social sciences, economics, labor, sociology, social work, politics, and government.
Classified: 1 Chief of Lib Dept; 1 Lib III; 4.5 Lib II; 1 Senior Clerk; 2 Clerk

13. TECH AND SCI DEPT
Providing reference and circulation service in the fields of technology and science, chemistry, physics, mathematics and all phases of engineering.
Classified: 1 Chief of Lib Dept; 2 Lib III; 4 Lib II; 3 Clerk

14. BROWSING LIBRARY
Providing broad general home reading and popular educational services, including fiction and non-fiction.
Classified: 1 Chief of Lib Dept; 1 Lib III; 2 Lib II; 1 Clerk

15. SPECIAL HISTORICAL COLLECTION
Providing reference and research service and a special research collection of books, periodicals, pictures and other information in the field of automotive history.
Classified: 1 Chief of Lib Dept; 1 Senior Clerk

16. BUSINESS AND FINANCE DEPT
Providing reference and circulation service in the field of business, finance and commerce; maintaining business and financial services.
Classified: 1 Chief of Lib Dept; 1 Lib III; 3 Lib II; 2 Clerk

17. INTERLIBRARY LOAN
Providing bibliographic and document exchange among libraries throughout the state and nation.
Classified: 1 Lib III; 1 Lib II; 2 Clerk

18. LOAN BUREAU
Making loans and keeping records of books loaned at main library; handling complaints and adjustments; making home calls and taking legal action to recover overdue books.
Classified: 1 Principal Clerk; 1 Senior Clerk; 4 Clerk

19. SWITCHBOARD
Operating main library switchboard.
Classified: 1 Senior Clerk

Library K, chart 3.

56

1. WEST SIDE BRANCH LIBRARIES

Provide home reading and reference service to adults, youths, and children; acting as neighborhood center for all book discussions, film forums, reading clubs, youth groups, and children's story hours. All west side branch libraries are under the coordination and direction of the Coord of Major Library Activity for the west side.
(See Chart K2)

12 BRANCHES

Classified: 7 Chief of Lib Dept; 7 Lib III; 6 Lib II; 5 Branch Lib Janitor; 6 Clerk; 1 Boiler Oper

Note: Staff rotates between two branches.

2. EAST SIDE BRANCH LIBRARIES

Providing home reading and reference service to adults, youths, and children; acting as neighborhood center for all book discussions, film forums, reading clubs, youth groups, and children's story hours. All east side branch libraries are under the coordination and direction of the Coord of Major Library Activity for the east side.
(See Chart K2)

10 BRANCHES

Classified: 5 Chief of Lib Dept; 5 Lib III; 4 Lib II; 3 Branch Lib Janitor; 5 Clerk; 2 Boiler Oper

Note: Staff rotates between two branches.

Library K, chart 4.

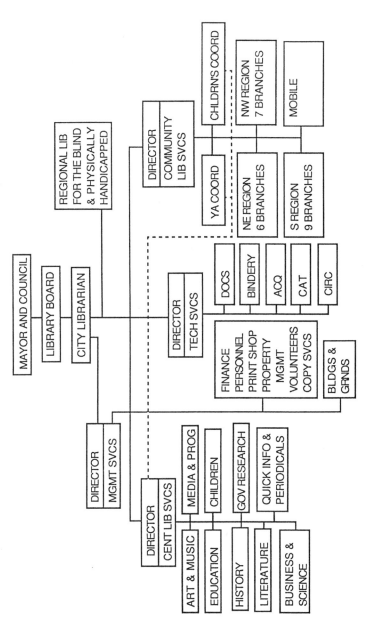

Library L, chart 1.

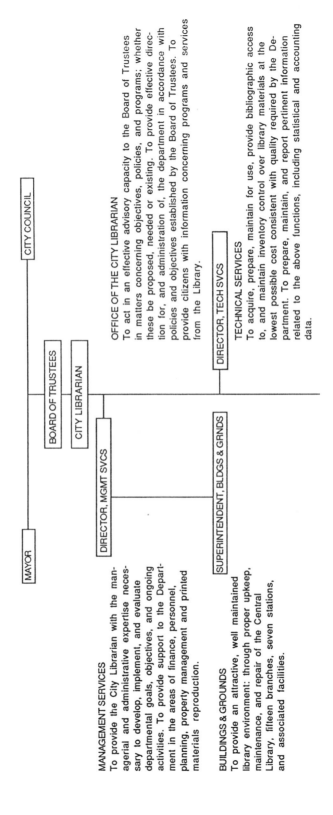

MAYOR

CITY COUNCIL

BOARD OF TRUSTEES

CITY LIBRARIAN

DIRECTOR, MGMT SVCS

SUPERINTENDENT, BLDGS & GRNDS

DIRECTOR, TECH SVCS

OFFICE OF THE CITY LIBRARIAN
To act in an effective advisory capacity to the Board of Trustees in matters concerning objectives, policies, and programs; whether these be proposed, needed or existing. To provide effective direction for, and administration of, the department in accordance with policies and objectives established by the Board of Trustees. To provide citizens with information concerning programs and services from the Library.

MANAGEMENT SERVICES
To provide the City Librarian with the managerial and administrative expertise necessary to develop, implement, and evaluate departmental goals, objectives, and ongoing activities. To provide support to the Department in the areas of finance, personnel, planning, property management and printed materials reproduction.

BUILDINGS & GROUNDS
To provide an attractive, well maintained library environment: through proper upkeep, maintenance, and repair of the Central Library, fifteen branches, seven stations, and associated facilities.

TECHNICAL SERVICES
To acquire, prepare, maintain for use, provide bibliographic access to, and maintain inventory control over library materials at the lowest possible cost consistent with quality required by the Department. To prepare, maintain, and report pertinent information related to the above functions, including statistical and accounting data.

DIRECTOR
CENTRAL LIBRARY SERVICES

ADMINISTRATION
To provide overall administration, planning evaluation and coordination of services and functions provided to the public by Subject Collections, Special Collections, and Quick Information and Periodicals services.

SUBJECT COLLECTIONS
To select, make accessible, and assist in the use of library materials in order to serve the informational, informal educational, cultural, and leisure time activity needs of citizens.

SPECIAL COLLECTIONS
To provide expertise, specialized collections of materials, and facilities to meet the needs of specific groups of library users. To enhance the Library's role as an informational educational resource by providing audio-visual information and materials for all users, and to back up the Library's community and outreach services.

QUICK INFORMATION AND PERIODICALS SERVICES
To answer short informational questions via telephone and provide accurate directional and catalog assistance. To evaluate in-depth inquiries so that these questions can be directed to the appropriate subject area. To provide centralized periodical service.

DIRECTOR
COMMUNITY LIBRARY SERVICES

ADMINISTRATION
To administer the Community Services program and provide coordination of Community Services elements' services, efforts, and activities for children and young adults.

REGIONS (NORTHEAST, NORTHWEST, SOUTH)
To select, make accessible, and assist in the use of general library materials for the cultural, recreational, and general information needs of the citizens in the regions of the community. To provide access to specialized informational service and materials through the Central Library. To increase community awareness of library resources and instruct in the use of library facilities through various library oriented programs.

DIRECTOR, BLIND AND PHYSICALLY HANDICAPPED SERVICES

READERS SERVICE
Circulates books, equipment, and materials provided by the National Service for the Blind and Physically Handicapped program (Library of Congress) to the print disabled.

RADIO READING SERVICE
Broadcasts current information and information of special interest to the blind and physically handicapped.

BRAILLE AND TAPING SERVICE
Transcribes materials not available elsewhere into taped or brailled format for the blind and physically handicapped.

Library L, chart 2.

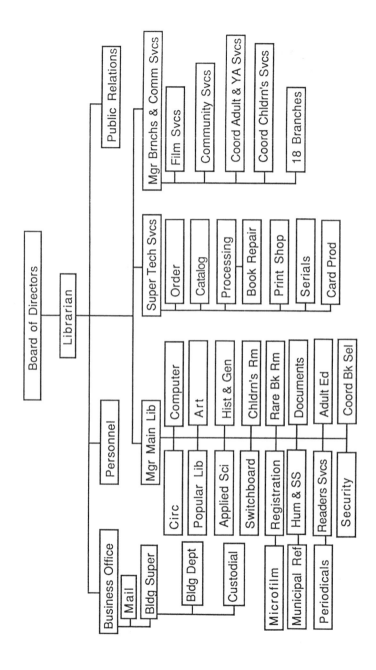

Library M.

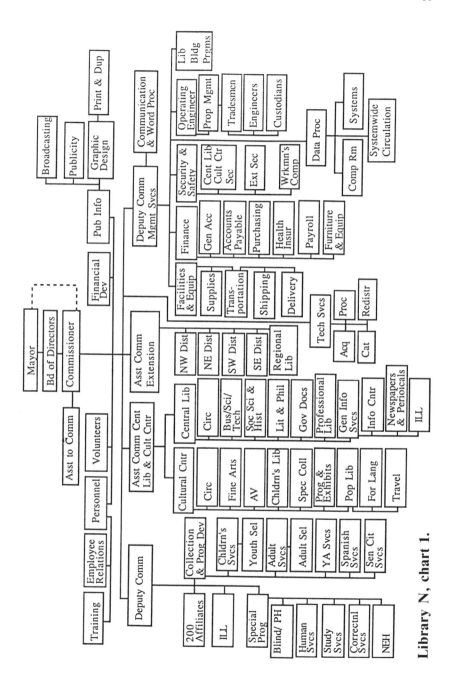

Library N, chart 1.

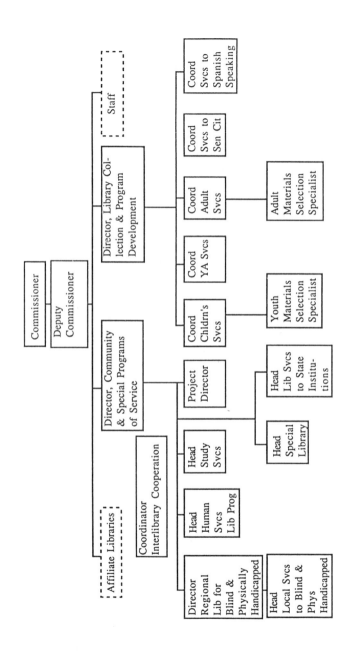

Library N, chart 2.

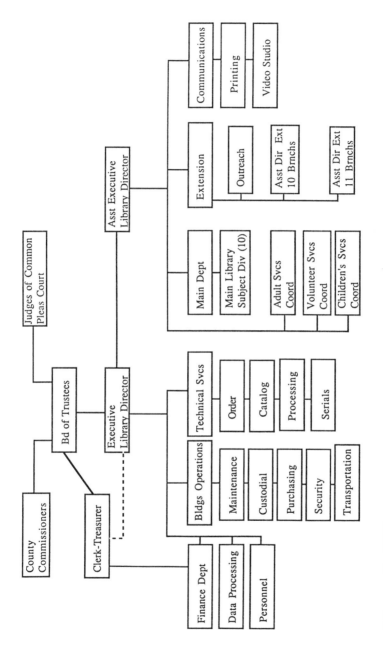

Library O, 1980.

64

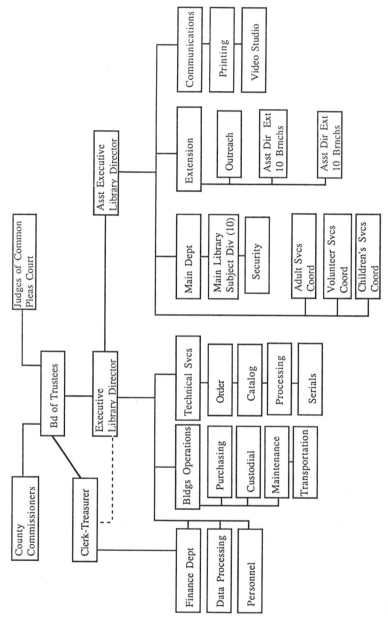

Library O, 1982.

65

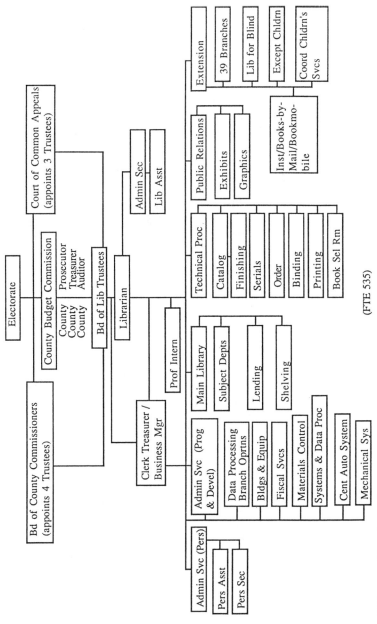

Library P, chart 1.

(FTE 535)

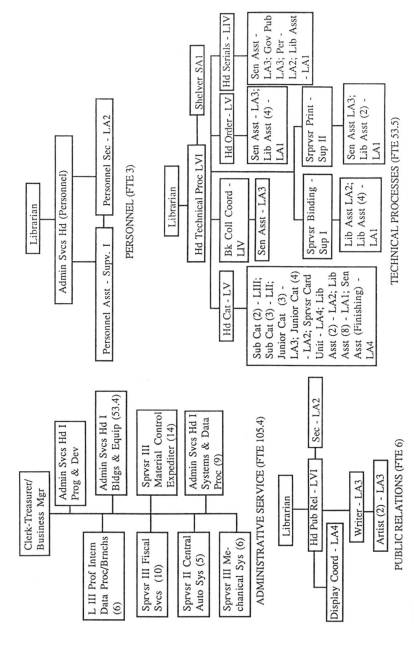

PERSONNEL (FTE 3)

TECHNICAL PROCESSES (FTE 53.5)

ADMINISTRATIVE SERVICE (FTE 105.4)

PUBLIC RELATIONS (FTE 6)

Library P, chart 2.

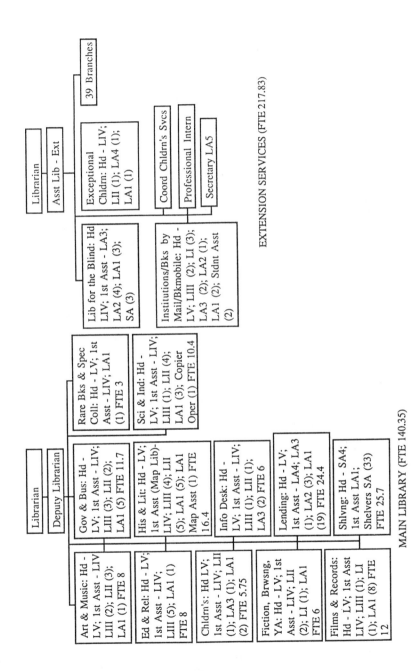

Librarian

Asst Lib - Ext

39 Branches

Exceptional Chldrn: Hd - LIV; LII (1); LA4 (1); LA1 (1)

Coord Chldrn's Svcs

Professional Intern

Secretary LA5

Lib for the Blind: Hd LIV; 1st Asst - LA3; LA2 (4); LA1 (3); SA (3)

Institutions/Bks by Mail/Bkmobile: Hd - LV; LIII (2); LI (3); LA3 (2); LA2 (1); LA1 (2); Stdnt Asst (2)

EXTENSION SERVICES (FTE 217.83)

Librarian

Deputy Librarian

Rare Bks & Spec Coll: Hd - LV; 1st Asst - LIV; LA1 (1) FTE 3

Sci & Ind: Hd - LV; 1st Asst - LIV; LIII (1); LII (4); LA1 (3); Copier Oper (1) FTE 10.4

Gov & Bus: Hd - LV; 1st Asst - LIV; LIII (3); LII (2); LA1 (5) FTE 11.7

His & Lit: Hd - LV; 1st Asst (Map Lib)- LIV; LIII (4); LII (5); LA1 (5); LA1 Map Asst (1) FTE 16.4

Info Desk: Hd - LV; 1st Asst - LIV; LIII (1); LII (1); LA3 (2) FTE 6

Lending: Hd - LV; 1st Asst - LA4; LA3 (1); LA2 (3); LA1 (19) FTE 24.4

Art & Music: Hd - LV; 1st Asst - LIV LIII (2); LII (3); LA1 (1) FTE 8

Ed & Rel: Hd - LV; 1st Asst - LIV; LIII (5); LA1 (1) FTE 8

Chldrn's: Hd LV; 1st Asst - LIV; LII (1); LA3 (1); LA1 (2) FTE 5.75

Fiction, Brwsng, YA: Hd - LV; 1st Asst - LIV; LII (2); LI (1); LA1 FTE 6

Films & Records: Hd - LV; 1st Asst LIV; LIII (1); LI (1); LA1 (8) FTE 12

Shlvng: Hd - SA4; 1st Asst LA1; Shelvers SA (33) FTE 25.7

MAIN LIBRARY (FTE 140.35)

Library P, chart 3.

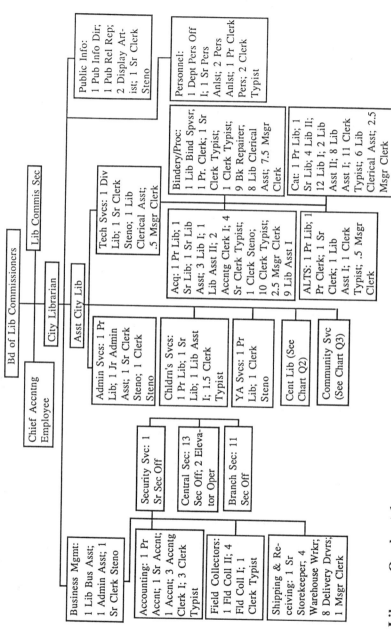

Library Q, chart 1.

Central Sub Depts: 1 Div Lib; 1 Admin Asst; 1 Sr Clerk Steno

Municipal Ref: 1 Pr Lib

City Hall: 1 Sr Lib; 1.5 Lib I; 1 LA I; 4 Clerk Typist; 1.5 Msgr Clerk

Planning: .5 Lib I; 1 Sr Clerk Typist

Police: 1 Sr Lib; 1 Lib I; 1 Clerk Typist; .5 Msgr Clerk

Water & Power: 1 Sr Lib; 3 Lib I; 1 LA II; 4 Clerk Typist; 1.5 Msgr Clerk

Asst to Dir of Cent: 1 Pr Lib; 1 Clerk Typist

Cent Tel Svc: 1 Sr Tel Oper; 3 Tel Oper

Gen Rdng Svcs*: 1 Sr Lib; 1 Lib I; 4 LA I; 1 Sr Clerk; 3.5 Clerk Typist; 7.5 Msgr Clerk

Circ & Reg: 1 Pr Clerk; 1 Sr Clerk; 1 Clerk Typist; 12 Lib Clerical Asst; 2.5 Msgr Clerk

* Includes:
Newspaper Room
Circulating Periodical Room
Magazine Pool
Information Desk
Popular Reading

Soc Sci: 1 Pr Lib; 1 Sr Lib; 1 Lib II; 4.5 Lib I; 1 LA I; 3 Clerk Typist; .5 Lib Clerical Asst; 5.25 Msgr Clerk

Phil & Rel: 1 Sr Lib; 3 Lib I; 1.5 Clerk Typist; 2.25 Msgr Clerk

Lit & Philology: 1 Pr Lib; 1 Sr Lib; 1 Lib II; 4.5 Lib I; 1 LA I; 2 Clerk Typist; 2 Lib Clerical Asst; 2 Msgr Clerk

Fiction: 1 Sr Lib; 3 Lib I; 1.5 Clerk Typist; 1 Lib Clerical Asst; 2 Msgr Clerk

Sci & Tech: 1 Pr Lib; 1 Sr Lib; 1 Lib II; 6.5 Lib I; 1 LA II; 2 LA I; 4.5 Clerk Typist; 1.5 Lib Clerical Asst; 7.75 Msgr Clerk

Chldrn's Lit: 1 Sr Lib; 1 Lib I; 1 Clerk Typist; .5 Lib Clerical Asst; 1 Msgr Clerk

For Lang: 1 Pr Lib; 1 Sr Lib; 2 Lib I; 1 LA I; 1 Clerk Tpist; 1 Lib Clerical Asst; 1.75 Msgr Clerk

His: 1 Pr Lib; 1 Sr Lib; 2 Lib II; 3 Lib I; 2 LA I; 1 Sr Clerk Typist; 2 Clerk Typist; .5 Lib Clerical Asst; 4.75 Msgr Clerk

Genealogy: 1 Sr Lib; 2 Lib I; .5 Lib Clerical Asst; 1.75 Msgr Clerk

Art & Mus: 1 Pr Lib; 1 Sr Lib; 1 Lib II; 5 Lib I; 1 LA II; 3 Clerk Typist; .5 Lib Clerical Asst; 4 Msgr Clerk

AV: 1 Pr Lib; 1 Sr Lib; 1 Sr Clerk; 4 Clerk Typist; 3.5 Lib Clerical Asst; 1 Film Inspector; 2.5 Msgr Clerk

Coll Dev Mgr: 1 Pr Lib; 1 LA I

Lib Mat Depository: 1 Sr Clerk

Bus & Econ: 1 Pr Lib; 1 Sr Lib; 1 Lib II; 4.5 Lib I; 1 LA I; 3 Clerk Typist; 1.5 Lib Clerical Asst; 3.5 Msgr Clerk

Library Q, chart 2.

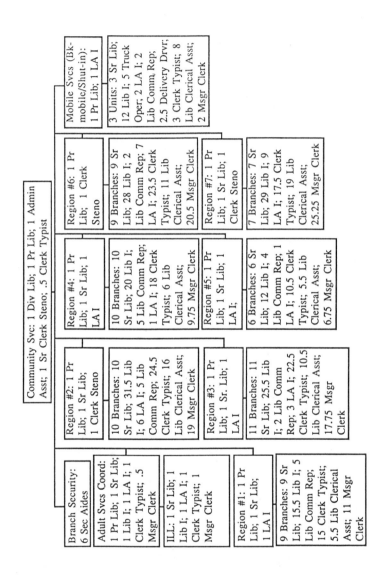

Library Q, chart 3.

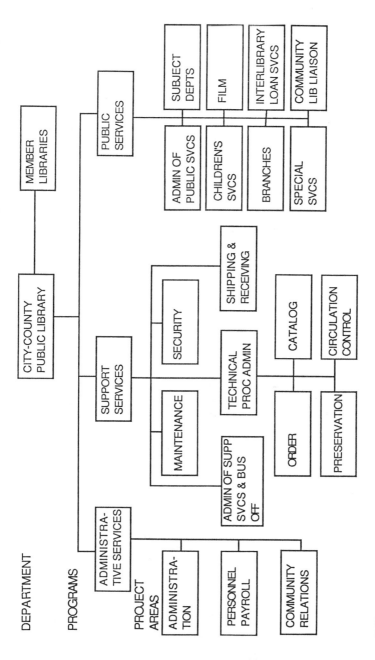

Library R, chart 1.

72

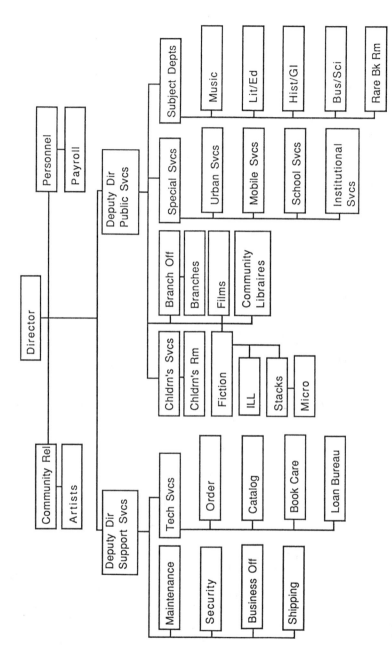

Library R, chart 2.

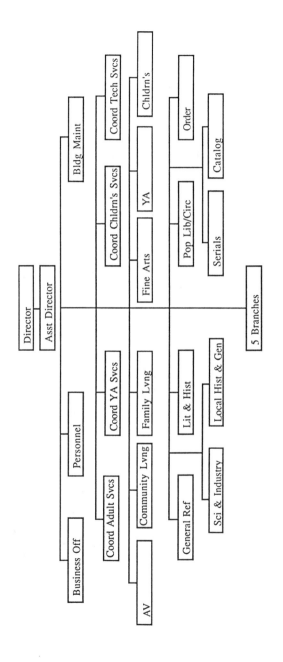

Library S, 1957.

74

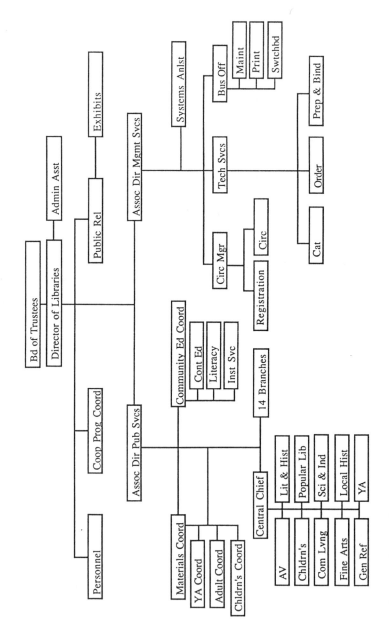

Library S, 1968.

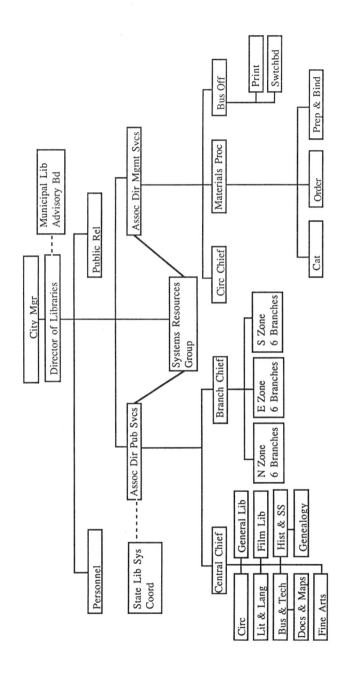

Library S, 1977/78.

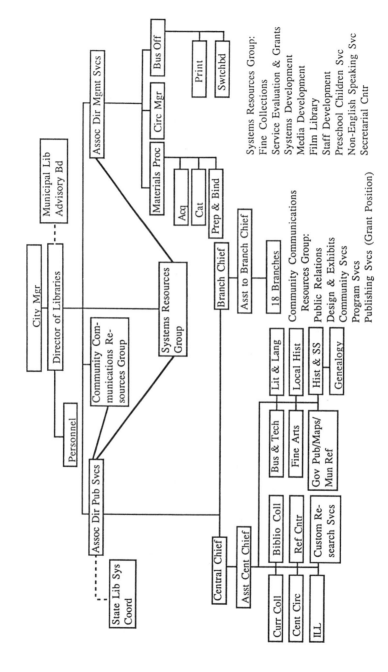

Library S, 1978/79.

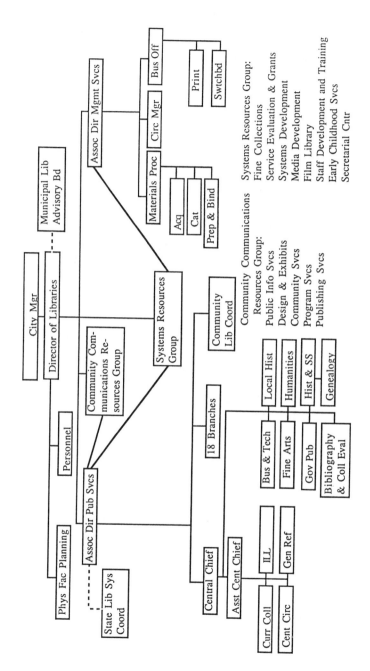

Library S, 1979/80.

78

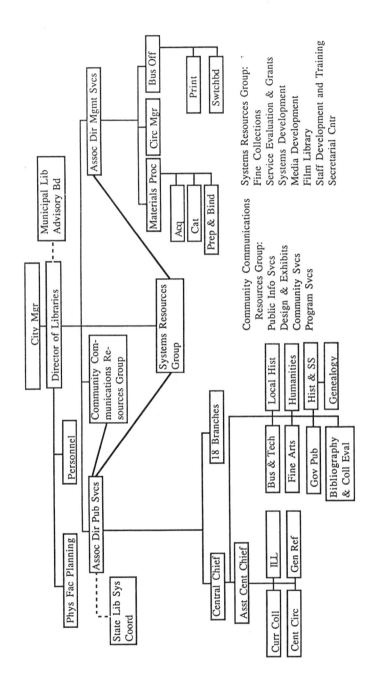

Library S, 1980/81.

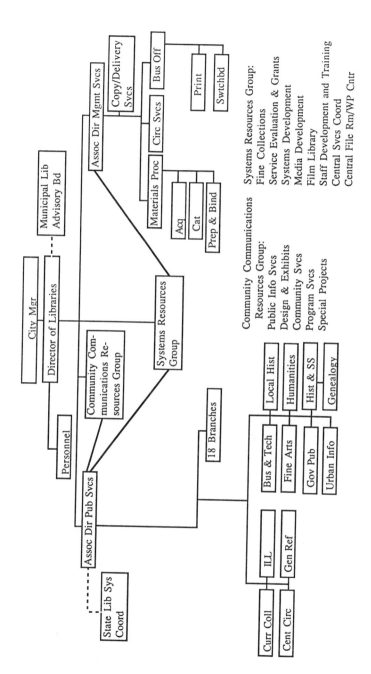

Library S, 1981/82.

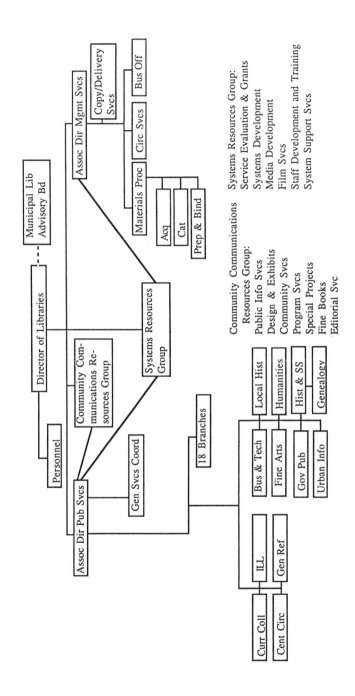

Library S, 1983/84.

Municipal Lib Advisory Bd

Director of Libraries

Personnel

Community Communications Re-sources Group

Systems Resources Group

Assoc Dir Mgmt Svcs

Copy/Delivery Svcs

Bus Off

Circ Svcs

Materials Proc

Acq

Cat

Prep & Bind

Assoc Dir Pub Svcs

Gen Svcs Coord

18 Branches

Local Hist

Humanities

Hist & SS

Genealogy

Bus & Tech

Fine Arts

Gov Pub

Urban Info

ILL

Gen Ref

Curr Coll

Cent Circ

Community Communications
Resources Group:
Public Info Svcs
Design & Exhibits
Community Svcs
Program Svcs
Special Projects
Fine Books
Editorial Svc

Systems Resources Group:
Service Evaluation & Grants
Systems Development
Media Development
Film Svcs
Staff Development and Training
System Support Svcs

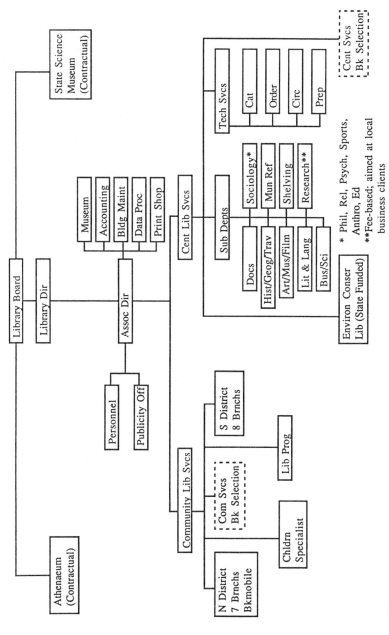

Library T, 1975.

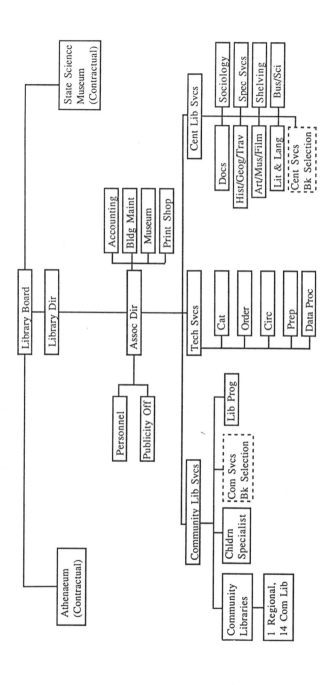

Library T, 1976.

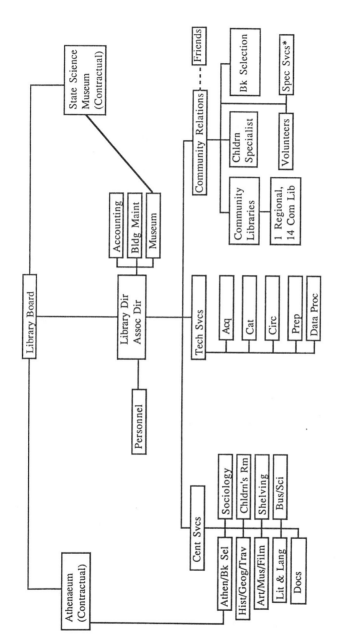

Library T, 1979.

*Environ Conser Lib; Research; Mun Info
Lib; Publicity; Print Shop

84

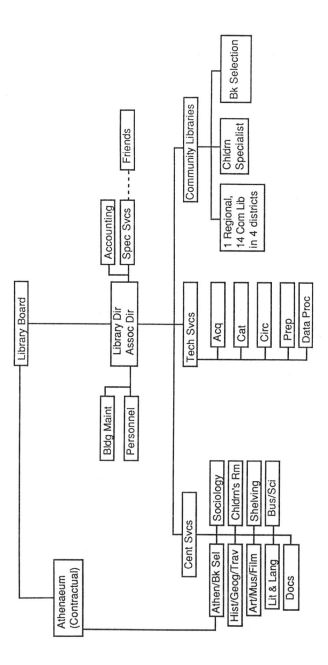

Library T, 1980.

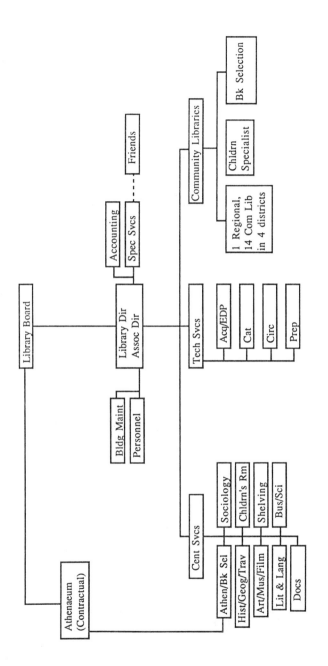

Library T, 1982.

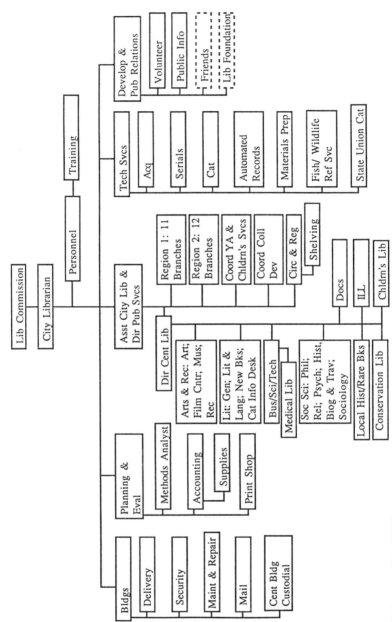

Library U, 1980.

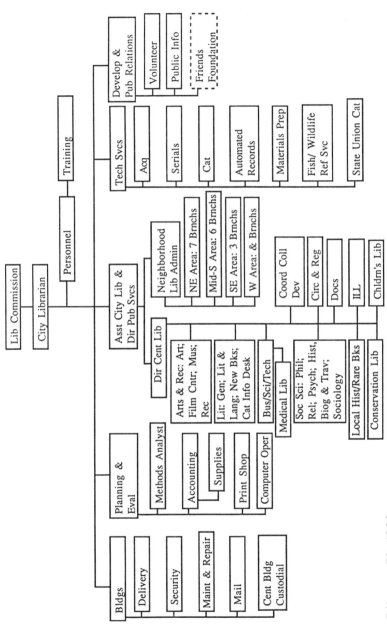

Library U, 1982.

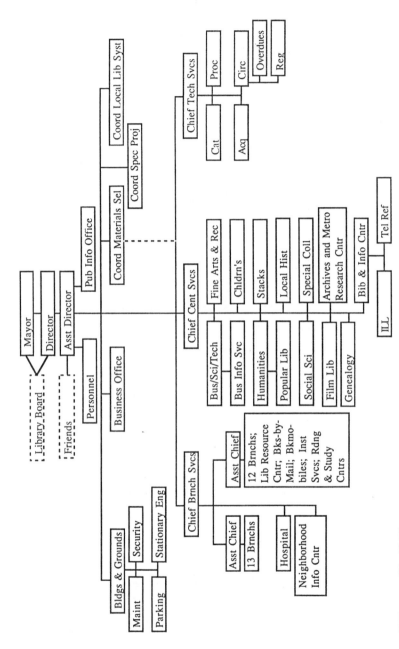

Library V, 1979.

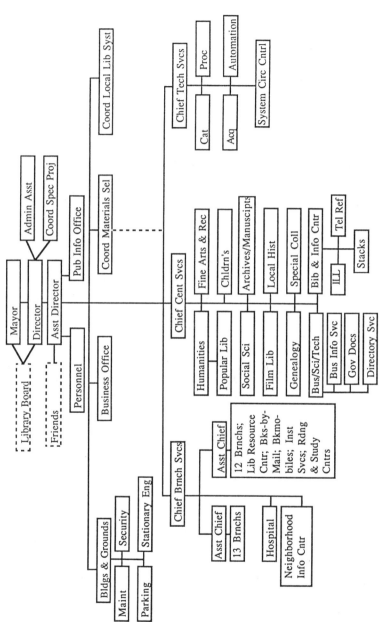

Library V, 1981.

II
Professionalism
in Public Librarianship

Librarians at times are preoccupied with asserting their professionalism and establishing librarianship as a genuine profession. But
what is a "profession"? The attributes that customarily have distinguished professions such as medicine and law from other types of occupations are in a state of reexamination at present due to such things
as frequent malpractice suits, consumerism, the introduction of adver-
tising into traditional professions, privacy legislation, intense media
scrutiny, and the accessibility of highly technical information to the
general public without the intervention of an expert. These and other
conditions are forcing changes in the way professionals conduct their
practice and in the way people think about the professions and their
relation to other lines of work.

Nevertheless, there remain a number of qualities that mark the
traditional professions and which librarians, and other groups who
aspire to professionalism, naturally feel compelled to emulate. These
include (1) lengthy specialized training, (2) access to privileged or confidential communication, (3) concern with matters of life and death, (4)
adherence to a set of self-regulating norms of behavior, (5) a commitment to public service, (6) proficiency in a core of systematic theoretical
knowledge, and (7) involvement in the discovery and application of
knowledge as opposed to its mere communication.[1]

The degree to which an occupation exhibits these qualities generally determines its stature as a profession. Librarianship is relatively
undeveloped in some of these areas and totally lacking in others. As a
result librarianship seems to fit into a category Etzioni describes as a
"semi-profession," and the public library into the category of a semi-
professional organization:

> Semi-professional organizations are more concerned with the com-
> munication and, to a lesser extent, the application of knowledge, their

professionals are less likely to be guaranteed the right of privileged communications, and they are rarely directly concerned with matters of life and death.[2]

As the charts illustrating Chapter 1 demonstrate, libraries are organized by the pyramid arrangement, an hierarchical multiplication of authority layers that narrows to the source of authority at the top of the hierarchical arrangement. This is typical of semi-professional organizations. Conversely, the presence of "full-fledged" professionals in an organization has several observable effects on the arrangement and operation of that organization. First, according to Hall, professional organizations tend toward minimal vertical complexity:

> The organization of the professional departments tends to be rather "flat." That is, the concept of equality among professionals (lawyers should be given equal status within a legal department) leads to little differentiation within a department. The model followed is the collegial, which is characterized by a few formal distinctions or norms and by little in the way of formalized vertical or horizontal differentiation.[3]

Second, while there may still be a complex division of labor in the activities performed in a professional organization, this complexity is "a consequence of the differentiation of the activities among the professionals and is thus not a formal organizational characteristic."[4] In other words, the differentiation is a result of the nature of the discipline itself and not a procedural differentiation imposed by the operation of the organization.

Third, professionalization diminishes the need for formalized organizational rules. Hall says, "Since professionals have internalized norms and standards, the imposition of organizational requirements is not only unnecessary; it is likely to lead to professional-organizational conflict."[5] Etzioni observes, "When people with strong professional orientations take over managerial roles, a conflict between the organizational goals and the professional orientation usually occurs."[6] Lynch addresses this conflict when she summarizes the differences between the authority of bureaucracy, or the formal organization, and professionalism:

> Bureaucratic authority rests not so much on technical skills or competencies as on official position. Bureaucratic authority requires subordinates to comply with directives under threat of some sanction. Professional authority rests upon possession of expertise. It requires an abstract body of knowledge to support the technical skills. Professional authority is

self-governing through an association of peers, professional standards of practice and ethical conduct. Professionalism has a service orientation.[7]

While it cannot be said that organizational formalization stifles professionalism, it may be argued that over-formalization produces a climate in which professionalism cannot flourish.

The personnel data, job classifications, and position descriptions assembled for study in this chapter are intended to measure the professionalism of librarianship by comparing formalization in the duties of public librarians with the professionalism of their public service duties of mediating the collection to individuals with widely varying needs.

Library Formalization

According to Hage,

> formalization, or standardization, is measured by the proportion of codified jobs and the range of variation that is tolerated within the rules defining the jobs. The higher the proportion of codified jobs and the less the range of variation allowed, the more formalized the organization.[8]

The classification documents and position descriptions following this chapter are intended to indicate (1) the typical duties performed in public libraries, (2) the differentiation between professional and non-professional duties, (3) the differentiation of duties between professional librarian levels, and (4) the methods by which labor is divided among professional librarians. They also indicate the degree of formality in the public library, which in turn will say a great deal about the professionalism of librarianship.

The position descriptions from Library C (pp. 104–141) are included to show complete rosters of jobs from a large public library. The descriptions indicate a clear demarcation between positions necessitated by the organization and those positions which perform the duties of professional librarianship. The organizationally imposed positions inlcude clerical as well as administrative positions. In other words, the functions of these positions are not involved directly in the practice of library science, and are similar to positions that exist in any other organization. They maintain an environment within which librarianship can be practiced.

The professional positions, on the other hand, are the locus of librarianship, as the job descriptions make plain. Yet within the range of professional positions we do not see the clear demarcation between the classifications that is so apparent between the professional and the nonprofessional groups.

This lack of differentiation is evident again in the descriptions contained in pages 141–174. The librarian I–III classifications from Library D (pp. 141–144), for instance, differentiate primarily on the basis of supervisory responsibility and experience. The same is true for the librarian positions of Library I (pp. 144–148), although the position titles and the relative criteria for each are different. Here also, and in other examples, classification is based on geographical departmentation.

The cataloger descriptions from Library U (pages 169–174) show an extreme case in which classification is assigned almost as a consequence of the cataloging procedure. Likewise, the other professional positions included from Library U are influenced heavily from a geographical division of labor.

The underlying assumptions of these classifications schemes, of course, is that longer professional experience makes a librarian better qualified as a cataloger, supervisor, or what have you. And civil service stipulations concerning seniority certainly enter into the devising of any job classification scheme.

Nevertheless, the librarian classifications have an appearance of artificiality. The division of labor among the professional classifications is more according to the typical methods of departmentation, as discussed in Chapter 1, than to those methods peculiar to librarianship. In short, the vertical complexity within the professional levels of the public library is largely a function of organizational formality, not of professionalism. For instance, that librarians catalog materials is professionally determined. But that the general practice of cataloging should be so finely divided into the hierarchy mandated by the job descriptions of Library U is an organizational, not a professional, development.

One result of this type of division may be an inefficient correlation of professional training and actual job duties in the public library. (This loosening of the connection between training and duties has been hastened by the recent increased use of paraprofessional categories, especially when they are inflated and formalized to the degree of the library technician and information specialist positions of Library C [pp. 118–123, 129–133].) Still another result may be diminishment of the stature of librarianship as a genuine profession.

As mentioned earlier, research has shown that the formalization of an organization is greatly affected by the relative number of professionals present. According to Hall,

> formalization and professionalization are actually designed to do the same thing — organize and regularize the behavior of the members of the organization. Formalization is a process in which the organization sets the rules and procedures and the means of ensuring that they are followed. Professionalization, on the other hand, is a nonorganizationally based means of doing the same thing.[9]

In other words, professionals belong to two occupational organizations simultaneously. The presence of professionals in an organization, especially in large numbers, represents the interaction of two organizations in the same environment. In highly professional organizations, formalization and professionalism are inversely related. Again, Hall:

> Studies of professionals in organizations have come up with quite consistent findings: The organizations involved are less formalized than organizations without professionals. As the level of professionalization of the employees increases, the level of formalization decreases. . . . The presence of professionals appears to cause a diminished need for formalized rules and procedures.[10]

As previously discussed, conflict can occur in highly formalized organizations that also employ a large complement or professionals. Because librarianship does not display all of the qualities customarily associated with professions, this conflict may be markedly reduced in its organizations. According to Etzioni, semi-professionals

> often have skills and personality traits more compatible with administration, especially since the qualities required for communication of knowledge are more like those needed for administration than those required for the creation and, to a degree, application of knowledge. Hence these organizations are run much more frequently by semi-professionals than by others.[11]

Indeed the job descriptions for library administrators in pages 174–190 show that in terms of administrative hierarchy, library managers for the most part are themselves librarians. This is the case in other semi-professions as well, such as teaching, social work, and nursing. In this regard, libraries resemble law firms, in which the directors tend to be attorneys, but they differ from clinics and hospitals, in which administrators typically are not physicians.

The question arises: Why must it be this way? In a large library, especially a large library system, it may be advantageous for the administrators to be professional managers instead of professional librarians. The assistant directors for management services of Library C (p. 105) and for nonpublic services of Library D (p. 174) indicate that nonlibrarians may fit well into library administrative positions that are, primarily at least, concerned with organizational formality as opposed to the duties of professional librarianship.

If the assertion is correct that an administrator's professional training often conflicts with organizational goals, increasing professionalization among librarians may make them less able administrators. Libraries are becoming increasingly dependent on non–library-trained experts such as programmers, systems analysts, and grantsmen. It may now be appropriate for the library profession to reconsider itself and pattern the library after a hospital, so that the business of sustaining the organization can be relegated to expert administrators, leaving librarians to ply the core skills of their profession. The core of librarianship, after all, is not library management, programming, or grant writing. Professional librarianship has to do with building and mediating the collection, as will be discussed below.

The job descriptions in pages 190–195 include a number of positions which deserve attention because they are so common to public libraries. Most of these positions fall into the categories of age-level or materials selection coordinators. These generally are closely related since a major function of age-level coordinators is selection, as the job descriptions show. To the extent that these positions perform mere selection, they are not peculiar to libraries, but are analogous to buyers for department stores and supermarkets, making sure that supplies keep pace with demand.

Actual collection development, however, is not the same as selection. Collection development proceeds less according to demand and more according to the logic of the discipline being developed. Yet few job descriptions gathered for this book addressed collection development. Even descriptions for the materials selection positions of libraries S and Y (pp. 194–195) fail to elaborate on the special nature of genuine collection development.

The coordinator of resources position from Library D (page 195), the materials selection positions at Library N (pp. 196–198) and the coordinator of collection development at Library U (pp. 204–205) come closer to collection development. As such, they suggest the professional task, peculiar to librarianship, of assembling a comprehensive collection that represents all the theoretical and practical positions that may be taken with regard to the disciplines contained in the collection.

The other descriptions in pages 195–216 illustrate positions that are also distinctive of the profession of librarianship in that they relate to methods of departmentation that are peculiar to libraries as discussed in Chapter 1, namely circulation and subject departmentation. Classification and cataloging were discussed earlier.

It is interesting that the function of circulation, being primarily clerical, is handled by nonprofessionals. This suggests that although a circulating inventory is unique to libraries, the task of circulating materials is not one of the distinguishing features of the practice of librarianship. Library U prefers trained professionals to perform the interlibrary loan function (pp. 206–207), which is an extension of circulation. But again, a professional degree is not required for this service, which is also unique to libraries.

The subject department job descriptions from libraries U (pp. 201–204) and V (pp. 207–216) demonstrate the scope that can be involved in library subject departmentation and the importance the public library as an organization places on this method of departmentation. Although these positions, like the cataloger positions discussed earlier, are overly formalized, they reflect the relative command of specialized knowledge among the librarians, and are less determined merely by organizational procedures. As will be discussed below, subject expertise may also have a significant bearing on librarians' claims to professionalism.

Judging from the job descriptions, then, it appears that at the preprofessional and administrative levels, libraries are no more formalized with respect to job classification than any other type of organization, including professions. But among professional librarian levels, the formalization may be overly drawn in comparison with other professional organizations. Often this involves an increase in rank with no appreciable increase in supervisory responsibility and barely discernible differences in duties among the four or five professional ranks. These minute, contrived distinctions, along with the more gross divisions between clerical, paraprofessional, and professional classifications, detract from the professionalism of librarianship. Excessive formalization in libraries is detrimental to the professionalism of librarians, and causes more conflict than would otherwise occur, especially among semi-professionals.

Complexity in Libraries

Organizational complexity is a result of the division of labor, and can be measured by the number of positions and subunits in the organization. The degree of horizontal complexity in an organization depends on the way tasks are divided among its units. Vertical complexity is apparent in the number of supervisory layers in the hierarchy of authority.

Research indicates that complexity, especially vertical complexity, is not necessarily inversely related to professionalism.[12] For instance, the presence of professionals in an organization, because they act with a high degree of autonomy, requires exacting organizational communication that may entail an increase in the number of hierarchical layers. Yet if organizational formalization differentiates duties beyond the norms of professional training and ethics, then we may say that the resulting complexity conflicts with the professional standards.

The job descriptions in this book show that the complexity of libraries, as depicted in preceding organizational charts and in contrast with the "flat" professional organizations described by Hall, is also organizationally and not professionally imposed. Based on the documentation assembled here, there is a lack of "equality" among librarians, and a tendency to horizontal and vertical complexity beyond what would normally be required in a professional organization, even one with services, clientele, and materials as diverse as those of the public library.

The organization of the public library is hardly flat. There is a good deal of vertical differentiation within departments, and this complexity is not directly atrributable to the norms, ethics, or training of librarianship, but to the formalization of the public library itself.

In light of these observations, then, we see in libraries more formalization than is present among full-fledged professions as well as more horizontal or vertical complexity. This formalization can have an adverse effect on the professional stature of librarians and on their ability to behave as professionals. But also, there is a greater propensity among librarians as semi-professionals toward self-administration, with a more limited likelihood of conflict between organizational and professional goals than would exist in a full-fledged professional organization.

The Interpersonal Nature of the Profession

One thing to be learned from the collection of job descriptions is that they are written with regard to bureaucratic, not professional, issues. They do not address strongly enough the service aspect of professional librarianship that requires deft interpersonal skills. To investigate this area of librarianship, we must turn to other sources than the job descriptions, primarily to the professional literature, which substantiates the common conception that librarianship is preeminently a service-oriented endeavor.

As Drake contends, the basic objective of the library is client-oriented information services.[13] The librarian's main purpose is to mediate a carefully developed collection to library users, usually in private, personalized consultations. Of course, this entails related functions such as acquisitions to secure the desired resources, cataloging to ensure the accessibility of materials, circulation control to extend to users the convenience of lending, and a host of others. These related functions must somehow be organizationally accommodated within the library's total operation. Nevertheless, they exist to support the librarian's task of negotiating information in terms of specific individual requests, however recurrent and commonplace they may at times be.

Two characteristics previously mentioned as distinguishing full-fledged professions from semi-professions are the presence or absence in interpersonal transactions of (1) a concern with matters of life and death, and (2) an intention to observe and protect confidentiality as part of a professional's duties. Reference departments of public libraries have their share of cases involving terminal diseases, spouse beatings, child abuse, euthanasia, suicide, homelessness, jurisprudence, and other life-and-death issues. Furthermore, reference librarians are trained to observe standards of privacy in conducting reference interviews and searches, and may be expected to object to invasions of their right to professional confidentiality as strenuously as any physician or attorney. On these issues, then, public librarianship approaches full professional standards.

The reference interview is perhaps the best indicator of the librarian's claim to professionalism and the essence of librarianship as collection mediation through interpersonal transaction. According to Taylor,[14] a library user may pass through as many as four successive levels while formulating a request for information: (1) the visceral, or unconscious; (2) the conscious; (3) the formalized; and (4) the compromised, which produces the final, rational form of the question structured in terms of the user's assessment of what the library may be able to deliver. Unfortunately, this final form may well be erroneous due to the user's misassessment of the library and its resources. The librarian's job, then, says Taylor, "is to work with the inquirer back to the formalized need, possibly even to the conscious need, and then to translate these needs into a useful search strategy."[15]

The librarian accomplishes this by passing the user's compromised question through five "filters": (1) the real subject of the inquiry; (2) objective and motivation of the inquirer; (3) personal characteristics of the inquirer; (4) relationship of the inquiry description to file organization; and (5) anticipated or acceptable answers.[16] These sophisticated and subtle maneuvers require an interpersonal expertise extending far beyond the mechanics of simply managing an overabundance of information and mastering the technologies developed for its handling. To mediate the collection effectively, the librarian must perform a dual feat of managing information, which the library's formal organization is intended to operationalize, and exercise an interpersonal finesse, which the formal organization all too often hinders, but which is the basis of a librarian's training, ethics, and professionalism.

Speaking of a process she calls "referral," Bates helps us understand better how the library's formal organization should function to allow the librarian to articulate his or her role as a collection mediator. She observes:

> With referral there is a leap from the whole body of information to the specific information desired, or at least a significantly smaller segment of the information than the whole body. The leap from the whole to the part is crucial to the idea of referral.[17]

We might add that leaping back again from the part to the whole is equally crucial, and may well involve leaps from one portion of the collection to another. Librarians know, for instance, that a reverse leap from specific data in the reference collection to a broad subject discipline in the general collection is not uncommon. One purpose of the reference collection is to provide introductory or background information on unfamiliar topics which the user may then research in the subject collections, very possibly with continued assistance from a librarian acting as a subject specialist.

Librarianship involves the ability to move with facility back and forth between the whole body of the collection and any of the segments thereof, always according to the needs of the individual user as they are carefully determined by the librarian. Thus there are three possible relationships between the user, the librarian, and the collection. First, the user may interact directly with the collection and have little or no assistance from the librarian. Second, the user may interact primarily with the librarian, who uses the collection as the resource for addressing the user's needs. Third, the user may interact with the collection and the librarian in a pattern of information retrieval or educational development appropriate to the situation.

Whenever the librarian actively enters into a relationship with a user, it is as a collection mediator responding to individual needs that are often quite complex. In this way, interpersonal transactions organize the practice of librarianship at least as much as organizational arrangements and job classifications. Indeed, the library's formalization complexity must not inhibit the librarian's ability to perform the interpersonal transactions. For it to do so would defeat the purpose of the library and librarianship.

Subject Departmentation

Subject departmentation was discussed as a method of organizational arrangement in Chapter 1. According to Wilkinson, it is also a measure of a librarian's professionalism. We recall his statement that librarians

> must choose between either offering services based upon independent, accountable judgments that arise from individual expertise and a body of specialized, expanding knowledge, or offering ingress to institutionally generated and controlled collections.[18]

Wilkinson is actually talking about the organizational-professional conflict that has already been mentioned, but he portrays it in the specific terms of an operational conflict between subject collection development and expertise as opposed to the library's organizational goal to build a broad, comprehensive collection.

To the extent that subject specialization constitutes the specialized knowledge base that characterizes professionalism, librarians may, following this line reasoning, lay additional claim to professionalism by becoming expert in specialized subject fields. And because subject specialization may vary widely between individual librarians, Wilkinson implies that library professionalism is a combination of expertise in library science and a content area.

This concept of library professionalism emphasizes the fact that quality librarianship ultimately depends on an individual effort, as is the case with all professions. Pursell says that there are three primary characteristics of professional work.[19] First:

> Professional work is concerned with investigation. Professional assignments always involve conducting investigations for the purpose of drawing scientific conclusions or solving technical problems.

Second:

> A professional worker is primarily concerned with the execution of technical work and secondarily with planning, organizing, and directing work carried out by others. Even though the individual may be the leader of a team or group attempting to reach a common objective, the professional worker will be making a substantial part of the contribution in an individual fashion.

Third, professional work is not repetitious or routine:

> It does not follow a pattern or cycle or consist of specialized duties and responsibilities as does the work of managerial or administrative positions. Professional work consists of a series of assignments, each having a beginning and end.

These characteristics are applicable to the reference interview as described by Taylor. A librarian, generally as an autonomous individual, investigates each user's request, each displaying some degree of uniqueness. The librarian then prescribes an item or obtains information that is suitable to the specific needs of the user. When the development of a subject expertise is added, as Wilkinson suggests, the professionalism of librarianship is further enhanced. Also, these characteristics clearly distinguish between the professional aspects of librarianship and the clerical and the administrative functions of running a library, which distinctions are apparent in the job descriptions included in this chapter.

Pursell's characteristics of professional work allow ample opportunity for increasing complexity within a professional organization. As mentioned before, organizational complexity is not necessarily contradictory to professionalism if that complexity is associated with the tasks required by the practice of the profession. But formalization, especially excessive formalization, would clearly upset the performance of professional work, as Pursell describes it. The formalization and much of the complexity in the public library is the result of bureaucracy and not professionalism, as the job descriptions indicate.

Conclusions

The documents discussed in Chapters 1 and 2 support Lynch's contention that the public library is highly bureaucratic, in the Weberian sense that much of its arrangement and many of its tasks exist primarily to maintain the organization itself. Organizational charts show that horizontal and vertical differentiation in public libraries are significant. Job descriptions show that these differentiations are due to an equally complex differentiation in job classifications, intense separation of duties, overly drawn rules and procedures, and artificial hierarchical ladders.

We have seen that the conflict existing between professionalism and formalism in professional organizations also exists in the public library, even though according to some criteria it may be classified as a semi-professional organization. In the public library, the conflict exists in terms of the organization's overly complex and formal distinctions between professional librarians and the librarian's professional calling to provide individualized collection mediation services. A secondary but related conflict exists between the librarian's need for subject specialization and the library's goal to build and mediate a collection that is broad and rather general.

These conflicts, while they detract from the professionalism of librarians, explain certain characteristics of librarianship such as (1) the "inherent difference of opinion between library managers and staff members over the type of organizational structure needed to achieve organizational goals,"[20] (2) the "prevailing attitude among librarians ... that the professional's work suffers from the constraints of bureaucratic conditions,"[21] and (3) the desire of librarians to be granted a more active role in decision making.[22]

Chapter 3 will relate these characteristics of conflict to the structure of the public library as a social institution, and demonstrate how they contribute to the meaning of the library in society.

Job Descriptions

Complete Job Description Set

The following job descriptions represent the complete range of positions for Library C.

Position Title: Account Clerk

NATURE OF WORK

This is varied and complex bookkeeping and related clerical work. An incumbent in this class is responsible for maintaining journals and ledgers involving a variety of accounts. Specific work details may vary with the nature of assignment but may include bookkeeping. This employee usually works with a considerable degree of independence on routine operations although on more difficult assignments, professional assistance is available. Judgment is limited to interpreting ordinances, State and Federal codes, or division/branch accounting regulations and classifications in terms of day-to-day transaction recording and preparation of the less complex financial reports. All work is subject to periodic audits and review.

This employee reports to and receives instructions from the Assistant Director, Management Services or other employee designated as supervisor.

ILLUSTRATIVE EXAMPLES OF WORK

- Processes bi-weekly payroll and verify time cards, audit payroll pre-run.
- Calculates vacation leave and severance pay for all employees.
- Prepares invoices and claim sheets for payment.
- Prepares receipts for remittance to City Treasurer.
- Maintains petty cash fund.
- Maintains Data Processing reports for necessary documentation.
- Verifies payment of invoices, file vouchers and supporting documents.
- Performs related work as requested.

KNOWLEDGE, SKILLS AND ABILITIES

- Considerable knowledge of bookkeeping principles, methods and techniques.
- Working knowledge of office methods and procedures.
- Some knowledge of government bookkeeping practices and of standard office equipment.
- Considerable knowledge of library policies and procedures.
- Skill and ability to calculate rapidly.

MINIMUM EXPERIENCE AND TRAINING

High school graduate including or supplemented by course work in accounting with three (3) years of accounting experience; or any equivalent combination of experience and training.

Position Title: Administrative Intern

NATURE OF WORK

Under close direction, may be assigned various areas of professional/technical support work in Public Services, Management Services, or Personnel.

ILLUSTRATIVE EXAMPLES OF WORK

- Collects, compiles and reports data.
- Reviews published material to gather information.
- Performs arithmetic calculations.
- Prepares statistical tabulations, analyzes results and prepares reports accordingly.
- Writes narrative and statistical reports on investigation and research studies.
- Assists in the development of studies and recommendations.
- Assists with the handling of minor administrative or technical details.
- May communicate verbally with a range of citizens and staff.

KNOWLEDGE, SKILLS AND ABILITIES. Ability and skill to:

- Gather information from written sources.
- Maintain neat, accurate records.
- Follow oral and written instructions.
- Communicate effectively both orally and in writing.
- Perform accurate mathematic computations.
- Work with various levels of staff.
- Complete assignments in a timely manner.
- Write clear and accurate reports.

MINIMUM EXPERIENCE AND TRAINING

Education: Equivalent to completion of the junior level of education (15 years) in an accredited four year college/university. Experience: None required.

Position Title: Assistant Director for Management Services

NATURE OF WORK

This is executive and administrative work involving advanced professional accounting duties, planning, evaluating and management. The Assistant Director—Management Services assists the Director in planning, fiscal management and control, facilities management, preparation of recommendations for Board action, and in representing the Library at civic, library-related and other meetings of benefit to the system. The Assistant Director — Management Services participates in the administrative team with the Assistant Director for Public Services and the Personnel Officer. The Assistant Director — Management Services acts for the Director when assigned.

This employee reports to and receives general instruction from the Director.

ILLUSTRATIVE EXAMPLES OF WORK

- Assists the Director in making studies and evaluation of library operations, and service programs from an administrative point of view and for the planning of system development.
- Prepares preliminary drafts of annual budgets which may include trust funds, federal and state grants, federal shared-revenue monies and city funds.
- Audits and maintains financial internal control within the Library and is responsible for the financial operation of the Library under the conditions set forth in the annual budget.
- Coordinates and supervises the operation of networking, facilities, technical services and the financial area of the Business Office of the Library.
- Acts in place of the Director when assigned.
- Prepares studies and recommendations on facilities management within the Library system.
- Prepares specifications and administers contracts for the purchases of services and supplies for the Library system.

KNOWLEDGE, SKILLS AND ABILITIES

- Extensive knowledge of accounting and business procedures to include indirect cost accounting and purchasing.
- Thorough knowledge of laws, rules and regulations governing accounting, auditing procedures and purchasing.
- Considerable knowledge of the operation of all system units for the purpose of assessing practical and administrative problems and recommending to the appropriate division/branch head action to improve the performance of public service.
- Ability and skill to assemble and correlate ideas and information relating to computerized accounting for library services for the formulation of plans, policies and procedures.
- Ability and skill to prepare technical bid documents and administer contracts.

MINIMUM EXPERIENCE AND TRAINING

Graduate of an accredited university with a major in a field relating to accounting and business management. Must have five years of progressively responsible experience in public/business administration with demonstrated ability to perform duties required.

Position Title: *Assistant Director for Public Services*

NATURE OF WORK

This is executive and administrative work. The Assistant Director for Public Services assists the Director in coordinating the work of employees, in making studies and evaluations of the Library's programs, in preparing recommendations to the Board, in staff and public relations, and in representing the Library at professional meetings. In conjunction with the Assistant Director, Management Services and the Personnel Officer, functions as the administrative team to the Director.

This employee reports to and receives general instruction from the Director.

ILLUSTRATIVE EXAMPLES OF WORK

* Supervises public services for the Library system.
* Provides direction for the Public Information Officer.
* Assists the Director in preparing and administering the annual budget.
* Maintains communications with the staff of supervisors, and assists the Director by recommending actions to improve performance and delivery of services.
* Represents the Library at civic, professional and other meetings as delegated by the Director and Board.
* Performs related work as assigned by the Director.
* Acts in place of the Director when assigned or when the Director is absent.

KNOWLEDGE, SKILLS AND ABILITIES

* Must have extensive knowledge, ability and skill in public relations, group leadership dynamics, and human resource management.
* Must have broad and comprehensive knowledge of current library theories and practices.
* Ability and skill required to assemble and correlate information and ideas relating to public library services for the formation of policies.
* Extensive knowledge of the operation of branches and divisions of the library for the purpose of assessing their practical and administrative problems and recommending actions to improve public services.
* Considerable knowledge of program planning and budgeting.

MINIMUM EXPERIENCE AND TRAINING

Must have at least six years of progressively responsible experience as a librarian with demonstrated ability and skill in planning, organizing and managing — particularly in the public library field. Must be a graduate of an accredited library school and be eligible for a certificate issued by the State Board for Certification of Librarians.

Position Title: Clerical Assistant

NATURE OF WORK

This is office and clerical work of a routine nature. An employee in this class is responsible for the performance, according to well established library procedures, of clerical tasks which can be readily learned by training on the job. Detailed instructions and close supervision are given at the beginning of the work and on subsequent new assignments; however, as employees become familiar with the particular procedures, they may work with independence of action on the more routine aspects of the work. Advice is given employee on unusual work problems and this work is usually reviewed or checked upon completion.

This employee reports to and receives general instruction from a librarian or other employee designated as supervisor.

ILLUSTRATIVE EXAMPLES OF WORK

- Maintains simple files; files materials alphabetically, numerically, or by other predetermined methods.
- May pick up, sort and send out mail including placing material in envelopes or packages, stamping mail, keeping postage records and operating postage machine.
- May deliver materials between branches, main library and/or other locations.
- Compiles tabulations from records at hand and prepares reports of a standardized and routine nature.
- Operates calculating and duplicating machines.
- Answers telephone. May assist the public in circulation and registration routines.
- Types correspondence, reports and other information.
- Answers directional questions and refers other questions to proper employee.
- Performs related work as required.

KNOWLEDGE, SKILLS AND ABILITIES

- Working knowledge of modern office practices and procedures, and of English and arithmetic.
- Skill and ability to understand and follow oral and written instructions.
- Good judgment in making minor decisions in accordance with policies and procedures of the library.
- Skill and ability to learn assigned clerical tasks.
- Skill and ability to type 35 words per minute.
- Evening and Saturday work may be required.

MINIMUM EXPERIENCE AND TRAINING

High school graduation or equivalent. Some experience in general office or clerical work is desirable. Drivers license and good driving record may be required.

Position Title: Clerk

NATURE OF WORK

This is advanced office and clerical work which may require skilled typing. An incumbent in this class performs moderately complex clerical operations requiring the application of judgment based on knowledge gained through experience. Decisions are made in accordance with established library policies and procedures. The variety and difficulty of the work is repetitive, there is an added responsibility for finality of action. The more difficult and important work is performed under close supervision. Advice is given the employee on unusual, difficult or important matters. This employee reports to and receives general instruction from a librarian or other employee delegated to supervise Clerks.

ILLUSTRATIVE EXAMPLES OF WORK

- Performs all duties of a Clerical Assistant plus additional responsibilities which may include the following:
- Types forms, accounting and financial statements, letters, vouchers, departmental reports and other materials requiring independent judgment.
- Maintains general department files and a variety of other records incidental to the more difficult work.
- May train subordinates in the same division in facets of the area.
- Records time worked by individual employees.
- Schedule may include evenings and Saturdays.
- Performs related work as required.
- Mends library books and magazines.

KNOWLEDGE, SKILLS AND ABILITIES

- Considerable knowledge of library policies and procedures, and of business English and arithmetic.
- Skill and ability to apply good judgment in making minor decisions in accordance with library policies.
- Skill and ability to understand and follow complex oral and written instructions.
- Ability and skill in performing computations, in filing, in maintaining other office records, and in operating common office equipment.
- Skill and ability to assign and supervise the work of subordinate if delegated to do so.

- Skill and ability to perform basic mathematics.
- Skill and ability to type 45 words per minute.
- Evening and Saturday work may be required.

MINIMUM EXPERIENCE AND TRAINING

High school graduation or equivalent plus experience in performing one year of library work. Drivers license and good driving record may be required.

Position Title: Community Relations Officer

NATURE OF WORK

This is skilled professional supervisory work and requires initiative, imagination and commitment to the overall goals and objectives of the organization. An incumbent in this class serves as the primary consultant to the Management staff of the Library in matters of communication and community relations.

ILLUSTRATIVE EXAMPLES OF WORK

- Assesses internal and external communication needs.
- Supervises and instructs community relations staff in publicity, printing, graphic arts and photography.
- Acts as a liaison with special interest groups as designated by the Assistant Director for Public Service.
- Speaks for management with the media.
- Assists managers in formulating programs to meet library needs.
- Implements communications/public relations programs.
- Represents the Library at public functions and/or on boards, commissions and committees, as designated by the Assistant Director for Public Service or Director.
- Conceives and designs informational materials (i.e., brochures, charts, pamphlets).
- Performs writing and editing assignments to develop and facilitate the dissemination of written informational materials.
- Provides technical assistance to branch/division librarians.
- Coordinates requests with available materials and facilities.
- Coordinates displays in the gallery.
- Performs related work as assigned.

KNOWLEDGE, SKILLS AND ABILITIES

- Extensive knowledge, ability and skill in the preparation and application of community relation methods and tools.
- Skill and ability to plan and direct work of others; instruct and supervise staff and confer and communicate with them to maintain good working production.

- Skill and ability to relate well to people and to understand and function within a complex organization.
- Express self clearly and concisely both in oral and written form.
- Self motivation and operation with a minimum of direction.

MINIMUM EXPERIENCE AND TRAINING

Should have a B.A. degree in English, journalism, communications, allied fields or equivalent four years experience in communication and inter-personal relations. Extensive work experience with the mass media is essential. Must have demonstrated ability and experience of previous public relations work.

Position Title: Computer Technician

NATURE OF WORK

This is skilled technical work involving most phases of operation of computer systems and related peripheral devices. The Computer Technician is responsible for monitoring the operation of the library computer systems, diagnosing problems, and working with maintenance vendors, suppliers of systems in use in the library, and library staff to maintain and improve day-to-day operation and performance. Duties are performed under general supervision of a higher classification. Assignments are evaluated for accuracy and completeness.

ILLUSTRATIVE EXAMPLES OF WORK

- Operates the Central site computer system, such as mounting tapes, setting up printers, backing up disc files, observing console, etc;
- Receives equipment for repair, clean and dispatch terminals;
- Inventories equipment and purchase necessary supplies;
- Diagnoses communication and terminal problems;
- Arranges for repair or replacement of equipment;
- Reviews equipment vendor manuals to determine operating principles of computer and related peripheral devices;
- Keeps current the Computer Operator manuals, reflecting changes in operating requirements and techniques;
- Trains other library staff in operation and use of the computer system and related peripheral devices;
- Performs related work as required, such as data entry, etc;
- Schedule may include evenings, weekends, and on-call work.

KNOWLEDGE, SKILLS AND ABILITIES

- Considerable knowledge of the practical application of computer operation and procedures;
- Working knowledge of data processing procedures and terminology;
- Ability to comprehend and apply the information found in technical

manuals and related literature with judgement and initiative to troubleshoot equipment and communication problems;
- Planning and scheduling skills;
- Ability and skill to establish and maintain effective communication and working relationships with other employees and system users;
- Ability and skill in training and communication;
- Ability and skill to organize work and carry through established procedures and work plans to meet scheduled deadlines;
- Data entry skills;
- Programming skills in some high-level language.

MINIMUM EXPERIENCE AND TRAINING

Must be a high school graduate or equivalent; two (2) years of experience in computer operation, preferably supplemented by vocational training in data processing, with some emphasis on basic hardware maintenance and trouble-shooting; or any equivalent combination of experience and training. Experience and training must include responsible work operating a combination of computer and auxiliary equipment, in equipment in an operating environment comparable to that in the Library.

Position Title: Confidential Secretary

NATURE OF WORK

This is confidential secretarial work for the principal administrative officials of the library. An incumbent is this class is responsible for the performance of confidential secretarial and related clerical duties in the Administrative Office. Work also involves additional secretarial duties for administrators, boards and other groups. This incumbent performs work which is distinguished from that of other clerical classifications by emphasis on secretarial duties or office management functions which require excellent judgment and reliability in acting for the superior on delegated administrative detail and maintaining the confidential integrity of subject matter. Employee must use independent judgment in determination on varied problems which do not involve major deviation from established policy or procedure. Though supervisory responsibilities are not ordinarily important, the employee may be responsible for the direction and coordination of delegated projects.

This employee reports to and receives general instruction from the Director.

ILLUSTRATIVE EXAMPLES OF WORK

- Types sometimes difficult dictaphone materials for letters, memoranda, speeches and reports.
- Answers correspondence which is of confidential nature.
- Follows up on reports and other clerical and administrative matters to assist

superior in the smooth operation of office or department.
- Sets up and maintains an efficient filing system and performs related work in connecton with supplying her/his employer with required information or data when needed.
- Performs related work as required.

KNOWLEDGE, SKILLS AND ABILITIES

- Considerable knowledge of Library operations and policies and procedures.
- Considerable knowledge of business English and modern office practices and procedures.
- Skill and ability to compose properly a variety of memoranda or letters with only general instructions.
- Skill and ability to understand and follow complex written or oral instruction.
- Skill and ability to receive, screen or admit, and give varied information to callers, many of whom are in professional, public or community groups.
- Skill and ability to take dictation/shorthand at 100 WPM.
- Skill and ability to type 80 WPM.

MINIMUM EXPERIENCE AND TRAINING

Considerable experience in performing progressively responsible clerical and secretarial work, preferably including some experience as secretary responsible to an executive or administrator. High school graduation preferably supplemented by graduation from a technical business school; or any equivalent combination of experience and training.

Position Title: Custodial Assistant

NATURE OF WORK

This is routine manual custodial work in library buildings. An employee in this class is responsible for the efficient performance of essentially routine janitorial services in and around library buildings. Specific instructions are received on unusual jobs and routine assignments are checked by spot inspections or as the result of complaints.

ILLUSTRATIVE EXAMPLES OF WORK

- Reports such damage to structure and equipment as requires repairs.
- Replaces light bulbs and cleans fixtures and washes windows.
- Dusts, polishes, arranges and moves furniture and equipment.
- Sweeps, mops, scrubs and polishes floors; dusts and cleans offices, washes woodwork and walls.
- Performs related work as required.

KNOWLEDGE, SKILLS AND ABILITIES

- Some knowledge of cleaning methods and equipment.
- Skill and ability to exercise care in the use of cleaning materials and equipment.
- Skill and ability to follow oral and written instructions.
- Skill and ability to perform routine operations involved in simple custodial duties without close supervision.
- Sufficient physical strength to withstand the strain of custodial work.
- May require the ability to work evenings and weekends as scheduled.

MINIMUM EXPERIENCE AND TRAINING

None is required.

Position Title: Custodian

NATURE OF WORK

This is routine and semi-skilled manual work in the cleaning and maintenance of library buildings and grounds on an assigned shift. An incumbent in this class is responsible to and receives general instructions from the crew leader or superintendent of maintenance.

ILLUSTRATIVE EXAMPLES OF WORK

- Cleans restrooms and replaces all supplies.
- Sweeps, mop scrubs, polishes floors; cleans ceilings, fixtures, walks, windows and other interior and exterior surfaces of buildings; dusts books, shelvings, furniture, etc.
- Relaces light bulbs and tubes.
- Cleans walks and grounds; may mow lawns, maintains neat appearance of planted areas, shrubbery, trees, etc.
- General painting of exterior and interior areas of library buildings.
- Maintains all supplies, tools, equipment used in his/her work in good order and requisitions their replacement through the crew leader.
- Reports in writing, promptly, to the crew leader all damage noticed in connection with the structure, grounds, equipment, furniture, or fixtures of the assigned area.
- Performs related work as required.

KNOWLEDGE, SKILLS AND ABILITIES

- Knowledge of housekeeping and cleaning methods and procedures.
- Working knowledge of the use of materials and supplies for custodial work, such as soaps, detergents, powders, polishes, oils and waxes.
- Working knowledge of safety rules in connection with ladders, tools, electrical and mechanical equipment.

- Skill and ability to understand oral and written instructions.
- Manual dexterity and physical strength necessary to do required work.
- Have the ability to work evenings and/or weekends.

MINIMUM EXPERIENCE AND TRAINING

One year (1) of experience in janitorial or related custodial work or any equivalent combination of experience and training.

Position Title: Crew Leader

NATURE OF WORK

This is supervisory and skilled work in connection with the maintenance and cleaning of library buildings and grounds on an assigned shift. An employee is this class is responsible for directing the activities of the fireman/custodian and custodians engaged in cleaning, maintenance and repair duties on a specific shift. Work includes the keeping of time and materials records as well as performing skilled maintenance tasks in carpentry, plumbing and the electrical area. General instructions are received from the Superintendent of Maintenance and the employee is responsible for the carrying out of these instructions. Work is reviewed through results attained and inspections by the Superintendent.

ILLUSTRATIVE EXAMPLES OF WORK

- Supervises and participates in semiskilled repair and maintenance tasks.
- Performs minor electrical repairs and installations.
- Performs carpentry work in restoration and construction.
- Performs plumbing repairs as needed.
- Inspects building, checking on the adequacy of the work of employees.
- Checks for the need of repair and maintenance.

KNOWLEDGE, SKILLS AND ABILITIES

- Considerable knowledge of the methods, tools and equipment used in building maintenance and repair work.
- Skill and ability to participate in and supervise personnel engaged in building cleaning and building heating systems.
- Skill and ability to conduct electrical inspections and make repairs as needed.
- Skill and ability to make plumbing repairs.
- Must have the knowledge, skill and ability to complete general repairs and maintenance in the library and its branches.
- Ability to work scheduled evenings and/or weekends.

MINIMUM EXPERIENCE AND TRAINING

Considerable proven experience, three (3) years or more, in building maintenance, repair and custodial work; completion of the eighth grade; or any equivalent combination of experience and training. Must hold a stationary (low pressure boiler) fireman's license issued to him/her in his/her name by the City.

Position Title: Fireman/Custodian

NATURE OF WORK

This is semi-skilled work in connection with the maintenance and custodial care of the library building facilities on assigned shifts. An employee in this class is responsible for the performance of routine cleaning operations, facility security, maintaining the heating system, and related custodial work. Duties also include the performance of varied building maintenance tasks. Work is subject to inspection and review at any time.

ILLUSTRATED EXAMPLES OF WORK

- Performs all duties and tasks of a custodian.
- Performs assigned repair and maintenance jobs relating to buildings, grounds, mechanical and electrical systems.
- Takes down boilers as required for the boiler inspector, and cleans and maintains the heating system for efficient operation.
- Observes, notes and reports conditions requiring attention.
- Performs related work as required.

KNOWLEDGE, SKILLS AND ABILITIES

- Must have the knowledge, abilities and skills required of a custodian.
- Skill and ability to make satisfactory minor repairs to buildings, grounds, mechanical and electrical systems and equipment.
- Ability to perform semi-skilled repair and maintenance tasks relating to plumbing and office furniture.
- Skill and ability to determine through inspection the adequacy of building maintenance and custodial work and to determine the need of repairs.
- Perform related work as required.

MINIMUM EXPERIENCE AND TRAINING

Completion of eighth grade of school, vocational instruction suited to building custodial maintenance work, or at least two (2) years of experience in custodial maintenance or any equivalent combination of experience and training. Within one year of date of initial employment in this class a fireman/custodian must hold a stationary (low pressure boiler) fireman's license issued to him/her in his/her name by the City.

Position Title: Graphics Specialist

NATURE OF WORK

This is skilled work in the preparation of graphically illustrated projects for all library uses. An incumbent in this class is responsible for providing repro-graphics technical advice and/or recommendations to the Public Information Officer. Assignments are received orally or in written form, affording an opportunity for independent judgment in planning work under general supervision.

ILLUSTRATIVE EXAMPLES OF WORK

- Prepares and illustrates graphs, charts, posters, brochures and other materials requiring artistic ability.
- Designs and sets up displays, exhibits and bulletin boards.
- Confers with persons requesting art work and consults with Public Information Officer regarding same.
- Explains problems involved in a project, makes alternative suggestions.
- May perform work of Graphics Technician or other employees in the Public Information Department.
- May supervise subordinates.
- Performs related work as required.

KNOWLEDGE, SKILLS AND ABILITIES

- Considerable knowledge of perspective, balance and color harmony as well as processes, materials and techniques used in preparing illustrations and making charts and graphs, and of the methods and materials used in composing layouts of printed and illustrated material.
- Skill and ability to design, construct and install three-dimensional displays and to work with limited supervision in the preparation of sketches, technical drawings and models.
- Skill and ability to work under pressure and to meet deadlines.

MINIMUM EXPERIENCE AND TRAINING

High school graduation or equivalent and two full years of experience or training, with emphasis in graphics, commercial art or related studies.

Position Title: Graphics Technician

NATURE OF WORK

This is moderately difficult and varied work frequently involving tasks requiring the application of judgment based on knowledge gained through experience. An incumbent in this class is responsible for implementation of graphic designs for forms, publications and displays.

ILLUSTRATIVE EXAMPLES OF WORK

- Adapts rough design work to finished layout including work and other needed materials.
- Creates and prepares design work for public relations or informational materials. Prepares layout and makes other preparations prior to the printing process.
- Changes the window displays monthly throughout main library and its branches (requiring stretching and lifting).
- Operates the Varitype-headliner.
- Maintains the microfilm equipment.
- Maintains a yearly paper supply for all in-house printing.

KNOWLEDGE, SKILLS AND ABILITIES

- Working knowledge of materials utilized in graphic arts.
- Good judgment in making minor decisions in accordance with regulations and departmental policies and procedures.
- Skill and ability to understand and follow complex oral and written instructions.
- Skill and ability to assign and supervise the work of clerical subordinates.
- Skill and ability to work under pressure and to meet deadlines.
- Must have physical ability to compose and move displays.

MINIMUM EXPERIENCE AND TRAINING

High school graduation or equivalent. Vocational training or experience in graphic arts is desirable.

Position Title: Information Specialist I

NATURE OF WORK

This is entry level information specialist work serving the public in answering questions of a basic nature, helping people select reading materials and work of a similar nature under supervision. Incumbents may work with children, adults or the elderly, or people in all of these age categories. Employees in this class must understand library policies and procedures, and are expected to ask their supervisor for assistance with unusual or difficult problems. This position does not have the authority or responsibility to supervise staff.

ILLUSTRATIVE EXAMPLES OF WORK

- Answers reference questions of a basic nature under supervision.
- Assists the public in locating specific books and magazine articles, as well as other materials found in the library.

- Schedules meeting rooms for public use and maintains record of same including recording number of people in attendance if job site is the branch.
- Maintains a record of all outgoing long distance calls.
- May operate audio-visual equipment.
- Schedule may include evenings and Saturdays.
- May do story telling or other programs.
- May perform technical and/or clerical duties as required.
- May operate the switchboard.
- Be able to perform the duties of clerks and clerical assistants.

KNOWLEDGE, SKILLS AND ABILITIES

- Skill and ability to adapt to changing situations.
- Skill and ability to perform basic mathematical computations.
- Skill and ability to communicate effectively, orally and in writing, with staff and patrons.
- Basic knowledge of manual and semi-automatic switchboards may be required.
- Initiative and ability in learning, have a retentive and acquisitive mind.
- Skill and ability to operate library equipment.

MINIMUM EXPERIENCE AND TRAINING

High school graduate or equivalent and two (2) years of equivalent full time library experience working with the public or an A.A. degree and one year of full time experience may substitute.

Position Title: Information Specialist II

NATURE OF WORK

This is complex Information Specialist work involving service to the public. Moderately difficult reference questions involving use of indexes and other reference materials are answered under supervision. The incumbent will also help the library user locate information on a topic and may instruct the library user in use of indexes, the catalog, the periodicals list, as well as equipment maintained for public use. Employees in this class must understand library policies and procedures and are expected to request assistance with unusual or difficult problems from their supervisor. This position does not have the authority or responsibility to supervise staff.

ILLUSTRATIVE EXAMPLES OF WORK

- Performs all duties of Information Specialist I plus additional responsibilities which may include the following:
- May assist library patrons in book selection.
- Assists in the use of library catalogs and other reference tools.

- Answers difficult reference questions under supervision.
- Conducts advanced bibliographic checks on materials requested by patrons.
- Schedule may include evenings and Saturdays.
- May speak to groups if assigned by supervisor.
- May perform technical and/or clerical duties as required.

KNOWLEDGE, SKILLS AND ABILITIES

- Skill and ability to file alphabetically and numerically.
- Skill and ability to perform basic mathematical computations.
- Adaptability to accept new tasks and suggestions relating to assignments.
- Good judgment in making decisions in conformance with policies and procedures.
- Skill and ability to operate library equipment.
- Skill and ability to communicate effectively, orally and in writing, with staff and patrons.
- Basic knowledge of manual and semi-automatic switchboards may be required.
- Initiative and ability in learning, have a retentive and acquisitive mind.

MINIMUM EXPERIENCE AND TRAINING

High school graduate or equivalent and three (3) years of full time library experience working with the public as an Information Specialist I or two years of experience equivalent to an Information Specialist I and possess an A.A. degree with a broad program of study.

Position Title: Information Specialist III

NATURE OF WORK

This is advanced Information Specialist work in serving the public. Difficult reference questions involving use of indexes and numerous other reference materials are answered with limited supervision. The employee will also aid the library user in locating information and may instruct in use of indexes, the card catalog, the periodicals list, as well as equipment maintained for the public. Employees in this class may assist a department/branch head; must be able to supervise subordinate employees, and have considerable knowledge of library policies and procedures. An Information Specialist III reports to and receives general instruction from a department/branch head and may be charged with the functioning of the department or branch in the absence of the supervisor.

ILLUSTRATIVE EXAMPLES OF WORK

- Performs all duties of Information Specialists I and II plus additional responsibilities which may include the following:

- Answers complex reference questions.
- Advises library users as to how and where to find the information they need or want.
- Devises workable schedules for branch or department employees.
- Trains and assist personnel in becoming familiar with library operations, policies and procedures.
- Schedule may include evenings and Saturdays.
- May perform technical and/or clerical duties as required.
- May assist with the budget for specific area.

KNOWLEDGE, SKILLS AND ABILITIES

- Considerable knowledge of supervisory methods and practices.
- Skill and ability to enforce library policies and procedures firmly, tactfully and impartially.
- Sufficient knowledge of special subjects to enable the incumbent to work effectively with little direct supervision.
- Skill and ability to operate library equipment.

MINIMUM EXPERIENCE AND TRAINING

Possess an A.A. degree with a broad program of study and three (3) years of equivalent full time work experience plus two (2) years at an Information Specialist II level, or a B.A. degree with broad liberal arts program and two years of library experience, or five years of progressively advanced library experience.

Position Title: Information Specialist IV

NATURE OF WORK

This is supervisory Information Specialist lead work in serving the public and training subordinate employees. Complex and difficult reference questions involving use of indexes and numerous other advanced reference inquiries requiring a great deal of initiative are answered by this employee with very general supervision. Incumbents at this level must be able to operate a division of the library working with the library administration and division staff. Employees in this class must have considerable knowledge of library policies and procedures.

ILLUSTRATIVE EXAMPLES OF WORK

- Performs all duties of Information Specialist I-III plus additional responsibilities which may include the following:
- Responsible for the training, supervision and performance of subordinate employees combined with participating in the work itself.
- Advising subordinates on complex questions.

- Schedule may include evenings and Saturdays.
- Assigns subordinates specific work areas and/or duties.
- May participate in the selection of staff.
- Performs related duties as required.
- Prepares a budget for a specific area of responsibility.

KNOWLEDGE, SKILLS AND ABILITIES

- Thorough knowledge of at least one subject field.
- Skill and ability to make decisions in compliance with library policies and procedures.
- Ability and skill in applying one's knowledge in the execution or performance of assigned tasks.
- Advanced knowledge of supervisory methods and practices.

MINIMUM EXPERIENCE AND TRAINING

Must possess a B.A./S. degree plus two (2) years of full time work experience at the Information Specialist III level, or an A.A. degree plus four (4) years as an Information Specialist with one year as a supervisor or seven (7) years of library experience with two years as a supervisor.

Position Title: Information Specialist V

NATURE OF WORK

This is management Information Specialist work and involves the planning, assigning and reviewing of the work of subordinates. Employees with this class may be responsible for the proper performance of more than one division and must have extensive knowledge of library policies and procedures.

ILLUSTRATIVE EXAMPLES OF WORK

- Performs all duties of Information Specialist I—IV in addition to responsibilities which may include the following:
- Assigning duties involving specialized knowledge combined with instructing, supervising and participating in the work itself.
- Duties may involve the integration and coordination of several functions.
- Schedule may include evenings and Saturdays.
- May do special research projects.
- Prepares the budget for an assigned area.

KNOWLEDGE, SKILLS AND ABILITIES

- Extensive knowledge of supervisory methods and practices.
- Considerable knowledge of specific subject and/or special skills related to work assigned.

- Skill and ability to assimilate and adjust to procedures unique to the library.
- Skill and ability to transmit plans and instructions of librarian/supervisor when training or supervising subordinates.
- Excellent judgment in making immediate decisions.

MINIMUM EXPERIENCE AND TRAINING

Must possess the B.A. or B.S. degree and two (2) years at the Information Specialist IV level or nine (9) years of varied and progressively more difficult library work with at least four (4) years as a supervisor.

Position Title: Librarian I

NATURE OF WORK

This is entry level librarian work involving media acquisitions, fine arts, circulation, cataloging and/or reference work. Incumbents in this class are responsible for the performance according to well established procedures, of professional tasks required. Advice is given to employees on unusual work problems. Work is reviewed through conferences, evaluations and performance. A Librarian I must have a working acquaintance with all branch/division routines. An employee in this class may be requested to supervise non-certified personnel.

ILLUSTRATIVE EXAMPLES OF WORK

- Assists library patrons in making effective use of the facilities and resources of the library, including audio visual services, card catalog and reference sources and materials.
- Assists in areas related to the employee's academic library speciality.
- Performs descriptive and subject cataloging of books and other library materials.
- Prepares reading lists and bibliographies.
- Gives general assistance and advisory service to readers.
- May visit schools and other institutions.
- May do storytelling, public speaking or lead discussions.
- Answers reference questions.
- Prepares miscellaneous library reports.
- Performs related work as required.

KNOWLEDGE, SKILLS AND ABILITIES

- Skill and ability to select materials in one or more subject areas.
- Skill and ability to assimilate and adjust to procedures unique to this library.
- Knowledge of the principles of Library Science and their application involving reader interest levels.
- Some knowledge of publishing and resources for library materials.

- Skill and ability to transmit plans and instructions of supervisor when training or supervising non-certified personnel.
- Schedule may include evenings and Saturdays.

MINIMUM EXPERIENCE AND TRAINING

Must be a graduate of an accredited library school and have obtained a certificate issued by the State Board for Certification of Librarians. An employee in this class need not have work experience as a librarian.

Position Title: Librarian II

NATURE OF WORK

This is library work involving the application of technical skills to a variety of work problems. An incumbent in this class is responsible for the application of library skills to a variety of technical or professional problems in cataloging, book selection, audio visual materials and reference service. A Librarian II in a specialized division must have interest and special knowledge related to the subject speciality. This employee receives general assignments from a Librarian III or other professional assigned as supervisor.

ILLUSTRATIVE EXAMPLES OF WORK

- Performs all duties of Librarian I plus additional responsibilities which may include the following:
- Answers difficult or technical reference questions.
- Reviews publications in a special field and orders books for a specific section of a division or a branch.
- Assists the library patrons in book selection.
- Demonstrates the use of library catalogs and other reference tools.
- Makes bibliographic searches.
- May prepare reports to a head librarian on activities in that section of the branch or division work which is his/her designated responsibility, and prepares branch or division reports in the absence of the head librarian.
- Interprets general policies and procedures and makes recommendations to superior for possible improvements.
- Analyzes and indexes scientific and technical reports and designates articles for inclusion in special bibliographies.

KNOWLEDGE, SKILLS AND ABILITIES

- Considerable knowledge of the principles and practices of modern library work.
- Thorough knowledge of the techniques used in library classifications and cataloging.
- Skill and ability to apply this knowledge to specific work problems.

- Good critical judgment in relation to books and knowledge of the book selection standards and policies of the library system.
- Demonstrated skill and ability to: maintain an overall view of the branch/division services; analyze the possibilities of library service to the particular community served; transmit plans and instructions of superior when training or supervising staff or non-certified personnel.
- Skill and ability to communicate, orally and in writing, with staff and patrons.
- Knowledge of policies and procedures of the library.

MINIMUM EXPERIENCE AND TRAINING

Must be a graduate of an accredited library school and have obtained a certificate issued by the State Board for Certification of Librarians. An employee in this class must have worked at least two years as a librarian, with demonstrated ability for professional service and public relations.

Position Title: Librarian III

NATURE OF WORK

This is management work wherein the employee is responsible for the operation of a division or a branch of the library. A Librarian III participates in the selection of staff for the department or branch and is responsible for their training and supervision. He/she is responsible for studying the services and facilities of the branch/division and for recommending improvements for inclusion in the annual budget. A head librarian is responsible to administration for the operation of the branch/division under the financial conditions set forth in the annual budget.

ILLUSTRATIVE EXAMPLES OF WORK

- Performs all duties of Librarian I and II plus additional responsibilities which may include the following:
- Supervises the selection of books and other library materials for the branch or division.
- Prepares reports as required by administration on activities in the branch or department.
- Supervises subordinate employees in the division or branch.
- Performs other professional library duties in addition to the supervisory ones.

KNOWLEDGE, SKILLS AND ABILITIES

- Thorough knowledge of library practice, policies and procedures.
- Skill and ability to assemble and coordinate data needed so that proper recommendations for improving the service of the branch or division can be made to the Director.

- Skill and ability to plan, assign, coordinate and supervise the work of all staff members in the division or branch.
- Skill and ability to analyze the possibilities of library service to the particular community served by his/her branch or division.
- Schedule may include evenings and Saturdays.

MINIMUM EXPERIENCE AND TRAINING

Must be a graduate of an accredited library school and have obtained a certificate issued by the State Board for Certification of Librarians. Must have served four years as a librarian with distinction for professional service and demonstrated ability for supervision of personnel and public relations.

Position Title: Librarian IV

NATURE OF WORK

This is management work wherein the employee is responsible for the coordinated operation of an area of service within the library system involving more than one branch or division. A Librarian IV participates in the selection of staff for the divisions associated with his/her field of responsibility and consults and advises on their training and supervision. He/she is responsible for studying the services and facilities within the field of responsibility assigned and for recommending improvements for inclusion in the annual budget. This librarian is responsible for the training, supervision and evaluation of personnel in his/her immediate area. She/he is responsible for the operation of units in his/her assigned field of responsibility.

ILLUSTRATIVE EXAMPLES OF WORK

- Assists with and coordinates the selection of books and other library materials for the service area assigned.
- Prepares reports as required by administration on activities in the special service area.
- Coordinates main library activities with system policies and procedures.
- Performs other professional library duties as necessary in addition to supervisory activities.
- Schedule may include evenings and Saturdays.

KNOWLEDGE, SKILLS AND ABILITIES

- Extensive knowledge of library practice, policies and procedures, inclusive of those performed by Librarians I through III.
- Skill and ability to assemble and coordinate data needed so that proper recommendation for improving the special service area can be made to the Director.
- Skill and ability to plan, assign, coordinate and supervise the work of other staff members.

- Skill and ability to analyze and recommend changes in the library service.

MINIMUM EXPERIENCE AND TRAINING

Must be a graduate of an accredited Library school and hold a certificate issued by the State Board for Certification of Librarians. Must have seven years of professional service and have demonstrated ability to manage and supervise. Should have special knowledge in the particular field of responsibility assigned.

Position Title: Librarian V

NATURE OF WORK

This is executive management work. The employee is responsible for the coordination and planning of all areas of public service in the main library. A Librarian V may participate in the selection of staff and consults and advises on training and supervision. This employee is responsible for studying services and facilities as assigned and for recommending changes for inclusion in the annual budget. This librarian is responsible for training, supervision and evaluation of personnel in his/her immediate area. This employee is responsible for the operation, planning and budgeting of that area and for the operation of divisions in his/her assigned field.

ILLUSTRATIVE EXAMPLES OF WORK

- Assists with and coordinates the selection of books and the budgeting of other library materials for the service area assigned.
- Prepares reports as required by administration.
- Consults with the Director and Assistant Directors to coordinate activities within system policies and procedures.
- Supervises Public Service areas of the Main Library.
- Performs other professional library duties as necessary.

KNOWLEDGE, SKILLS AND ABILITIES

- Extensive knowledge of library practices, policies and procedures.
- Skill and ability to assemble and coordinate data.
- Skill and ability to plan, budget, assign, coordinate and supervise the work of all staff members assigned to his/her area of supervision.
- Skill and ability to analyze and do research and planning.

MINIMUM EXPERIENCE AND TRAINING

Must be a graduate of an accredited Library School and holder of a certificate issued by the State Board for Certification of Librarians. Must have served as a librarian for ten years and demonstrate ability for management and supervision. Should have special knowledge in the particular field of responsibility assigned.

Position Title: Library Page

NATURE OF WORK

This is hourly manual library and messenger work. A Library Page is responsible to the head of a branch, department, or to a Librarian or other employee delegated to supervise the Library Page. Sorts, moves, shelves, locates and retrieves library materials to contribute to efficient and effective library service. The position is located throughout the library in all library divisions and provides services that vary according to the assignment.

ILLUSTRATIVE EXAMPLES OF WORK

- May deliver mail in the Main Library Building or retrieve materials from outside the building.
- Sorts and puts in order on shelves in any established filing arrangement books, periodicals, maps, pamphlets, pictures, clippings, phonograph records, films and other library materials.
- "Reads shelves" to put back into proper order and arrangement all books and other materials.
- Files government documents after use or when received and marked for filing.
- Moves and arranges collections of library materials under supervision.
- Rewinds, splices and repairs 8mm and 16mm motion picture films: operates film projector.
- Obtains and returns library materials from shelves or stacks as required.
- Performs elementary tasks and duties of registration and circulation under direct supervision.
- Receives instruction in mending and elementary binding of materials and performs these tasks with a minimum of supervision, subject to inspection.
- Performs related work required by supervisor.

KNOWLEDGE, SKILLS AND ABILITIES

- Knowledge of alphabetical, numerical and decimal system of arrangement.
- Ability and skill to understand oral and written instructions and carry out the instructions.
- Must be able to read English.
- Ability and skill to operate library equipment as assigned.
- Must have physical ability to lift up to fifty (50) pounds and climb stairs.
- Ability and skill to adapt to changing procedures and situations.

MINIMUM EXPERIENCE AND TRAINING

If under 18 years of age, a Library Page must obtain from the office and complete a "Parent/School Authorization for Employment of a Minor required by the Department of Labor and Industries of the State." No experience is required but a filing and/or shelving test will be given.

Position Title: Library Technician I

NATURE OF WORK

This is entry level library technical work involving cataloging, networking or mending, following prescribed or standardized methods where some judgment may be exercised. The position reports to a Library Technician IV or V or a Librarian in the library services divisions. This position does not have the authority or responsibility to supervise. The position provides technical support at the work site including typing and filing. Further, the position may develop special files and indexes and operates library computer terminals and equipment.

ILLUSTRATIVE EXAMPLES OF WORK

- Searches on-line data base for cataloging copy.
- Enters local data into on-line cataloging system.
- Conducts basic bibliographic checking.
- Prepares uncataloged materials for release, types catalog cards matching materials with appropriate set of cards.
- Receives books, films, tapes, microfilms, microfiche, newspapers and other materials from publishers and vendors.
- Maintains records and inventory of items received, missing or in need of repair.
- Searches for requested books or other materials under technical direction.
- Assists in the collection of statistics regarding use and inventory of library materials, facilities and holdings.
- Participates in circulation/networking operations.
- Types orders for publications, such as books, A-V materials, library supplies and equipment.
- May do mending and mailing of library materials and correspondence.

KNOWLEDGE, SKILLS AND ABILITIES

- Skill and ability to type forty-five (45) words per minute.
- Skill and ability to communicate effectively orally and in writing with staff and the public.
- Skill and ability to operate and maintain library equipment, to type proficiently and file alphabetically, numerically, and perform basic computations.
- General knowledge of library policies, procedures and equipment.
- Perform related work as required.

MINIMUM EXPERIENCE AND TRAINING

High school graduation or equivalent or two years of full time clerical experience related to library acquisitions, networking, cataloging, mending or records work. A degree in library technology may substitute for one year of experience.

Position Title: Library Technician II

NATURE OF WORK

This is complex Library Technician work involving cataloging, networking or mending work within the library system. Incumbents must exercise considerable judgment in their duties. Assignments are distinguished from the I level in that incumbents have a functional responsibility as opposed to detailed repetitive tasks within an activity. This position does not have the authority or responsibility of supervision. This employee reports to and receives general instruction from a librarian or other employee designated as supervisor.

ILLUSTRATIVE EXAMPLES OF WORK

- Performs all duties of Library Technician I plus additional responsibilities which may include the following:
- Prepares bibliographic indexes, catalog files, and abstract services under direction of a librarian or superior.
- Conducts advanced checks on materials requested for purchase.
- Maintains periodicals, standing orders and other serial subscriptions and initiates renewals.
- Assists in searching and verifying book and serials orders, using Library of Congress catalogs and similar bibliographic tools.
- Does simple cataloging of books and/or non-book materials.
- Prepares the computer for programmed operations utilizing computer set up sheets.
- Verifies correct computer input.
- Does other computer duties as assigned.
- Supervises work of other library technicians and clerks in any of the above jobs when delegated.
- Enters original cataloging prepared for on-line cataloging database.
- Selects from variant forms appropriate cataloging copy from an on-line cataloging database.

KNOWLEDGE, SKILLS AND ABILITIES

- Working knowledge of library policies, procedures and equipment.
- Ability to type forty five (45) words per minute.
- Some knowledge of the practical application of computer operations procedures as they apply to the library.
- Adaptability and ability to accept corrections and suggestions.
- Ability and skill to transmit plans and instructions of supervisor when training or supervising other employees.

MINIMUM EXPERIENCE AND TRAINING

Three (3) years of experience as a Library Technician I, or an A.A. degree in

Library Technology and two years of full time experience as a Library Technician I or equivalent experience and education.

Position Title: Library Technician III

NATURE OF WORK

This is advanced library technical work involving acquisitions, cataloging, networking or mending. Incumbents are expected to perform complex technical procedures under professional direction. This position may be assigned to supervise other staff members.

ILLUSTRATIVE EXAMPLES OF WORK

- Performs all duties of Library Technicians I and II plus additional responsibilities which may include the following:
- Leads work of other library technicians, clerical and library aides in acquisitions, cataloging, mending or computer operations.
- May be in charge of a specific function.
- Organizes work assignments and schedule the work of subordinte personnel.
- Trains and assists personnel in becoming familiar with library operations and routines.
- Assists other employees in the use of various library files and records, referring them to a librarian for professional services.
- Classifies and catalogs books, periodicals, and/or non-book materials which meet standard criteria.
- Catalogs common forms of materials using MARC formats.
- May assume temporary responsibilities in the absence of supervisor.
- Answers correspondence and questions pertaining to networking, cataloging and acquisition, including, interpreting policies and procedures.

KNOWLEDGE, SKILLS AND ABILITIES

- Comprehensive knowledge of library policies, procedures and work relating to both print or non-print materials.
- Adaptability to accept corrections and suggestions.
- Good judgment in making decisions in conformance with policies and procedures.
- Considerable knowledge of supervisory methods and practices.
- Working knowledge of the practical application of computer operations procedures as they apply to the library.
- Ability to type 45 words a minute.

MINIMUM EXPERIENCE AND TRAINING

Three (3) years of experience as a Library Technician II, or an A.A. degree in Library Technology and two (2) years of full time experience as a Library Technician II or equivalent experience and education.

Position Title: Library Technician IV

NATURE OF WORK

This is specialized library technical work involving acquisitions, cataloging and/or networking requiring extensive subject or technical knowledge. Incumbents in this class work within guidelines established by professional librarians and supervise activities of assigned subordinates, and may serve as a division head.

ILLUSTRATIVE EXAMPLES OF WORK

- Performs all duties of Library Technicians I through III plus additional responsibilities which may include the following:
- Serves as supervisor of a division.
- Coordinates non-professional responsibilities and functions in a division.
- Trains subordinates and assign work.
- Prepares work schedules and adapt shift patterns to work flow.
- Evaluates and monitor work processes.
- Makes suggestions and recommendations for alteration and improvements of specific routines.
- May be responsible for preliminary budget preparation for an area.
- Performs related duties as required.

KNOWLEDGE, SKILLS AND ABILITIES

- Skill and ability to perform assigned tasks with a high level of competence.
- Thorough knowledge of supervisory methods and practices.
- Extensive knowledge of library policies and procedures.
- Considerable knowledge of the practical application of computer operations may be required.
- Skill and ability to type forty five (45) words a minute.
- Skill and ability to communicate effectively orally and in writing with staff and the public.

MINIMUM EXPERIENCE AND TRAINING

A degree in Library Technology and four years of full time Library Technician III experience. Six years of full time library technician experience or equivalent experience and education may be substituted.

Position Title: Library Technician V

NATURE OF WORK

This is difficult and varied work performed by a specialist involving responsible technical supervisory work. Incumbents in this class are responsible for the performance, according to established policies and procedures, of tasks required or assigned. This is a management position.

ILLUSTRATIVE EXAMPLES OF WORK

- Performs all duties of Library Technicians I through IV plus additional responsibilities which may include the following:
- Serves as supervisor for one or more areas.
- Trains, assigns and supervises the work of subordinates performing difficult clerical or technical operations.
- Develops library procedures designed to simplify and expedite work flow.
- Participates in the selection of staff for the division.
- Coordinates, evaluates and analyzes work processes.
- Performs related duties as required.

KNOWLEDGE, SKILLS AND ABILITIES

- Extensive knowledge of the policies and procedures of the library and/or the specific skills related to the work assigned.
- An understanding of the service goals of the library and the capacity to foster those aims through tasks assigned.
- Skill and ability to perform assigned tasks with a high level of competence.
- Skill and ability to recognize problems and assess situations; to gather and evaluate information from a variety of sources relevant to the problem; and to take appropriate action based on this information.

MINIMUM EXPERIENCE AND TRAINING

The A.A. degree in Library Technology and five years of full time Library Technician IV experience. Full time Library Technician experience may substitute for required education.

Position Title: Library Director

NATURE OF WORK

This is highly responsible administrative work directing the operations of the library system.

An employee of this class enforces and administers the provisions of the Revised Code, of the laws and ordinances governing the library, and the rules and regulations established by the Board of Trustees. Within the framework of general policy established by the Board of Trustees, duties are performed with a wide latitude of action in planning and directing library functions so as to establish and maintain effective management of the administrative affairs of the library. Work is subject to review for results obtained and conformance with policies by the Board of Trustees through discussion and analysis of recommendations and reports.

ILLUSTRATIVE EXAMPLES OF WORK

- Plans the future welfare of the Library.
- Reviews all departmental programs and provides general leadership and direction.
- Reports to, and advises, the Board of Trustees on Library problems.
- Holds staff meetings and conferences to consider and determine policy issues.
- Meets with other libraries and city government officials to arrive at solutions to mutual problems.

KNOWLEDGE, SKILLS AND ABILITIES

- Extensive knowledge of management theory and practices.
- Extensive knowledge of library organization and practices.
- Ability and skill to plan and enforce a balanced budget.
- Ability and skill to plan, direct and co-ordinate a varied work program on a large scale.
- Ability to gain and retain effective working relationships with the community at large, the Board and other public officials.
- Ability to maintain effective public relations.

MINIMUM EXPERIENCE AND TRAINING

Extensive administrative experience, eight years in the planning, co-ordination and financing of libraries; graduation from an accredited school for librarianship with an MLS degree.

Position Title: Parking Lot Attendant

NATURE OF WORK

This is work of routine nature, semi-skilled, in the issuing and receiving of parking permits, and making change for the use of the Library parking lot. This work also entails the cleaning up of the parking lot and maintaining the attendant office. An incumbent in this class is responsible to and receives general instructions from the Crew Leader or Superintendent of Maintenance.

ILLUSTRATIVE EXAMPLES OF WORK

- Issues and receives daily/hourly parking permits to users of the parking lot.
- Makes change for hourly, daily parking permits as needed;
- Makes up a daily revenue sheet, to be submitted to Management Services, on a daily basis, of all receipts.
- Sweeps and cleans the parking lot as needed.
- Polices the grounds, removing and bagging debris around the parking lot.
- Reports in writing to the Superintendent of Maintenance all damage to the facilities and grounds.

- Reports all accidents involving parking lot users to the Superintendent of Maintenance.
- Properly cleans and maintains the parking lot attendant's office.
- Maintains landscaping adjacent to and on the parking lot.
- Reports and logs all complaints of service.
- Performs other related work as assigned.

KNOWLEDGE, SKILLS AND ABILITIES

- Skill and ability to do elementary mathematics, including adding, subtraction, multiplication and division.
- Skill and ability to understand oral and written instructions.
- The ability to sweep, pick up debris, and to clean the attendant office.
- Skill and ability to maintain good relations with the public and staff.

MINIMUM EXPERIENCE AND TRAINING

Some experience (one year), in the handling of cash and dealing with the public. Experience in working as a parking lot attendant is highly desirable.

Position Title: Personnel Officer

NATURE OF WORK

This is responsible professional and technical work administering the Library's personnel policies and programs. This employee is responsible for a wide variety of tasks necessary to plan, recommend and implement the personnel policies as established by the Board of Trustees.

This employee must use discretion and judgement but has wide latitude for independent action under the general supervision of the Director.

ILLUSTRATIVE EXAMPLES OF WORK

- Administers the Library's personnel policies including Affirmative Action, Safety, Training and Development, etc.
- Participates in negotiations, prepares contracts and related documents, and administers such agreements.
- Confers with Branch/Division Heads and other supervisory personnel on matters relating to personnel including interviewing, discipline, evaluations, classifications, etc.
- Assigns, supervises and evaluates personnel staff.
- Prepares wage and benefit, classification and related studies.
- Conducts long and short term analysis of Library manpower requirements and recommends plans to meet anticipated needs.
- Initiates statistical and analytical studies of personnel practices.
- Supervises personnel records and the preparation of periodic and annual reports.
- Performs related work as required.

KNOWLEDGE, SKILLS AND ABILITIES

- Thorough knowledge of the principles and practices of public personnel administration.
- Thorough knowledge of personnel techniques employed in recruitment, classification, testing, job analysis, wage and salary administration, record-keeping and staff development and training.
- Considerable knowledge of the principles, practices and techniques of personnel training and related technical phases of personnel administration.
- Considerable knowledge of governmental organization, rules, regulations and procedures.
- Extensive knowledge of labor relations and techniques of labor negotiations in the public sector including applicable laws.
- Ability and skill to write clear and accurate reports and specifications.
- Ability and skill to establish and maintain effective working relationships with City and departmental officials, Library employees and their representatives, job applicants and the general public.
- Ability to supervise and lay out the work of subordinate employees.

MINIMUM EXPERIENCE AND TRAINING

Four year degree in Public Administration, Business Administration or closely related field is desired. Three to five years of progressively responsible experience in Public Personnel Administration and supervisory experience is required. Must have thorough knowledge of the technical aspects of the personnel process acquired through both practical experience and education.

Position Title: Personnel Specialist

NATURE OF WORK

This is specialized technical work in the field of public personnel administration. An employee in this class is responsible for the application of technical knowledge and skills to personnel problems in such areas as recruiting, positions classification and other personnel transactions. The incumbent may be assigned to a single personnel function or may provide technical assistance in several phases of the Library's personnel program. Work involves considerable contact with managers and supervisors. Assignments are received orally and in writing and the incumbent is expected to exercise independent judgment in planning work details and making technical determinations. The incumbent is responsible for completing assignments in accordance with established policies and procedures with work being performed under general direction and subject to review by superior.

This employee reports to and receives general instruction from the Personnel Officer of the Library.

ILLUSTRATIVE EXAMPLES OF WORK

- Prepares announcements and other informational material to recruit candidates.
- Reviews and processes various personnel actions concerning classification, pay and performance appraisals.
- Performs routine technical personnel tasks, organizes and maintains personnel records, conducts basic research from files, compiles summaries.
- Researches information regarding rules, policies and procedures as requested.
- Provides information regarding rules, policies and procedures to employees, employee representatives and institutions as requested.
- Participates in staff conferences and various committee meetings concerning personnel activities and problems.
- Coordinates federally funded personnel programs under direction of superior.

KNOWLEDGE, SKILLS AND ABILITIES

- Working knowledge of the fundamentals of public personnel administration.
- Working knowledge of the principles or organization, recruitment, tests and measurements, position classification and compensation.
- Considerable knowledge of the qualifications and characteristics of a wide variety of occupations.
- Skill and ability to relate well to people and to understand and function within a complex organization.
- Working knowledge of governmental organization, rules, regulations and procedures.
- Skill and ability to write clear and accurate reports.

MINIMUM EXPERIENCE AND TRAINING

Four years of experience in performing progressively responsible personnel work and graduation from high school. Graduation from college with specialization in personnel and one year of experience; or any equivalent combination of experience and training.

Position Title: Press Operator

NATURE OF WORK

This is moderately difficult and varied work frequently involving tasks requiring the application of judgment based on knowledge gained through experience. An employee in this class is responsible for the operation of an offset printing machine, preparation of printing materials prior to the printing process and light maintenance of machine.

ILLUSTRATIVE EXAMPLES OF WORK

- Operates an offset printing machine such as Multilith 1000, 1250, 1273 or AB Dick 350 and has a working knowledge of Varityper 730.
- Prepares paper, plastic and metal master plates.
- Mixes and applies dampening solutions, inks and protective coatings.
- Adjusts rollers, feeds regulating devices and paper guides to maintain correct ratios during operation.
- Operates a collator and power paper cutter.
- May operate photo camera equipment and exposure frames in making negatives or direct image masters.
- Prepares layout work and makes other preparations prior to the printing process.
- Operates and maintains microfilm reader/printers.
- May be delegated other responsibilities in absence of Public Information Officer.

KNOWLEDGE, SKILLS AND ABILITIES

- Considerable knowledge of printing machines and printing materials.
- Working knowledge of library policies and procedures, and of business English and arithmetic.
- Skill and ability in operating common office equipment.
- Good judgment in making minor decisions in accordance with regulations and departmental policies and procedures.
- Skill and ability to understand and follow complex oral and written instructions.
- Skill and ability to assign and supervise the work of subordinates.
- Skill and ability to work under pressure and meet deadlines.

MINIMUM EXPERIENCE AND TRAINING

High school graduate or equivalent. Vocational training and one (1) year of experience in a related field is desired.

Position Title: Secretary

NATURE OF WORK

This is difficult and varied secretarial work in providing secretarial services to the Assistant Director for Public Services. Work involves responsibility for directly providing secretarial services to the Assistant Director for Public Services, administrative office, and occasionally filling in for the Confidential Secretary in his/her absence. Included in the work is the exercise of independent judgment and discretion in screening calls, visitors, mail; arranging conferences and meetings; maintaining appointment schedules. Changes in procedures and policies and new assignments are received in general outline and employee is expected to proceed with minimum supervision. Work is reviewed for the achievement of desired results and adherence to established procedures and policies.

ILLUSTRATIVE EXAMPLES OF WORK

- Takes, transcribes, checks, and proofreads dictation, using shorthand or dictaphone, consisting of correspondence, memoranda, reports and minutes.
- Maintains relatively complex fiscal, administrative general records; reviews various reports and forms for accuracy and completeness.
- Compiles and completes data for administrative and public reports, bulletins, questionnaires and other documents;
- Prepares complex work sheets and tables from standardized raw data, and makes varied arithmetical computations.
- May take and transcribe minutes of committees, labor or Board meetings.
- Composes routine letters and articles; proofreads reports, forms, and other typed material for mathematical accuracy and correct grammatical usage.
- Performs related work as assigned.

KNOWLEDGE, SKILLS AND ABILITIES

- Skill and ability to type accurately at 70 words per minute.
- Skill and ability to take shorthand at 80 words per minute.
- Skill and ability to operate and transcribe dictation from the dictaphone.
- Skill and ability to operate a 10-key adding machine.
- Skill and ability to communicate effectively with the staff and the public.
- Skill and ability to maintain administrative, fiscal and general records.

MINIMUM EXPERIENCE AND TRAINING

Experience in performing progressively responsible clerical and stenographic work. Graduation from an accredited institution plus supplemental course work in office practices or any equivalent combination of experience and training.

Position Title: Superintendent of Maintenance

NATURE OF WORK

This is responsible management work in the field of building maintenance, repair and development of library owned facilities. An employee in this class is responsible for designs, estimates, coordination of trades and supervision of construction projects and maintenance or development of library owned facilities. Duties include planning, assigning work schedules and evaluation of building repair, maintenance, custodial and security programs. An employee in this class may prepare or assist in the preparation of drawings, specifications and cost estimates for diversified building maintenance projects, and develops maintenance programs for the library facilities. Supervision and direction received is in the form of general direction from an administrative superior and work is subject to review by evaluation of results obtained.

ILLUSTRATIVE EXAMPLES OF WORK

* Establishes and maintains preventive maintenance programs.
* Coordinates service requests and work orders.
* Conducts feasibility studies and makes recommendations.
* Maintains inventory, budgetary and related records.
* Participates in the preparation of plans, specifications, time and cost estimates and scheduling of construction projects and services including carpentry, painting, electrical, plumbing and heating, equipment installation, floor covering, roofing and drainage.
* Orders materials and supplies as needed and budgeted.
* May be required to attend Board meetings.

KNOWLEDGE, SKILLS AND ABILITIES

* Considerable knowledge of all construction trades.
* Knowledge of occupational hazards and construction safety standards.
* Ability and skill to develop plans, specifications, cost and time estimates and recommendations for maintenance and development projects.
* Ability and skill to prepare and maintain records and reports, including yearly budget of maintenance and construction costs.
* Ability and skill to establish and maintain effectively relations with administrative superiors, other employees, contractors and the general public.
* Perform related work as required.

MINIMUM EXPERIENCE AND TRAINING

Four years of experience in building maintenance, repair and custodial work, including some experience in a supervisory capacity. Must hold a license from the City as a stationary (low pressure boiler) fireman. Graduation from a standard high school, vocational school supplemented by training in the construction trades, or any equivalent combination of experience and training.

Position Title: Switchboard Operator

NATURE OF WORK

This is routine work in the operation of a telephone switchboard. An incumbent in this class is responsible for accurate and speedy operation of a telephone switchboard with a heavy traffic load and requires ability to remember names and the extensions of those served and to react quickly in the prompt placing and receiving of calls. Work normally includes the performance of incidental and related clerical tasks and may include basic questions which can be readily answered. Incumbents in this class work independently once procedures have been learned.

This employee reports to and receives general instructions from a supervisor and work is reviewed through observation.

ILLUSTRATIVE EXAMPLES OF WORK

- On an assigned shift, operates semi-automatic switchboard having a large number of trunklines and extensions.
- Answers all incoming local and long distance telephone calls and makes proper connection to person or office required.
- Places all calls requiring the use of the lines and receives calls coming to switchboard over these lines.
- Places outgoing long distance calls when requested.
- May give routine, non-technical information upon request and refers all other questions to the proper person.
- Maintains a record as directed, of all outgoing long distance calls.
- Performs related work as required.

KNOWLEDGE, SKILLS AND ABILITIES

- Some knowledge and skill in the operation of semi-automatic switchboards.
- Physical and mental ability to operate a complicated switchboard under stress with accuracy in a calm and efficient manner.
- Skill and ability to answer calls with a well-modulated, pleasant voice using good grammatical construction in choice of words.
- Skill and ability to remember the names and locations of personnel employed and to understand emergency operational procedures.
- Skill and ability to perform simple clerical tasks.

MINIMUM EXPERIENCE AND TRAINING

Graduation from high school or equivalent plus experience and/or training in the operation of a switchboard.

Librarian Classifications

Library D

LIBRARIAN I

Nature of Work: This is professional library work in one or more specialized fields in the city-county library system. Employees perform duties involving the general application of professional library techniques and procedures. Fields of assignment include cataloging and classification, general and technical reference, readers' advisory service, children's library services, and general duties in the main library or as supervisor of a branch library. The work is performed under the direction of an administrative superior, who exercises general supervision and assists with difficult or unusual problems; all work is performed according to established policies and procedures. Supervision may be exercised over a small staff of clerical and sub-professional employees.

Illustrative Examples of Work: Supervises the work of a branch library, interpreting area needs and interests.

Performs readers' advisory work assisting patrons in the use of library facilities; advises parents in selection of reading material for children.

Catalogs books.

Prepares general book lists and bibliographies, does general reference work; processes government documents; maintains pamphlet and clipping files.

Supervises specialized reading rooms and service facilities.

Performs related work as required.

Knowledges, Abilities and Skills: Knowledge of modern library principles, methods, and practices.

Knowledge of reader interest levels and of books and authors.

Knowledge of library reference materials, aids, and procedures.

Ability to supervise the work of a small group of clerical employees.

Ability to establish and maintain effective working relationships with library patrons and with other employees.

Desirable Experience and Training: Graduation from an accredited college or university with undergraduate courses in Library Science and some experience in professional library work. Desirable courses are: Reference, Book Selection, the Library in the Social Order, and Cataloging.

LIBRARIAN II

Nature of Work: This is professional work requiring experience and special training in library science. An employee of this class is responsible for professional duties involving administrative or supervisory responsibilities, or in-depth subject specialization. Modern library techniques must be applied normally without direct supervision although work is subject to review by an administrative superior who is consulted on difficult problems.

Illustrative Examples of Work: Acts as a principal assistant in a large department and/or contributing in-depth subject specialization.

Trains personnel in library routines; catalogs books; answers reference questions; assists in the selection of materials for the library or one or more of its special collections.

Performs varied reference work including research on difficult technical questions; prepares book lists and bibliographies; handles correspondence of research questions done by mail; classifies and assigns subject heading for pamphlets for various sections of the library.

Assists supervising librarians in division management; prepares work schedules, and gives departmental orientation and training to new clerical and professional employees.

Performs related work as required.

Knowledges, Abilities and Skills: Considerable knowledge of modern library purposes, professional policies, methods and techniques.

Considerable knowledge of reference, cataloging, and circulation procedures, materials, aids and skill in their application.

Knowledge of reader interest levels and in-depth knowledge of books and authors.

Ability to perform specialized research on historical, technical or other questions.

Ability to establish and maintain good work relationships with community groups, the public, and with other employees.

Ability to analyze professional and administrative problems and assist in their solution.

Desirable Experience and Training: Graduation from an accredited college or university and attainment of a graduate degree from an accredited school of library science or a Masters Degree in another field of specialization required by the library. Experience in professional library work including some experience in a progressively responsible supervisory position.

LIBRARIAN III

Nature of Work: This is professional library work in administration of a major function of the library system. The work is performed under general supervision, and considerable latitude for initiative and independent judgment is present. Supervision may be exercised over a large staff of professional, subprofessional, and clerical employees.

Illustrative Examples of Work: Manages a major department or group of branches of the library system.

Trains and directs professional and clerical staff.

Develops, installs and supervises procedures to assist the division in more effectively performing its work.

Provides consultant services to organizations and general public.

Plans and participates in special activities designed to inform the public on library facilities or to expand the scope of services being offered.

Attends staff meetings and workshops.

Knowledges, Abilities and Skills: Considerable knowledge of modern library principles, methods, and practices.

Considerable knowledge of the acquisition and organization of library materials.

Considerable knowledge of patron interest levels and a wide knowledge of a variety of books, and other library materials, print and non-print.

Considerable knowledge of the techniques of library service, services to individuals and to groups, and library program planning.

Ability to establish and maintain good work relationships with community groups, the public, and to provide constructive leadership and supervision of a large staff of employees.

Ability to analyze problems and determine most appropriate solution.

Ability to set goals, plan for achieving the goals, and secure cooperation of others in attaining them.

Desirable Experience and Training: Graduation from an accredited college or university with a Masters in Library Science; and at least three years of successful employment in a professional capacity, including some supervisory experience.

Library I

CLASS TITLE: Librarian

DEFINITION: Under direction; performs work of moderate difficulty at a beginning professional level.

EXAMPLES OF DUTIES: Researches and answers reference questions; prepares bibliographies; suggests titles of interest in subject areas indicated by patrons; assists in the selection of materials for appropriate age and developmental level; recommends materials for addition to the collection in assigned fields or subjects; provides or assists in providing instruction and training in library methods and techniques to non-professional employees; catalogs print and audio-visual materials subject to review; maintains cataloging authority data and resolves complex problems related to input and correction of machine-readable bibliographic data; plans exhibits; maintains pamphlet collections; weeds the materials collection; may supervise community library during absence of the head librarian; may serve as first assistant in a large community library; performs related work as required.

EMPLOYMENT STANDARDS:

Education and Experience. Bachelor's Degree including or supplemented by 28 semester or 42 quarter credits distributed among specified library science courses plus two years of professional library experience or an approved equivalent of education and experience.

Knowledge, Abilities, and Skills. Good knowledge of library policies, methods, and procedures; good knowledge of materials in several broad subject fields; good knowledge of cataloging and classification.

Working ability to use reference materials; working ability to select appropriate materials for patrons of all ages; working ability to classify materials according to Dewey Decimal Classification; working ability to perform subject and descriptive cataloging; working ability to learn Marc format and to edit bibliographic data; working ability to instruct and train non-professional library staff in methods and procedures; working ability to establish and maintain effective working relationships with others; some ability to write reviews, prepare bibliographies, and interpret library resources and services to the public.

CLASS TITLE: Senior Librarian

DEFINITION: Under general direction; performs work of moderate difficulty in supervising the operation of a medium sized community library providing a full-time program of library services; or serves as first assistant librarian in a large community library where the program and schedule require such assignment; or provides a full range of library services in one or more of the professional functional areas for the library system.

EXAMPLES OF DUTIES: Plans in consultation with supervisors the program and services of all subordinate personnel; assists in the planning and operation of an assigned specialized library program in an area library; performs complex or specialized cataloging or book cataloging or book catalog editing; provides assistance to patrons in the selection and location of appropriate material; selects additions to the collection in assigned fields, subject to review; weeds the materials collection; writes reviews and explains library services to community groups; prepares bibliographies; researches and answers reference questions; trains and supervises subordinate personnel in library policies and procedures; keeps records and prepares regular and special reports; performs related work as required.

EMPLOYMENT STANDARDS:

Education and Experience. Bachelor's Degree including or supplemented by 28 semester or 42 quarter credits distributed among specified library science courses plus three years professional library experience or an approved equivalent of education and experience. (Some positions may require experience in a specialized area.)

Knowledge, Abilities, and Skills. Considerable knowledge of library policies, methods, and procedures; considerable knowledge of materials in several broad subject fields; considerable knowledge of specialized activities and materials involved in children's work; considerable knowledge of cataloging and classification.

Marked ability to select appropriate materials for patrons of all ages; considerable ability to use reference materials; considerable ability to instruct and train library staff in methods and procedures; considerable ability to write reviews, prepare bibliographies and interpret library resources and services to the public; considerable ability to establish and maintain effective working relationships with others; working ability to maintain records and prepare reports.

Working skill in planning the work of others.

CLASS TITLE: Principal Librarian

DEFINITION: Under general direction; performs work of moderate difficulty in supervising the operation of a large community library; provides a full-time program of library services; or performs responsible, professional duties in a highly specialized field.

EXAMPLES OF DUTIES: Plans in consultation with supervisors the program and services; plans and supervises the work of all community library or department personnel; advises patrons concerning the library and its services and resources; if working in a specialized field, supervises professional staff engaged in that specialized capacity, for example, information services or cataloging; provides assistance to patrons in the selection of appropriate materials; researches and answers reference questions; performs related work as required.

EMPLOYMENT STANDARDS:

Education and Experience. Bachelor's Degree including or supplemented by 28 semester or 42 quarter credits distributed among specified library science courses plus four years of professional library experience or an approved equivalent of education and experience. (Some positions may require experience in a specialized area.)

Knowledge, Abilities, and Skills. Comprehensive knowledge of library methods, procedures and policies; comprehensive knowledge of materials; comprehensive knowledge of material classification; comprehensive knowledge of cataloging.

Marked ability to use reference materials; marked ability to interpret library resources and services to the public; considerable ability to instruct and supervise others; considerable ability to maintain discipline; considerable ability to maintain records and prepare reports; considerable ability to establish and maintain effective working relationships with others.

Considerable skill in performing full range of librarian functions; considerable skill in planning and supervising the work of others.

CLASS TITLE: Coordinating Librarian

DEFINITION: Under direction; performs work of considerable difficulty in supervising the activities of a group of community libraries or an Area Library.

EXAMPLES OF DUTIES: Coordinates and directs the activities of a group of community libraries or an Area Library; evaluates activities of assigned community libraries and sets priorities for staffing, scheduling, and equipment needs; participates in planning new facilities and services within geographic area; directs implementation of system-wide policies, procedures, and services within assigned community libraries; meets with other area supervisors to exchange information, develop cooperative services, and promote consistent application of system-wide policies and programs; plans and directs the activities of an Area Library; may direct the system-wide reference support service; prepares budgets; trains, supervises, and evaluates staff; develops community awareness of library services; assists in establishing standards for material collections and services and devises controls to ensure attainment of standards; assists patrons in selection of appropriate material; researches and answers reference questions; performs related work as required.

EMPLOYMENT STANDARDS:

Education and Experience. Bachelor's Degree including or supplemented by 28 semester or 42 quarter credits distributed among specified library science courses plus six years of professional library experience or an approved equivalent of education and experience. (Some positions may require experience in a specialized area.)

Knowledge, Abilities, and Skills. Comprehensive knowledge of the principles and methods of professional library work; considerable knowledge of the principles of management and supervision.

Considerable ability to plan and organize workloads and schedules; considerable ability to evaluate performance, to set objectives and priorities, and to prepare budgets.

Considerable skill in developing and implementing operating policies and procedures; considerable skill in communicating with others, both orally and in writing.

CLASS TITLE: Library Division Manager

DEFINITION: Under general direction; performs work of considerable difficulty in planning, supervising and evaluating the work of a library division.

EXAMPLES OF DUTIES: Directs, through supervisors, the activities of highly specialized, system-wide and support services and programs including: acquisition, cataloging, and circulation; analyzes needs and recommends or implements appropriate methods and procedures for improving services; interprets services to schools, the public, and community organizations; assists in establishing standards and minimum essentials for collections and services and devises control procedures to assure attainment of standards; trains, supervises, and evaluates personnel; confers with library management in providing a coordinated program of library services; prepares budget estimates; gives information or answers complaints; prepares regular and special reports; develops or supervises the maintenance of records and statistics; performs related work as required.

EMPLOYMENT STANDARDS:

Education and Experience. Master's Degree in Library Science from ALA accredited school, and 8 years of post degree professional experience *OR* Bachelor's Degree with 42 quarter credits in Library Science and 10 years of post degree professional experience *OR* Bachelor's Degree including or supplemented by 15 quarter credits in library science and 12 years of post degree professional experience. Library Science requirements may be replaced by media/audio-visual or information or Computer Science when appropriate to the position. When position is in specialized area, a minimum of five years must be in the specialty, including four years of supervisory experience.

Knowledge, Abilities, and Skills. Comprehensive knowledge of the principles and methods of professional library work; comprehensive knowledge of the processes of management and supervision.

Considerable ability to plan and organize workloads and schedules; considerable ability to evaluate performance and needs, and to set priorities and prepare budgets.

Considerable skill in developing and implementing operating policies and procedures; considerable skill in planning and supervising the work of others; considerable skill in communicating with others, both orally and in writing.

Library O

POSITION TITLE: Librarian I. DEPARTMENT: As assigned. DIVISION: As assigned. TITLE OF IMMEDIATE SUPERVISOR: Lib. IV or V—Division or Branch Head.

1. PURPOSE OF WORK

Under the general supervision of the Division or Branch Head, performs professional service without specialized subject, service, or administrative responsibility and with immediate professional supervision. Keeps informed of developments and participates in activities of professional and community organizations related to the library's mission.

2. MINIMUM QUALIFICATIONS

1. Graduate degree in library science from an ALA accredited school, no prior experience necessary.
2. Organizational skill.
3. Ability to meet and deal with people effectively.
4. Knowledge of principles and practices of professional library work.
5. Possession of a valid drivers license and ready access to suitable transportation or a personal vehicle appropriate for use in the transaction of library business and performance of job related duties (approved mileage reimbursed at prescribed rate).

3. TYPICAL DUTIES

1. Answers reference questions.
2. Assists readers in the selection, organization, and interpretation of library material.
3. Catalogs and classifies materials.
4. Conducts programs for adults and children, including outreach programs.
5. Instructs patrons in the use of basic reference tools and catalogs.
6. Participates in materials selection and evaluation.
7. Supervises, maintains, or assists with special files and indexes.
8. Assists branch or division head in the initiation and implementation of an active program of educational, cultural and informational services relevant to the clientele of the branch or division.
9. Performs other duties as assigned.

POSITION TITLE: Librarian II*. DEPARTMENT: As assigned.
DIVISION: As assigned. TITLE OF IMMEDIATE SUPERVISOR:
Lib. IV or V — Division or Branch Head.

1. PURPOSE OF WORK

Under the general supervision of Librarian IV or V — Division or Branch Head, performs specialized services, minor administrative duties, and program responsibilities in a small branch or division. Keeps informed of developments and participates in activities of professional and community organizations related to the library's mission.

2. MINIMUM QUALIFICATIONS

1. Graduate degree from an ALA accredited school with a minimum of one year of relevant professional experience in library work.
2. Organizational and supervisory skills.
3. Ability to meet and deal with people effectively.
4. Familiarity with specialized bibliographic and reference tools.
5. Possession of a valid drivers license and ready access to suitable transportation or a personal vehicle appropriate for use in the transaction of Library business and performance of job related duties (approved mileage reimbursed at prescribed rate).

3. TYPICAL DUTIES

1. Provides professional library services above that of a Librarian I involving minor administrative duties as an assistant head in a small branch or small division.
2. Interprets library services and activities.
3. Participates in collection development.

4. Performs original subject cataloging.
5. Performs reference services for individuals, groups, or organizations.
6. Presents programs for community groups.
7. Provides in-depth assistance in a specialized subject field when appropriate.
8. Is responsible for preparation of administrative reports and budgetary requests, and selection, evaluation, and training of assigned personnel.
9. Performs other duties as assigned.

* LIBN II
* LIBN II—ASST HD—SM BR
  LIBN II—ASST HD—SM DIV

POSITION TITLE: Librarian III*. DEPARTMENT: As assigned. DIVISION: As assigned. TITLE OF IMMEDIATE SUPERVISOR: Lib. V—Division or Branch Head.

1. PURPOSE OF WORK

Under the general supervision of a Librarian V—Division or Branch Head, performs specialized services, minor administrative duties, and program responsibilities in a large branch or division. Keeps informed of developments and participates in activities of professional and community organizations related to the library's mission.

2. MINIMUM QUALIFICATIONS

1. Graduate degree from an ALA accredited school with a minimum of one year of relevant professional experience in library work.
2. Ability to communicate effectively.
3. Ability to establish and maintain effective relationships with community groups.
4. Ability to lead and direct staff.
5. Reading background and knowledge of bibliographic sources in a specialized subject field when appropriate.
6. Possession of a valid drivers license and ready access to suitable transportation or a personal vehicle appropriate for use in the transacton of Library business and performance of job related duties (approved mileage reimbursed at prescribed rate).

3. TYPICAL DUTIES

1. Provides professional library services above that of a Librarian II involving minor administrative duties as an assistant head of a large branch or large division.
2. Assists in the selection and evaluation of personnel.
3. Coordinates the use of media in the library program.

4. Plans and supervises the work of subordinates.

5. Assists branch or division head in the initiation and implementation of an active program of educational, cultural and informational services relevant to the clientele of the branch or division.

6. Performs other duties as assigned.

* LIBN III – ASST HD – LG BR
* LIBN III – ASST HD – LG DIV

POSITION TITLE: Librarian IV*. DEPARTMENT: As assigned. DIVISION: As assigned. TITLE OF IMMEDIATE SUPERVISOR: Asst. Dir. of Extn. Srvcs./Asst. Dir. Main Lib.

1. PURPOSE OF WORK

Under the direct supervision of the Assistant Director of Extension Services or the Assistant Director of Main Library, performs major administrative and program responsibilities. Keeps informed of developments and participates in activities of professional and community organizations related to the library's mission.

2. MINIMUM QUALIFICATIONS

1. Graduate degree from an ALA accredited school with minimum of two years of professional experience in library work.

2. Ability to communicate effectively.

3. Ability to establish and maintain effective working relationships with community groups.

4. Ability to lead and direct staff.

5. Knowledge of current management practices.

6. Possession of a valid drivers license and ready access to suitable transportation or a personal vehicle appropriate for use in the transaction of Library business and performance of job related duties (approved mileage reimbursed at prescribed rate).

3. TYPICAL DUTIES

1. Provides professional library service above that of a Librarian III involving the primary administration of a small branch or small division.

2. Assigns library materials for review and evaluation.

3. Prepares replies to requests for information.

4. Selects materials and/or advises on the acquisition of materials.

5. Initiates and implements an active program of educational, cultural and informational services in concert with the Children's and Adult Services Coordinators relevant to the clientele of the branch or division.

6. Is responsible for the preparation of administrative reports and

budgetary requests, and selection, evaluation, and training of assigned personnel.

7. Performs other duties as assigned.

* LIB IV – HD – SM BR

POSITION TITLE: Librarian V*. DEPARTMENT: As assigned. DIVISION: As assigned. TITLE OF IMMEDIATE SUPERVISOR: Asst. Dir. Extn. Srvcs./Asst. Dir. Main Library.

1. PURPOSE OF WORK

Under the general supervision of the Assistant Director of Extension Services or the Assistant Director of Main Library, performs major administrative and program responsibilities involving the coordination of activities in a large branch or large division. Keeps informed of developments and participates in activities of professional and community organizations related to the library's mission.

2. MINIMUM QUALIFICATIONS

1. Graduate degree from an ALA accredited school with three years of progressively more responsible experience in library work.

2. Ability to lead and direct staff and communicate effectively.

3. Ability to establish and maintain effective relationship with community groups.

4. Knowledge of current management practices.

5. Possession of a valid drivers license and ready access to suitable transportation or a personal vehicle appropriate for use in the transaction of Library business and performance of job related duties (approved mileage reimbursed at prescribed rate).

3. TYPICAL DUTIES

1. Provides professional library service above that of a Librarian IV involving the primary administration of a large branch or large division.

2. Plans and executes public relations program in concert with Director of Communications.

3. Initiates and implements an active program of educational, cultural, and informational services in concert with the Children's and Adult Services Coordinators relevant to the clientele of the branch or division.

4. Is responsible for preparation of administrative reports and budgetary requests, and selection, evaluation, and training of assigned personnel.

5. Performs other duties as assigned.

* LIB V – HD – LG BR
  LIB V – HD – LG DIV

Library Q

LIBRARIAN
SENIOR LIBRARIAN
PRINCIPAL LIBRARIAN

Summary of Duties: Does reference work and readers' guidance for adults, young adults, and children and provides other professional library services to patrons; selects, reviews, indexes, classifies, and catalogs books and other library materials; or supervises a group of professional, subprofessional, and clerical employees and does the more difficult professional work; or directs the daily operation of a library unit; or directs a central library subject department, a library region, a technical services agency, or the mobile services department; or coordinates a system wide service; or does responsible specialized library administrative work; and does related work.

Distinguishing Features: Employees of these classes are primarily concerned with making library resources and facilities available to the public. This includes practical arrangement of library materials, giving professional assistance to library patrons, apprising the public of available library resources, and maintaining up-to-date collections of books and other library materials. Much of their work is performed without close supervision and requires considerable judgment and tact in dealing with the public.

A Librarian represents the first level of professional library work. Although an employee of this class may have charge of a sub-branch library or a subdivision of a Central Library section, a Librarian ordinarily works under the immediate direction of a Senior Librarian. An employee of this class frequently functionally supervises and, occasionally, completely supervises clerical employees.

A Senior Librarian supervises a branch library or a bookmobile unit, assists in administering a larger unit, or gives staff direction to other library functions. Additionally, a Senior Librarian does more responsible professional work than that ordinarily assigned to Librarians. A Senior Librarian normally reports to a Principal Librarian.

A Principal Librarian is responsible for the operation of a library region consisting of several branch libraries, or the mobile services department or a Central Library subject department, or for high-level staff services in a specialized library function. In addition to administrative and supervisory responsibilities, an employee of this class solves highly technical problems in professional library work. A Principal Librarian reports to a Division Librarian who is available for consultation on difficult problems.

Examples of Duties: Librarian: Explains the nature and extent of library resources and guides children, young adults, and adults in the selection and location of library materials and the use of card catalogs, indexes, and other library tools; gives book talks to juvenile, young adult, and adult groups in libraries, schools, and other agencies; resolves problems and complaints of patrons; analyzes reference questions and selects sources to be consulted;

makes extended searches for information not available in obvious reference sources and adds citations for these to information files; prepares displays, exhibits, and other library publicity materials; takes and fills reserve and interlibrary loan requests after making necessary bibliographic and subject searches;

Maintains special library materials collections for children or young adults; advises teachers and parents on the choice of reading matter for these groups; organizes and works with young adults or children's groups and conducts programs; scans new periodicals for usable book reviews and information for reference files; reviews materials and recommends their purchase;

Makes bibliographic searches and prepares orders for serials and new titles and editions of books; catalogs books and other materials, including the assignment of classification and Cutter numbers, main entries, and cross references; assigns subject headings and indexes of uncataloged materials such as documents, pamphlets, and pictures; makes material counts and takes inventory of assigned sections; serves on book evaluation, young adults advisory, and other committees; reads library journals, book reviews, and other materials to keep abreast of current trends and literature in assigned subject fields; assists in the selection of library materials for binding, mending, replacement, and withdrawal;

Maintains information, pamphlet, picture, or clipping files, maintains a popular library section; prepares reading lists, bibliographies, indexes, analytics, and other library aids; reviews clerical work such as filing and typing; keeps records and prepares reports of activities; may supervise and work in a bookmobile to provide service to schools or areas not served by library branches; and may act for a Senior Librarian in that employee's absence.

Senior Librarian: Supervises a library branch, bookmobile unit, or unit of a Central Library subject department, or a unit of the Technical Services Division, or assists a Principal Librarian in managing a Central Library subject department; prepares work schedules; selects, trains, and supervises professional, subprofessional, and clerical employees; assures that agency facilities, equipment, and vehicles are in proper condition; makes recommendations for the arrangement of material collections; determines priorities for processing incoming library materials; answers difficult reference questions and adjusts complaints unresolved by Librarians; directs searches for missing books;

Selects or makes recommendations for acquiring, binding, mending, withdrawing, and replacing library materials; identifies agency needs for budget requests; requisitions supplies and equipment; serves on committees and personnel interview boards; helps organize programs; gives book talks to community groups, writes articles for newspapers, and uses other methods of publicizing services and resources of a library branch or unit; prepares reports of branch or unit operations; may act as regional children's librarian and advise all children's librarians in a region; may coordinate interlibrary loan activities for the Library Department; may supervise a book order or serial order unit; may coordinate the transfer of books among branches and between branches and the Central Library; and may act for a Principal Librarian in that employee's absence.

Principal Librarian: Plans, directs, coordinates, and supervises the work of a Central Library subject department, a technical services agency, the mobile services division, or a library region; establishes operating policies and procedures; assures that the department or region is properly staffed; instructs subordinates in library policies and procedures and resolves problems and questions; evaluates operations to ensure full public service and utilization of personnel; coordinates and develops library services and administers the maintenance and development of an up-to-date materials collection; approves the development of special collections; approves recommendations for purchasing, withdrawing, binding, mending, and replacing library materials; determines if the last copy of a book may be removed, if gifts should be added to the collection, and if reference books may circulate; identifies major new informational resources of library-wide importance; identifies rare and valuable materials for retention in the library's special collections; plans for seasonal demands on the library section or region; determines the most advantageous use of available space; investigates sources of potential grant funds for library functions; makes surveys and prepares reports on library functions; assists in revising the Department procedures manual; serves on committees and personnel interview boards; cooperates with schools and community organizations in determining library needs and explaining library policies, procedures, and goals; speaks to groups and writes articles on library services and materials; keeps local officials informed of library activities; directs the preparation and publication of catalogs, newsletters, booklists and other informational material; may serve as subject expert and establish policies for the loan of specialized material to other libraries; surveys communities and makes recommendations on location of library facilities; makes recommendations on physical size and layout of branch facilities; works with the building and planning units to determine the best utilization and planning of facilities for patrons' desks and collection housing;

May coordinate the selection of adult materials for branches, coordinate and supervise the purchase of materials collections for new and expanding branches, and supervise centralized interlibrary loan services and transfer of materials among branches; may coordinate the activities of Librarians and Senior Librarians assigned to work with children, young adults, and adults; coordinates the selection of children's materials, conducts regular conferences to review children's materials, and discusses general problems in the field; and may coordinate the activities of Librarians assigned to work with young adults, select young adult material for Central Library sections and coordinate the selection of such material for branches;

May direct the classification and cataloging of all types of library materials, decide difficult technical problems, direct the recataloging of transferred and other library material, and oversee the maintenance of official authority files, card catalogs, shelf lists, and other cataloging records; may serve as an aide to the Division Librarian in charge of the Central Library subject departments and to the Division Librarian in charge of branch libraries; may direct the activities of an order section engaged in purchasing books, serials, and other materials selected by operating units, see that orders are placed to obtain the best discounts, and direct the receiving and processing of library materials prior to cataloging, approving of invoices, and maintenance of book order records and current information on publishers; may direct the activities of the Mobile Services Unit, including bookmobile units and library service to shut-ins; may plan, coordinate, and direct the Automated Library Technical Services Department; may interact with other City Departments to assure proper operation of supervised units; and may act for a Division Librarian in that employee's absence.

Employees in all three classes occasionally may be assigned to other duties for training purposes or to meet technological changes or emergencies.

Qualifications:

Knowledges:	Librarian	Senior Librarian	Principal Librarian
Technical reference procedures and problems, including standard and specialized reference and bibliographic sources;	Good	Good	Good
General public library activities, policies, aims and services;	Good	Good	Good
Standards for selecting out-standing and distinguished books in the children, young adult and adult fields;	Good	Good	Good
Books that most authorities agree are of distinguished literary value;	Good	Good	Good
Professional library techniques;	Working	Good	Good
Organization, activities, procedures, policies, rules, aims, and services of the Library Department;		Good	Good
Clerical procedures and techniques of the library;		Good	Good
Books currently and generally in demand in the City and local subject reading interests;		Good	Good
City personnel rules, policies and practices;		Good	Good
Memoranda of understanding as they apply to subordinate personnel;		Good	Good

Knowledges:	Librarian	Senior Librarian	Principal Librarian
Technical classification and cataloging procedures and problems, including the Dewey decimal classification system, Library of Congress subject heading plan, and Cutter numbers;	Working	Good	Good
Techniques used in work with children and young adults;	Working	Good	Good
Procedures involved in centralized ordering, receiving, and processing of books, serials, and other library materials;		Working	Good
Safety principles and practices;	Some	Good	Good
Supervisory principles and practices;	Some	Working	Good
Laws and regulations related to equal employment opportunity and affirmative action;		Working	Good
Administrative and professional problems encountered in furnishing library services to the public and techniques for their solution;	Some	General	Good
Preparation of budget estimates for the library unit concerned;		General	Good
Abilities:			
Do technical reference work and bibliographic research;	x	x	x
Furnish reading guidance to library patrons;	x	x	x
Review and analyze books;	x	x	x
Evaluate and select books and other library materials for acquisition or discard;	x	x	x
Speak effectively before groups of children, young adults, and adults;	x	x	x

Abilities	Librarian	Senior Librarian	Principal Librarian
Deal tactfully and effectively with other employees and the public;	x	x	x
Train and evaluate subordinates;		x	x
Supervise difficult technical reference work and bioliographic research;		x	x
Analyze facts and make decisions		x	x
Prepare correspondence and accurate and concise reports.		x	x

A Master's degree in Library Science or comparable fifth-year degree in Library Science is required for Librarian.

Two years of professional library experience as a Librarian is required for Senior Librarian.

Two years of professional library experience as a Senior Librarian is required for Principal Librarian.

License: All Classes: A valid driver's license may be required.

Physical Requirements: All Classes: Strength to perform average lifting of less than 5 pounds and occasionally over 30 pounds; arm, hand, and finger dexterity involved in activities such as reaching, handling, and feeling; good speaking and hearing ability; and good eyesight.

Persons with handicaps may be capable of performing the duties of some of the positions in this class. Such determination must be made by the medical examiner on an individual basis.

As provided in Civil Service Commission Rules and the Administrative Code, this specification is descriptive, explanatory and not restrictive. It is not intended to declare what the duties and responsibilities of any position shall be.

DIVISION LIBRARIAN

Summary of Duties: Directs a major library division consisting of the central library service to the public, the branch library system, or the library technical services; and does related work.

Distinguishing Features: A Division Librarian is responsible for the activities of a large library division concerned with services such as acquiring, processing, and circulating books and other library materials, or giving reference and readers' advisory services to the public. He assists in departmental administration by planning, developing, recommending, testing, and administering policies, procedures, and standards for professional library service, and by insuring uniformity in the interpretation of policies and the application of rules.

He exercises supervision through Principal Librarians and other subordinate supervisors. He receives supervision from the Assistant City Librarian in the form of directives, policy statements, and administrative conferences, and his work is evaluated on the basis of results obtained.

Examples of Duties: Plans, organizes, directs, coordinates, and reviews the activities of a major library division, such as the central library service to the public, branch library system, or library technical services; interviews job applicants; assures that personnel have adequate training in their work; spot checks division activities and reviews activity reports; confers with subordinate supervisory and professional personnel and conducts periodic staff meetings to resolve problems, clarify policy interpretations and procedures, and improve coordination of library services; occasionally handles difficult complaints of library patrons which have not been resolved elsewhere;

Supervises the preparation of, and determines priorities for division budget requests; makes recommendations regarding furniture and equipment needs and improvements in the physical layout of sections of the library; supervises the maintenance of book collections, including selecting, ordering, cataloging, repairing, and weeding of books; helps determine public service policies; maintains good public relations with civic groups and informs them of special services offered by the library; supervises the maintenance of library records and the preparation of periodic and special reports about division activities; and may have charge of forms control for the Library Department.

Qualifications: A thorough knowledge of the activities, aims, and services of the Library Department; a thorough knowledge of administrative and professional problems encountered in furnishing library service to the public and techniques for their solutions, a thorough knowledge of library reference methods; a good knowledge of principles and procedures of library organization and administration, including policy formulation, budget preparation, employee selection, and coordination of activities and services; a good knowledge of the policies, principles and practices of the Library Department affecting book selection, ordering, cataloging, circulation, repairing, and weeding; a general knowledge of supervisory principles and practices; a general knowledge of the City Charter provisions relating to the Library Department; a general knowledge of the Civil Service Commission Rules; the ability to plan, organize, and direct the activities of a major library division; the ability to deal tactfully and effectively with other employees and the public; the ability to prepare correspondence and accurate and concise reports; and the ability to speak effectively before groups.

A Master's Degree or comparable fifth-year degree in Library Science and seven years of professional librarian experience, five years of which was as a Senior Librarian, or in a class which is at least at that level and provides supervisory experience as a professional librarian in a public library, are required.

License: A valid driver's license is required.

Physical Requirements: Strength to perform lifting up to five pounds and occasionally over fifteen pounds; good speaking and hearing ability; and good eyesight.

Library T

Librarian II, Catalog Department

Grade: Librarian II
Title: Librarian II, Catalog Department
Reports to: Department Head, Catalog

Description: Is responsible for assisting in the professional work of the department; implements goals and objectives for Technical Services; maintains standards for professional activities of the department; does original cataloging and classifies materials in assigned subject areas for which Library of Congress cataloging is not available; works on special projects as assigned; increases knowledge and background in cataloging and classification, in machine-based systems and in subject areas assigned.

Supervisory responsibility: In the absence of the Department Head may supervise day to day operations.

Requirements: Library School degree.

Librarian II, Central Library

Grade: Librarian II
Title: Librarian II, Subject Department, Government Documents, or Special Services
Reports to: Department Head

Description: Is responsible for assisting in the reading guidance and reference services and other professional work in the department; implements goals and objectives for Central Library Services; maintains standards for public service and internal professional activities; provides person to person reading guidance and reference assistance, including on-line searching; works with and supervises staff assisting at the service desk; informs the department supervisor regarding books and other materials needed in the collection; increases knowledge and background in subject areas of the department.

Supervisory responsibility: In the absence of the Department Head may supervise day to day operations.

Requirements: Library School degree.

Librarian II, Community Library Services

Grade: Librarian II
Title: Community Librarian
Reports to: Assistant Chief, Community Libraries

Description: Under the supervision of the Assistant Chief, Community Libraries, is responsible for the day to day operations of the community library; implements goals and objectives for Community Library Services; maintains standards for public service and internal professional activities; provides person to person reading guidance and reference assistance; evaluates performance of personnel at the community library; studies the community to become aware of the needs of present and potential patrons; represents the Library to the community and interprets the Library's role as a cultural, educational and recreational agency; consults Assistant Chief on equipment, furnishings and related needs of the community library; sees that communications from the Assistant Chief and other Library offices reach staff members and transmits staff suggestions to the Assistant Chief; knows the resources of the community library collection, recommends title or subject needs, maintains records and prepares reports; increases knowledge and background in public library service.

The Community Librarian functions in accord with established policies under supervision of the Assistant Chief with some latitude for independent judgment; refers out-of-the-ordinary questions to the Assistant Chief for decision.

Supervisory responsibility: Supervision of personnel in the community library excepting the building staff.

Requirements: Library School degree.

Librarian III, Films Specialist

Grade: Librarian III
Title: Films Specialist
Reports to: Department Head, Art, Music and Films

Description: Under the supervision of the Head of Art-Music-Films is responsible for the daily operation of films service; implements goals and objectives of Central Library Services; maintains standards of public service and internal professional activities; provides reference assistance and guidance to patrons in use of films and related materials; assists the Department Head in training and scheduling of personnel and selection of developments in the field; assists in the maintenance of records and the preparation of reports.

Supervisory responsibility: Under the direction of the Department Head supervises personnel assigned to the Films Desk.

Requirements: Library School degree, three years of professional library experience, a thorough knowledge of the subject area.

Librarian III, Subject Departments

Grade: Librarian III
Title: Assistant Department Head
Reports to: Department Head, Subject Departments

Description: Under the supervision of the Department Head is responsible for assisting in the administration of the department; provides person to person reading guidance and reference assistance; implements goals and objectives for Central Library Services; maintains standards of public service and internal professional activities; assists Deaprtment Head in such activities as training, supervising and scheduling of personnel, selection of materials for the collection, planning and policy development and other activities as assigned; assists in the maintenance of records and the preparation of reports; increases knowledge and background in subject areas of the department.

Supervisory responsibility: Assists in the supervision of personnel in the department; supervises the department in absence of the Department Head.

Requirements: Library School degree, three years of professional library experience, a thorough knowledge of the subject areas of the department.

Librarian IV, Catalog Department

Grade: Librarian IV
Title: Department Head, Catalog
Reports to: Chief of Technical Services

Description: Is responsible for the administration of the department, for the maintenance of the book, card, and microfilm catalogs and the cataloging and classification of books and other library materials; implements goals and objectives for Technical Services; maintains high standards for the department; recommends changes in policy or procedure to increase the effectiveness and service of the department; organizes, assigns and supervises the work of the department, orients new staff to the department, supervises training, evaluates performance of personnel; maintains necessary records, prepares reports; sees that communications from the Chief and other Library offices reach staff members and that staff suggestions are transmitted to the Chief and other offices; consults and cooperates with others on the Library staff; keeps informed on cataloging developments in the Library of Congress and other libraries and in catalog theory and practice, and is alert to new trends such as automated catalogs.

Supervisory responsibility: Supervision of personnel in the department.

Requirements: Library School degree, four years of professional library experience including supervisory responsibility, broad knowledge of the field including cataloging experience with the Library of Congress classification scheme.

Librarian IV, Central Library

Grade: Librarian IV
Title: Department Head, Subject Departments
Reports to: Chief of Central Library Services

Description: Is responsible for the administration of the department, for the selection of books and other materials, and for the maintenance of a high standard of reference service; implements goals and objectives for Central Library Services; maintains standards of public service and internal professional activities; recommends changes in policy or procedure to increase the effectiveness and service of the department; organizes, assigns and supervises the work of the department; orients new staff to the department, supervises training, evaluates performance of personnel; sees that communications from the Chief and other Library offices reach staff members and that staff suggestions are transmitted to the Chief and other offices, consults and cooperates with others on the Library staff; establishes contacts with individuals and organizations in related fields in the community, promotes the use of the department's resources and services; maintains necessary records and prepares reports, increases knowledge and background in public library service and in the subject area.

Supervisory responsibility: Supervision of personnel in the department.

Requirements: Library School degree, four years of professional library experience including supervisory responsibility, broad knowledge of the subject fields.

Librarian IV, Community Library Services

Grade: Librarian IV
Title: North Regional Librarian
Reports to: Assistant Chief, Community Libraries

Description: Under the general supervision of the Assistant Chief, Community Libraries is responsible for the supervision of the North Regional Library including bookmobile service; develops suitable procedures for the maintenance of a high standard of reference service in the North Regional Library and to other community library agencies; supervises intra-library loans of materials from North Regional Library to other community library agencies; implements goals and objectives for Community Library Services; maintains standards for public service and internal professional activities; evaluates performance of personnel at North Regional Library; studies the community to become aware of the needs of present and potential patrons; represents the Library to the community and interprets the Library's role as a cultural, educational and recreatonal agency; consults with the Assistant Chief on equipment, furnishings and related needs of the North Regional Library; sees that communications from the Assistant Chief and other Library offices reach staff members and transmits staff suggestions to the Assistant Chief; knows the resources of the regional library collection and recommends subject or title needs to fulfill the function of a regional agency; maintains records, prepares reports; increases knowledge and background in public library service.

Supervisory responsibility: Supervision of personnel at North Regional Library excepting the building staff.

Requirements: Library School degree, at least four years of professional library experience including supervisory responsibility.

Librarian IV, Government Documents

Grade: Librarian IV
Title: Department Head, Government Documents
Reports to: Chief of Central Library Services

Description: Is responsible for the administration of the department, for the acquisition and organization of materials, and for the maintenance of a high standard of reference service; implements goals and objectives for Central Library Services; maintains standards of public service and internal professional activities; recommends changes in policy or procedure to increase the effectiveness and service of the department, orients new staff to the department, supervises training, evaluates performance of personnel; sees that communications from the Chief and other Library offices reach staff members and that staff suggestions are transmitted to the Chief and other offices; consults and cooperates with others on the Library staff; establishes contacts with individuals and organizations in related fields in the community, promotes the use of the department's resources and services; maintains necessary records and prepares reports; increases knowledge and background in public library service and in government documents.

Supervisory responsibility: Supervision of personnel in the department.

Requirements: Library School degree, four years of professional library experience, including supervisory responsibility, broad knowledge of government documents.

Librarian V, Order Department

Grade: Librarian V
Title: Department Head, Acquisitions/EDP*
Reports to: Chief of Technical Services

Description: Is responsible for the administration of the department, for the ordering of books, serials, periodicals, phonograph records, cassettes, and other such materials for Library collections; implements goals and objectives for Technical Services; maintains high standards for the department; recommends changes in policy or procedure to increase the effectiveness and service of the department; organizes, assigns and supervises the work of the department, orients new staff to the department, supervises training, evaluates performance of personnel; maintains necessary records, prepares reports; sees that communications from the Chief and other Library offices reach staff members and that staff suggestions are transmitted to the Chief and other offices; consults and cooperates with others on the Library staff; keeps informed on developments in other libraries and in the publishing and book selling world, and is alert to new trends in the acquisition field and in automation.

Supervisory responsibility: Supervision of personnel in the department.

Requirements: Library School degree, four years of professional library experience including supervisory responsibility, broad knowledge of the field.

* This job description does not include responsibilities associated with EDP.

Librarian V, Central Library

Grade: Librarian V
Title: Department Head, Business and Science or Art/Music/Films
Reports to: Chief of Central Library Services

Description: Is responsible for the administration of the department, for the selection of books and other materials, and for the maintenance of a high standard of reference service; implements goals and objectives for Central Library Services; maintains standards of public service and internal professional activities; recommends changes in policy or procedure to increase the effectiveness and service of the department; organizes, assigns, and supervises the work of the department, orients new staff to the department, supervises training, evaluates performance of personnel; sees that communications from the Chief and other library offices reach staff members and that staff suggestions are transmitted to the Chief and other offices, consults and cooperates with others on the library staff; establishes contacts with individuals and organizations in related fields in the community, promotes the use of the department's resources and services; maintains necessary records and prepares reports, increases knowledge and background in public library service and in the subject areas.

Supervisory responsibility: Supervision of personnel in the department.

Requirements: Library School degree, five years of professional library experience including supervisory responsibility, broad knowledge of the subject fields.

Librarian V, Community Library Sciences

Grade: Librarian V
Title: Community Services Book Selection Librarian
Reports to: Chief of Community Library Services

Description: Is responsible for implementing the Library's book selection policies for community library collections and for supervising the work of intra-library loans; recommends changes in policies or procedure to improve service or increase efficiency in the area of responsibility; serves as resource authority for community library collections; participates in developing recommendations on book budget allocations; maintains close relationships with central library book selection activity; keeps informed on resources of the central collection, is alert to trends in publishing, in reader interests and new forms for the communication of ideas; maintains statistics and prepares reports.

The Community Services Book Selection Librarian functions in accord with established policies under general supervision of the Chief of Community Library Services with latitude for independent judgment subject to prior approval only in complex circumstances.

Supervisory responsibility: Direct supervision of office staff.

Advisory responsibility: To the Chief of Community Library Services and to the Assistant Chief, Community Libraries.

Requirements: Library School degree, five years of professional library service including a variety of experiences in public service.

Librarian VI, Central Library

Grade: Librarian VI
Title: Central Library Services Book Selection Librarian
Reports to: Chief of Central Library Services   ⌐

Description: Is responsible for the administration of the Central Book Selection Office; implements goals and objectives for Central Library Services; maintains high standards in special collections; responsible for selection overview for central subject departments, collects and maintains rare books, special collections, popular library; serves the public as reference resource in the areas of rare books and special collections; recommends changes in policy or procedure to increase effectiveness; assists in making recommendations for book selection policy and for book budget allocations; organizes, assigns and supervises the work of the agency, maintains necessary records, prepares reports; consults and cooperates with others on the staff, particularly the Community Services Book Selection Librarian, keeps informed on developments in bibliography in the rare book world.

Supervisory responsibility: Direct supervision of office staff.

Advisory responsibility: To the Chief of Central Library Services.

Requirements: Library School degree, six years of professional library service including a variety of experience in public service.

Librarian VII, Community Library Services

Grade: Librarian VII
Title: Chief of Community Library Services
Reports to: Associate Director/Director

Description: Is responsible for the overall administration of Community Library Services; community libraries, bookmobile, Children's Department, programs office, homebound service; develops goals and objectives for Community Library Services; develops standards for public service and internal professional activities; recommends changes in policies that will increase the effectiveness of Community Library Services; encourages staff contacts with community leaders and a program of library related activities for all segments of the community; participates in the selection of personnel and approves staff assignments within the area of responsibility; prepares specifications, evaluates bids, and participates in budget allocations for library materials, equipment and services, and is responsible for approving expenditures and requisitions against the budget allocation; participates in developing long range plans for Community Library Services in determining needs in collections, services, and physical facilities for the delivery of optimum library services.

The Chief, in accord with general Library policy, functions under the direction of the Director or Associate Director with latitude for independent judgment subject to prior approval only in the most complex or unusual circumstances.

Supervisory responsibility: Direct supervision of Assistant Chief, Community Library Book Selection Librarian, Head of Children's Department, Library Programs Librarian and Library Technician; Homebound, community libraries office staff; general supervision of all Community Library Services personnel.

Advisory responsibility: To Director and Associate Director on Community Library Services.

Requirements: Library School degree, 10 years of professional public library experience including demonstrated supervisory experience and administrative management capacity with at least three years of experience in community libraries.

Librarian VII, Central Library Services

Grade: Librarian VII
Title: Chief of Central Library Services
Reports to: Associate Director/Director

Description: Is responsible for the overall administration of Central Library Services; Central Services Book Selection Office, subject departments, Special Services Department, Shelving and stack allocations; develops goals and objectives for Central Library Services; develops standards for public service and internal professional activities; recommends changes in policies that will increase the effectiveness of Central Library Services; encourages staff contacts with community leaders; participates in the selection of personnel and approves staff assignments within the area of responsibility; prepares specifications, evaluates bids and participates in budget allocations for library materials, equipment and services and is responsible for approving expenditures and requisitions against the budget allocations; participates in developing long range plans for Central Library Services and describes needs in collections, services and physical facilities for the delivery of optimum library service.

The Chief, in accord with general Library policy, functions under the direction of the Director or Associate Director with latitude for independent judgment subject to prior approval only in the most complex or unusual circumstances.

Supervisory responsibility: Direct supervision of Central Library Services Book Selection Librarian, department supervisors, police officer, central library office staff; general supervision of all Central Library Services personnel.

Advisory responsibility: To Director and Associate Director on Central Library Services.

Requirements: Library School degree, 10 years of professional public library service including demonstrated supervisory experience and administrative management capacity with at least three years of experience in reference and readers advisory service.

Librarian VII, Technical Services

Grade: Librarian VII
Title: Chief of Technical Services
Reports to: Associate Director/Director

Description: Is responsible for the overall administration of Technical Services: Catalog, Circulation, Data Processing, Order, Preparations; develops goals and objectives for Technical Services, develops standards for public service and internal professional activities; recommends changes in policies that will increase the effectiveness of Technical Services; participates in the selection of personnel and approves staff assignments within the area of responsibility; prepares specifications, evaluates bids and participates in budget allocations for materials, equipment and services and is responsible for approving expenditures and requisitions against the budget allocations; participates in developing long range plans for Technical Services and describes needs in services, equipment and physical facilities for the delivery of optimum library service.

The Chief, in accord with general Library policy, functions under the direction of the Director or Associate Director with latitude for independent judgment subject to prior approval only in the most complex or unusual circumstances.

Supervisory responsibility: Direct supervision of department supervisors, general supervision of all Technical Services personnel.

Advisory responsibility: To Director and Associate Director on Technical Services.

Requirements: Library School degree, 10 years of professional public library service including demonstrated supervisory experience and administrative management capacity with at least three years of experience in cataloging, acquisitions or data processing or a combination thereof.

Library U

CATALOGING LIBRARIAN

General Statement of Duties: Performs professional library work cataloging for specialized new title materials with machine readable copy, including serials, periodicals, local history, genealogy and rare book items.

Supervision Received: Works under the supervision of the Original Cataloging Supervisor or other professional as assigned.

Supervision Exercised: None.

EXAMPLES OF DUTIES:

Catalogs specialized materials, serials, periodicals, and books for western history and genealogy using OCLC copy. Compares the copy with the item to verify that the description is absolutely accurate. Verifies fixed fields and variable tags, codes and indicators. Makes changes as needed. Checks all names, series and subjects against current authority files to assure consistency.

Validates suggested Dewey classification numbers and creates call numbers. Refers problems and non-matches to the appropriate Original Cataloger.

Prepares preliminary cataloging (descriptive and authority checking) for items forwarded to the Original Cataloger, and for those with National Union Catalog (NUC) or other copy.

Prepares descriptive cataloging of AV materials without cataloging copy. Forwards to the appropriate Original Cataloger.

Performs preliminary searching for name authority work.

Searches a variety of on-line data bases for cataloging information. Edits OCLC on-line for retrospective conversion.

Performs related work as required.

QUALIFICATIONS FOR APPOINTMENT

Knowledges, Skills and Abilities: Working knowledge of Machine Readable Cataloging (MARC) tags. Working knowledge of current and past cataloging rules. Working knowledge of publishing practices related to periodicals and non-print materials. Working knowledge of periodical and serials control methods. Working knowledge of Dewey Decimal Classification and Library of Congress subject headings. Some subject knowledge. Ability to establish and maintain effective working relationships with other employees.

Education: Graduation from an American Library Association accredited university with a Master of Library Science degree.

Experience: None.

Alternative to the Minimum Education and Experience Requirements: Graduation from a college or university with a Masters degree in any subject area and one year of professional or paraprofessional experience in a library; or graduation from a college or university with a Baccalaureate degree in any subject area and two (2) years of professional or paraprofessional experience in a library.

CATALOGING SPECIALIST

General Statement of Duties: Performs professional library work cataloging all new titles without OCLC copy and specialized materials such as periodicals, serials, rare books, non-print materials and materials for western history and genealogy.

Supervision Received: Works under the supervision of the Original Cataloging Supervisor or other supervisor.

Supervision Exercised: None.

EXAMPLES OF DUTIES:

(Any one position may not include all of the duties listed, nor do the listed examples include all tasks which may be found in positions of this class.)

Prepares original cataloging for new titles which have no cataloging copy. Develops descriptive cataloging, assigns Dewey classification numbers and Library of Congress subject headings, and selects added entries.

Prepares original input work forms for new and retrospective titles lacking OCLC copy.

Catalogs specialized materials such as serials, periodicals, non-print materials and materials for western history and genealogy which are passed on from the Cataloging Librarian; catalogs foreign language materials.

Determines the need for catalog data base maintenance and updating and initiates changes.

Maintains awareness of current developments in classification, cataloging and OCLC procedures.

Searches a variety of on-line data bases for cataloging information and data base building.

Performs related work as required.

QUALIFICATION FOR APPOINTMENT

Knowledges, Skills and Abilities: Considerable knowledge of current and past cataloging rules and Dewey classification system. Considerable knowledge of Machine Readable Cataloging (MARC) tags and bibliographic searching techniques. Considerable knowledge of Library of Congress subject heading practice and of publishing practices and patterns. Working knowledge of Library of Congress classification. Working knowledge of at least one foreign language. Ability to establish and maintain effective working relationships with other employees.

Education: Graduation from an American Library Association accredited college or university with a Master of Library Science degree.

Experience: One year of professional or paraprofessional experience cataloging and classifying library materials.

Alternatives to the Minimum Education and Experience Requirements: Graduation from a college or university with a Masters Degree in any subject area and two years of professional or paraprofessional experience cataloging and classifying library materials or graduation from a college or university with a Baccalaureate degree in any subject area and three years of professional or paraprofessional experience cataloging and classifying library materials.

CATALOGING SUPERVISOR I

General Statement of Duties: Performs supervisory and professional work directing a group of Cataloging Assistants in performing cataloging with machine readable copy.

Supervision Received: Works under the direction of the Cataloging Department Manager.

Supervision Exercised: Supervises Cataloging Assistants.

EXAMPLES OF DUTIES:

Supervises cataloging and classification of routine new titles with OCLC copy. Prepares and revises procedures, trains, monitors work flow, and maintains quality control.

Trains Cataloging Assistants in developing cataloging skills such as identifying variant editions, consulting the Dewey schedules, updating Library of Congress subject headings.

Makes professional decisions regarding all aspects of cataloging when problems are identified by the Cataloging Assistants. Resolves conflicts and assigns Dewey classification numbers and Library of Congress subject headings as needed. Forwards unusual problems to the Original Cataloging Supervisor.

Supervises the maintenance of authority files, official revision, and OCLC error reporting.

Assists the Department Manager in interviewing and evaluating employee performance and in the formulation of department goals and objectives.

Maintains awareness of current professional literature, changes in cataloging rules and changes in OCLC procedures.

Searches a variety of on-line data bases for cataloging information. Edits cataloging on-line as needed.

Performs related work as required.

QUALIFICATIONS FOR APPOINTMENT

Knowledges, Skills and Abilities: Considerable knowledge of past and present cataloging rules, Library of Congress Subject headings, and Dewey Decimal Classification. Considerable knowledge of Machine Readable Cataloging (MARC) tags, and OCLC procedures. Ability to communicate effectively both orally and in writing. Ability to establish and maintain effective working relationships with other employees.

Education: Graduation from an American Library Association accredited college or university with a Master of Library Science degree.

Experience: One year of professional or paraprofessional experience cataloging and classifying library materials.

Alternatives to the Minimum Education and Experience Requirements: Graduation from a college or university with a Masters Degree in any subject area and two years of professional or paraprofessional experience cataloging and classifying library materials or graduation from a college or university with a Baccalaureate degree in any subject area and three years of professional or paraprofessional experience cataloging and classifying library materials.

CATALOGING SUPERVISOR II

General Statement of Duties: Performs professional and supervisory work directing Cataloging Librarians and Original Catalogers in preparing original input to OCLC and in cataloging special materials.

Supervision Received: Works under the direction of the Cataloging Department Manager.

Supervision Exercised: Supervises Original Catalogers and Cataloging Librarians.

EXAMPLES OF DUTIES:

Supervises Original Catalogers in preparing original input for new titles which have no cataloging copy and preparing original input workforms as needed.

Supervises Original Catalogers and Cataloging Librarians in the cataloging of specialized materials such as serials, periodicals, non-print materials, rare books and materials for western history and genealogy.

Serves as primary resource person for decisions on classification, subject analysis, and name authority work. Provides support training and written procedures for the original and copy cataloging groups.

Maintains contact with appropriate Public Services departments for exchange of information on current developments, and to maximize public access to materials.

Selects, interviews and evaluates the personnel supervised. Monitors workflow, statistics and quality control.

Develops and updates cataloging manuals. Provides necessary information on Library of Congress rule interpretations.

Assists the Department Manager in the formulation of goals and objectives and serves as back-up for the Department Manager.

Searches a variety of on-line data bases for information for decision making.

Maintains awareness of current professional literature, changes in cataloging rules and Library of Congress practice, and changes in OCLC procedures.

Performs related work as required.

QUALIFICATIONS FOR APPOINTMENT

Knowledges, Skills and Abilities: Thorough knowledge of current and past cataloging rules. Thorough knowledge of Machine Readable Cataloging (MARC) tags and bibliographic searching techniques. Thorough knowledge of Library of Congress classifications, subject heading policy and practices. Thorough knowledge of Dewey Classification system. Working knowledge of at least one foreign language and of rare books cataloging. Ability to establish and maintain effective working relationships with other employees and other departments. Ability to communicate effectively both orally and in writing.

Education: Graduation from an American Library Association accredited college or university with a Master of Library Science degree.

Experience: Two years of experience performing original cataloging in a library.

Alternatives to the Minimum Education and Experience Requirements: Graduation from a college or university with a Masters Degree in any subject area and four years of experience performing original cataloging, or graduation from a college or university with a Baccalaureate degree in any subject area and five years of experience performing original cataloging.

Library Administrators

Library D

LIBRARY DIRECTOR

Nature of Work: This is administrative and professional library work in managing the county library system. As chief administrative officer, the employee has responsibility for planning, directing, coordinating and supervising all activities of the library system. Subject to general policies established by the Library Commission, the employee has full responsibility for developing a detailed library program and for maintaining standards in professional and related activities adequate for the attainment of the objectives of the library system. He will concentrate on external relations, the direction and development of the library, evaluation of progress and performance.

Illustrative Examples of Work: Plans and directs all phases of the operations of the library system.
   Supervises and participates in the preparation of library budget.
   Prepares building programs, coordinates building planning for construction and renovation with architects.
   Instructs supervisory personnel in general policies and procedures and conducts general staff conferences and meetings.
   Supervises preparation of recommendations on personnel and policy. Reviews recommendations by library staff for personnel appointments, classification, promotion, and makes final determination of personnel actions.

Supervises preparation of reports, newsletters, releases for governmental officials, staff and communications media.

Reviews and makes final approval of recommendations by library staff for the expenditure of funds including purchase of books and other materials.

Recommends approval of contractual services to the Library Commission.

Repesents the library in civic, educational and library affairs of the city and county and in its relationships at state and national levels.

Meets with community organizations and others in explaining library system objectives and policies and in extending library services.

Performs related work as required.

Knowledges, Abilities and Skills: Extensive knowledge of the principles, methods, and practices of modern library administration. Thorough knowledge of community needs and interests in relation to library services.

Thorough knowledge of reader interest levels and a wide knowledge of books and authors.

Thorough knowledge of sound methods of management in relation to the operation of a large public library system.

Considerable ability in establishing and maintaining effective working relationships with community leaders, public officials, professional groups, and the general public.

Considerable ability in analyzing library needs and evaluating library services.

Ability to speak and write effectively.

Desirable Experience and Training: Considerable professional library experience in an administrative capacity; and graduation from an accredited college or university and attainment of a graduate degree from an accredited school of library science.

ASSISTANT DIRECTOR OF PUBLIC SERVICES

Nature of Work: This is administrative and professional library work assisting the Director in the general management of the City-County Library System. As an assistant to the chief administrative officer of the library system, the employee participates in the planning, coordinating, supervising, and directing of the public service activities in the library system. May direct all phases of the library system in the absence of the Director.

Administers the Central Library, the branch libraries and the bookmobiles, schedules and assigns personnel, interprets library policy, resolves staff relationships, maintains quality of reference and reader's advisory services to community and professional groups. Plans, recommends, and executes changes in organization, methods, and procedures for improvement in efficiency and service to the system.

Illustrative examples of work: Develops public service program, instructs and supervises the department heads of the Central Library, the regional librarians and the bookmobile librarians. Maintains effective relationships between programs and personnel of the Central Library, the branches and bookmobiles.

Represents the library in civic, educational and library affairs of the City and County and in its relationships at state and national levels.

Meets with community organizations and others in explaining library system objectives and policies and in extending library services.

Knowledges, abilities and skills: Wide knowledge of modern library organization, procedures, policy, aims and service.

Skill in coordinating various departments and directing staff. Considerable ability in analyzing library needs and evaluating library service.

Initiative, resourcefulness, good judgment and tact.

Considerable knowledge of reader interest levels and wide knowledge of books and authors.

Ability to establish and maintain effective working relationships with community groups, the public and with other employees.

Desirable experience and training: Considerable professional experience in an administrative capacity; graduation from an accredited college or university and attainment of a graduate degree from an accredited school of library science.

ASSISTANT DIRECTOR FOR NON-PUBLIC SERVICES

Nature of Work: This is responsible administrative and supervisory work in directing the budgeting, accounting, purchasing, personnel, training, collection, acquisition and technical processing of the library system. Supervision is received from the Library Director, but considerable latitude is allowed for independent judgment and initiative in carrying on the work for non-public services.

Illustrative Examples of Work: Makes forecasts of income and expenses for use in budgeting and financial planning; directs regular and special financial reporting; makes surveys and special reports to aid Library Director and Commission.

Receives and verifies requisitions and determines priority of purchases; consults with appropriate vendors; receives and analyzes quotations and bids for prices and consistency with specifications; prepares specifications; issues purchase orders.

Interviews prospective employees; contacts sources of applicants; schedules appointments for supervisors; maintains records of current and former personnel.

Coordinates and arranges for in-service training for staff members of a variety of subjects as determined by analyzing needs.

Serves as custodian of all money collected by the various departments and branches.

Supervises the preparation of financial reports monthly.

Negotiates building leases and service contracts such as for cleaning, printing, equipment maintenance.

Prepares proposals for special funding such as Revenue Sharing, LSCA, or related sources.

Works with local agencies in obtaining additional staff from work-study, work-training, and youth programs.

Acts as Affirmative Action officer for the Library.

Knowledges, Abilities and Skills: Knowledge of current methods of business management and their application.

General knowledge of library philosophy, purposes and functions.

Knowledge of personnel practices and procedures.

General knowledge and familiarity with automation, its principles, and potential for library applications.

Ability to establish and maintain effective working relationships with other governmental agencies, with other employees, and with vendors, contractors and service representatives.

Desirable Experience and Training: Graduation from an accredited college or university with a degree in business or related fields. Experience in public administration, business management and systems analysis.

Library I

CLASS TITLE: Library Director

DEFINITION: Under administrative direction; performs work of unusual difficulty in planning and directing the operations of the County Library system.

EXAMPLES OF DUTIES: Develops system wide policies and procedures for library operations; plans, organizes, and directs all activities concerned with the administration and operation of the library system; establishes objectives, policies, and procedures for the system; coordinates and administers library programs and operations; develops and coordinates programs for new or revised services and facilities to meet the changing needs of the community; determines need for and recommends additions or changes of location or services of branch libraries; supervises the selection and training of personnel; represents the library in professional associations and in dealing with other governments and library committees; supervises division operations and matters concerning personnel, buildings, equipment, and policy; supervises the preparations and administration of the library budget; coordinates library operations with other County departmental functions; does special research and reading in library functions and administration; makes policy recommendations to library board; makes site recommendations for new library facilities and directs the library building program; performs related work as required.

EMPLOYMENT STANDARDS:

Education and Experience. Master's Degree in Library Science and five years of experience in a library administrative capacity; or an equivalent combination of training and experience.

Knowledge, Abilities, and Skills. Comprehensive knowledge of specialized professional library principles, methods, techniques and procedures; comprehensive knowledge of laws and regulations relating to library operations; comprehensive knowledge of administrative and personnel management methods and techniques; considerable knowledge of technical advances in library processes and library services including information retrieval.

Marked ability to analyze trends and to develop and maintain a good book collection; marked ability to evaluate community needs and to develop the best methods of providing services; considerable ability to establish and maintain effective relationships with the public and other administrative personnel.

Comprehensive skill in planning and directing library system operations; considerable skill in directing and coordinating building programs.

CLASS TITLE: Associate Library Director

DEFINITION: Under administrative direction; performs work of unusual difficulty in directing the public service of the County Library.

EXAMPLES OF DUTIES: Through Coordinating Librarians and special service staff directs and coordinates the service of community and area libraries; directs the activities of system-wide services and programs to include bookmobiles, outreach services and varied community programming; assists Director in planning library facilities; analyzes community library services and needs; recommends or implements appropriate methods to improve service; interprets library service to schools, community organizations and other interested parties; assists in establishing standards and minimums for collection and services; devises control procedures to assure attainment of standards; trains, supervises and evaluates staff; participates in devising a coordinated program of system-wide library service; prepares budget estimates; advises the public, e.g., giving information and answering complaints; develops and supervises the maintenance of public service related records and statistics; assumes final responsibility for specific assignments delegated by the Director; performs related work as required.

EMPLOYMENT STANDARDS:

Education and Experience: Master's Degree in Library Science from ALA accredited school and a minimum of two years of professional experience in a public library system. Additionally, five years of experience in a library administrative capacity or in the supervision of professional library staff is required.

Knowledge, Abilities and Skills. Comprehensive knowledge of specialized library principles, techniques and procedures; comprehensive knowledge of management principles and techniques; comprehensive knowledge of the concepts of library service; considerable knowledge of public relations techniques.

Marked ability to evaluate performance of staff; marked ability to develop program recommendations and effect program changes; marked ability to establish and maintain effective communication in the community and with administrative staff; considerable ability to define needs, set priorities and prepare budgets; considerable ability to plan and coordinate system-wide programs and schedules.

Comprehensive skill in developing and effecting changes in operating policies and procedures; comprehensive skill in staff training and supervision.

CLASS TITLE: Deputy Library Director

DEFINITION: Under administrative direction; performs work of unusual difficulty assisting in the direction and coordination of the library system; provides administrative support to Associate Director and Division Managers.

EXAMPLES OF DUTIES: Coordinates and supervises library operations; directs the collection development program and establishes standards and minimums for the collection; supervises library public information program; supervises library personnel function; analyzes and evaluates department's service policies and procedures through staff consultations; reviews recommendations on the expansion or revision of community library facilities; makes policy change recommendations to the Director for more effective implementation of the activities of various divisions; explains departmental policies to the public and other interested parties; represents the department in negotiations with local community officials concerning library related problems within the County; trains, supervises and evaluates staff; prepares budget estimates; assumes final responsibility for specific assignments delegated by the Director; serves as Director in the absence of the Director; performs related work as required.

EMPLOYMENT STANDARDS:

Education and Experience. Master's Degree in library science from ALA accredited school; and a minimum of two years of professional experience in a public library system; additionally, five years of experience in a library administrative capacity or in the supervision of professional library staff is required.

Knowledge, Abilities, and Skills. Comprehensive knowledge of specialized library principles, techniques and procedures; comprehensive knowledge of management principles and techniques; comprehensive knowledge of technical aspects of library processes and library service, including information retrieval; considerable knowledge of laws and regulations relating to library operations; considerable knowledge of public relations techniques.

Marked ability to analyze trends and to develop and maintain collections; marked ability to establish and maintain effective communication in the community and with other public officials; considerable ability to evaluate community needs, set priorities and develop methods of providing service.

Comprehensive skill in the use of specialized library principles, techniques and procedures; comprehensive skill in staff training and supervision; considerable skill in evaluating community needs and in developing methods of providing service.

Library O

POSITION TITLE: Executive Director. DEPARTMENT: Administrative Services. DIVISION: Administrative Services. TITLE OF IMMEDIATE SUPERVISOR: Board of Trustees.

1. PURPOSE OF WORK

With the assistance of the administrative staff, designs, implements and evaluates an active program of educational, cultural, and informational services relevant to the people of the City and County, in accordance with the policies, goals and objectives of the Board of Trustees. Advises the Board on library services and development, administers their policies, and coordinates the operation of the library through the various departments of the institution.

2. MINIMUM QUALIFICATIONS

1. Graduate degree in library science from an ALA accredited school.
2. Minimum of ten years of progressively more responsible professional library experience.
3. Ability to communicate effectively with public.
4. Demonstrated knowledge of budgeting and public library finance.
5. Possession of a valid drivers license and ready access to suitable transportation or a personal vehicle appropriate for use in the transaction of Library business and performance of job related duties (approved mileage reimbursed at prescribed rate).

3. TYPICAL DUTIES

1. Meets with the Board of Trustees and its committees to consider their policies and implements their directives.
2. Communicates the library's services, resources, and programs to the community.
3. Coordinates the administrative operation of the library in concert with the department heads.

4. Develops new services and programs to better serve the community.

5. Works with other community and government groups to coordinate the delivery of services to the city and county.

6. Evaluates existing services and programs with regard to their effectiveness, and modifies them or recommends modifications as required.

7. Resolves complaints from the public, Board, and staff.

8. Is responsible for preparation of administrative reports and budgetary requests, and selection, evaluation, and training of assigned personnel.

9. Performs other duties as assigned.

POSITION TITLE: Assistant Executive Director of the Library. DEPARTMENT: Administrative Services. DIVISION: Administrative Services. TITLE OF IMMEDIATE SUPERVISOR: Executive Director.

1. PURPOSE OF WORK

Under the general supervision of the Executive Director, is responsible for major administrative responsibilities in carrying out the policies and attaining objectives established by the Board of Trustees. Directs personnel, develops and maintains liaison with key governmental, civic and community groups and generally assists the Executive Director in all areas as assigned.

2. MINIMUM QUALIFICATIONS

1. Graduate degree in Library Science from an ALA accredited school.

2. Minimum of eight years of progressively more responsible administrative experience sufficient to perform the assigned responsibilities.

3. Demonstrated administrative, managerial, and communicative skills.

4. Demonstrated ability to write lucid reports, letters, memoranda and other communications; ability to speak well in one-to-one situations, as well as in large meeting; ability to communicate effectively with various socioeconomic and ethnic groups; participation in regional, state and national professional organizations and activities.

5. Possession of a valid drivers license and ready access to suitable transportation or a personal vehicle appropriate for use in the transaction of Library business and performance of job related duties (approved mileage reimbursed at prescribed rate).

3. TYPICAL DUTIES

1. Acts in the absence of the Director, assuming all those duties and authorities of the Executive Director's position.

2. Assists the Executive Director in carrying out the directives of the Board of Trustees.

3. May gather facts and information for the Board of Trustees and the Executive Director to expedite and improve the decision-making process.

4. Directly supervises assigned personnel.

5. May serve as a liaison and representative for the Library with community, professional, and civic groups.

6. May be responsible for preparation of administrative reports, special projects, requests and review, evaluation and training of assigned personnel.

7. Performs other duties as assigned.

POSITION TITLE: Director of Extension Services. DEPARTMENT: Extension. DIVISION: Extension. TITLE OF IMMEDIATE SUPERVISOR: Executive Director of the Library.

1. PURPOSE OF WORK

Under the general supervision of the Executive Director, performs major administrative responsibilities involving the planning, coordination, and supervision of activities in the branch libraries, hospital, and bookmobile departments.

2. MINIMUM QUALIFICATIONS

1. Graduate degree in library science from an ALA accredited school.

2. Minimum of eight years of progressively more responsible professional library experience.

3. Demonstrated administrative, managerial, and communicative skills with sound public relations capabilities.

4. Flexible with respect to work schedule.

5. Possession of a valid drivers license and ready access to suitable transportation or a personal vehicle appropriate for use in the transaction of library business and performance of job related duties (approved mileage reimbursed at prescribed rate).

3. TYPICAL DUTIES

1. Schedules and conducts branch meetings.

2. Interprets library goals and objectives and aids in planning appropriate library services.

3. Formulates and administers branch policies.

4. Advises staff on acquisition of materials.

5. Is responsible for preparation of administrative reports, budgetary requests, and selection, evaluation, and training of assigned personnel.

6. Plans in concert with the Coordinator of Children's and Young Adult Services and the branch or division heads; stimulates these heads; and subsequently evaluates their development of a program of educational, cultural, and informational services relevant to the clientele of the individual branches or divisions.

7. Performs other duties as assigned.

POSITION TITLE: Director of Main Library. DEPARTMENT: Main. DIVISION: Main. TITLE OF IMMEDIATE SUPERVISOR: Assistant Executive Director of the Library.

1. PURPOSE OF WORK

Under the general supervision of the Assistant Executive Director of the library, performs major administrative responsibilities involving the planning, coordination, and supervision of the activities in the Main Library and Divisions.

2. MINIMUM QUALIFICATIONS

1. Graduate degree in library science from an ALA accredited school.
2. Minimum of eight years of progressively more responsible professional library experience.
3. Demonstrated administrative, managerial, and communicative skills with sound public relations capabilities.
4. Flexible with respect to work schedule.
5. Possession of a valid drivers license and ready access to suitable transportation or a personal vehicle appropriate for use in the transaction of Library business and performance of job related duties (approved mileage reimbursed at prescribed rate).

3. TYPICAL DUTIES

1. Schedules and conducts division meetings.
2. Interprets library goals and objectives and aids in planning appropriate library services.
3. Formulates and administers divisional policies, procedures, and budgets.
4. Advises staff on acquisition of materials.
5. Plans in concert with the coordinator of Children's and Young Adult Services and the branch or division heads; stimulates these heads; and subsequently evaluates their development of a program of educational, cultural and informational services relevant to the clientele of the individual branches or divisions.
6. Is responsible for preparation of administrative reports and budgetary requests, and selection, evaluation and training of assigned personnel.
7. Performs other duties as assigned.

POSITION TITLE: Director of Technical Services. DEPART-MENT: Technical Services. DIVISION: Technical Services. TITLE OF IMMEDIATE SUPERVISOR: Executive Director of the Library.

PURPOSE OF WORK

Under the general supervision of the Executive Director of the Library, plans, coordinates, and supervises the acquisition, cataloging, and processing of books, periodicals, and other materials.

2. MINIMUM QUALIFICATIONS

1. Graduate degree in library science from an ALA accredited school.

2. Minimum of eight years of progressively more responsible professional library experience.

3. Demonstrated administrative, managerial, and communicative skills, preferable in technical services.

4. Working knowledge of OCLC and other library automation procedures.

5. Possession of a valid drivers license and ready access to suitable transportation or a personal vehicle appropriate for use in the transaction of Library business and performance of job related duties (approved mileage reimbursed at prescribe rate).

3. TYPICAL DUTIES

1. Plans, coordinates, and supervises the overall operation of the Technical Services Department.

2. Reviews and evaluates current and proposed policies and procedures and related activities within the department.

3. Participates in the acquisition and evaluation of personnel.

4. Provides supervisory assistance to the Technical Services Division Heads.

5. Describes and explains Technical Services policies and procedures to Public Services Agency Heads.

6. Is responsible for preparation of administrative reports and budgetary requests, and selection, evaluation, and training of assigned personnel.

7. Performs other duties as assigned.

Library S

POSITION TITLE: Director of Libraries

POSITION REPORTS TO: City Manager through Assistant City Manager

SUMMARY

The Director of Libraries acts as the Chief Administrator for the Municipal Library System. This position encompasses the Central Research Library, Branch Libraries, Bookmobiles and Deposit Stations within the system.

EDUCATION AND EXPERIENCE

Education: Master's degree in Library Science.

Experience: Ten years or more of experience in municipal library procedures and administration.

DUTIES AND RESPONSIBILITIES

1. Participates in long range planning including identification and presentation of goals and objectives.
2. Participates in the planning and approval of the operating budget and reviews periodic reports and identifies significant variances.
3. Reviews and approves personnel management tasks such as hiring, firing, promotions and transfers.
4. Reviews the policies and techniques relating to selection, acquisition, classifying and cataloging of books, films, maps, documents and others.
5. Participates in the evaluation of current services and in long range plans for facilities development.
6. Works with Municipal Library Advisory Board and serves as communication channel to City Council.
7. Helps secure grants for experimental and innovative programs.
8. Coordinates the regional efforts of cooperative ventures for extension of library services among communities.
9. Represents the library system on state, regional and national levels. Often given the opportunity to interpret the library as a user-oriented agency.
10. Works with Friends of the Library, auxiliary supporting library's role and functions in the community.
11. Oversees the preparation of the annual report.
12. Supports fund raising activities from private sources for projects not included in the City budget.

MEASURES OF PERFORMANCE

Objective:

1. Amount of citizen usage of library facilities.
2. Adherence to budget performance.
3. Personnel performance evaluation records.
4. Production of work on other City assignments.
5. Obtaining grants as recognition of proficiency.
6. Preparation and publication of reports, professional articles, etc.
7. Offices held on state, regional, national and international levels.

Subjective:

1. Citizen compliments or complaints.
2. Citizen support in bond programs and other library projects.
3. Innovative programs for new educational methods.
4. Professional staff stability re turnover in responsible positions.
5. Professional recognition of staff trained at the Library.
6. Degree to which library serves all citizens in all parts of the City.

POSITION TITLE: Associate Director of Libraries – Management Services

POSITION REPORTS TO: Director of Libraries

SUMMARY

The Associate Director of Libraries – Management Services is responsible for directing the business operations of the library system for the management of the centralized, internal services that have system-wide impact.

EDUCATION AND EXPERIENCE

Education: Master's degree in Library Science.

Experience: Seven to ten years of administrative experience, preferably in a public-service oriented institution. Knowledge of data processing systems and budget administration, with some knowledge of grant funding procedures.

DUTIES AND RESPONSIBILITIES

1. Directs operations of the Materials Processing and Circulation Control units and the Business Office.

2. Participates in the fact-finding, analysis, and long range planning phases of library policy and procedure development, revision, and implementation.

3. Evaluates, formulates, and recommends annual budget requirements. Reviews for significant variances actual versus budget.

4. Administers operations, capital improvement, and revenue-sharing budgets.

5. Prepares statistical and financial reports for management use and to meet legal, contractual, and public requirements for information about library operations.

6. Prepares and reviews contract specifications for materials, maintenance work, and other services.

7. Reviews professional journals to keep up-to-date on innovative library programs and administrative systems. Directs the preparation of responses to questionnaires and correspondence on library operations.

8. Reviews monthly operating reports from all units.

9. Directs purchases of all library materials, and establishes control procedures for their processing and initial circulation into the system.

10. Reviews building design, construction, and maintenance plans for cost feasibility.

11. Works with other libraries to originate cooperative library services.

12. Deals with vendors and suppliers of items purchased by the library.

MEASURES OF PERFORMANCE

Objective:

1. Accuracy of budget forecasts and ability to operate within budget limitations.

2. More accurate information for management on operations costs, circulation, and other service data.

Subjective:

1. Fewer patron complaints.

POSITION TITLE: Associate Director of Libraries — Public Services

POSITION REPORTS TO: Director of Libraries

SUMMARY

The Associate Director of Libraries — Public Services is the administrator of the Central and branch libraries and their sub-units. This position is responsible for setting public service program goals, planning for expansion of services and facilities, and providing for expansion of services and facilities, and providing for the recruitment and development of the professional staff.

EDUCATION AND EXPERIENCE

Education: Master's degree in Library Science.
Experience: Seven to ten years of progressive administrative experience in a public library system.

DUTIES AND RESPONSIBILITIES

1. Plans personnel staffing requirements to meet specific public service needs and future growth patterns of the library system.
2. Evaluates circulation data, program impact, and budget expenditures to measure cost effectiveness of all public services.
3. Joins with the Director and other Associate Director of Libraries to establish and evaluate departmental goals, policies, and procedures, and to determine program priorities.
4. Recruits donations of funds, private collections of other unique resource materials to enhance the scope of the library's permanent collection.
5. Works with public and private citizen groups to develop special interest collections.
6. Directs and approves the work of Materials Specialists who review and select book and non-book items for the entire library system for adult and youth users.
7. Cooperates with other libraries and library systems to plan cooperative programs and centralized support services for participating institutions.
8. Approves the staffing and operation of all branch libraries and mobile units to meet specific local community needs and interests. Approves the staffing and operation of the library's outreach efforts to special community groups.

9. Approves the staffing and operations of the Central Library in its function as a source of highly specialized collections and centralized information services.

10. Acts in the capacity of Department Head when the Director of Libraries is absent.

11. Reviews subordinate performance and recommends promotions, salary increases, or disciplinary action as appropriate.

MEASURES OF PERFORMANCE

Objective:

1. Increased circulation of materials.
2. Increased usage, in-person and by telephone, of reference and research services.
3. Adherence to schedules and budgets.

Subjective:

1. A better public image resulting from improved and new services.
2. Improved quality of service.
3. Improved employee morale.

Library V

LIBRARY DIRECTOR

FUNCTION:

Under the general direction of the Mayor, directs the administration of all activities of the Library Department.

PRIMARY TASKS PERFORMED:

Plans, establishes, directs and controls, through division heads, administrative and supervisory policies of the department.

Advises and assists the Mayor and City Council in developing programs and practices which are consistent with City Charter and ordinance requirements.

Directs the coordination and implementation of departmental operations to assure the delivery of City services.

Meets with employee, governmental, business, professional, civic and other groups to discuss, interpret and explain departmental policies, programs and objectives as they relate to the community.

SECONDARY TASKS PERFORMED:

Composes correspondence and prepares drafts on sundry departmental matters and edits material as needed.

Prepares and issues press releases and prepares and presents other material for public information in regard to various activities of the department.

QUALIFICATIONS:

Appointment by the Mayor.
Majority approval of City Council.

ASSISTANT DIRECTOR

SCOPE

The Assistant Director works with the Director in administering the Public Library System which serves as an information center and an agency for informal education by furnishing reference, advisory, research and bibliographic service and by providing books and other materials for education, information, cultural enrichment, and recreation. Incumbent assists and advises the director in guiding operations of the system which at present are composed of a Central Library, Library for Genealogical Research, the Library Resources Center (which includes the Extension Office, 3 bookmobiles and Children's Carousel) and 23 branches. The Assistant Director aids the Director in directing such activities as (1) developing and maintaining the Library collection of reference and circulating books, periodicals, pamphlets, phonograph records, microfilms, documents, maps, pictures, etc.; (2) furnishing reference, advisory and bibliographic services; (3) ordering, cataloging and maintenance of books and other library materials; (4) promoting library public relations and educational activities; (5) planning library budget; (6) recruiting and training personnel; (7) maintaining library buildings and equipment; and (8) planning new library agencies and extending Library service.

POSITION CONTROLS

The Public Library operates as a department of the City and is under the direction of Mayor and Council. The Public Library board consists of thirteen members nominated by the Mayor and confirmed by Council. It is an advisory Board whose recommendations are referred to Mayor and Council for approval. The selection of the Director is made by the Library Board and is confirmed by Mayor and Council. As a department head of the City, he is responsible to the Mayor, works directly with other city officials and is advised in policy matters by the Library Board. When the Assistant Director serves in the Director's stead, she assumes these same responsibilities and relationships. At other times she works under the Director's general direction. As the Director's chief assistant, the incumbent has a wide scope for using independent judgment, imagination and initiative for making decisions.

SUMMARY OF DUTIES AND RESPONSIBILITIES

The Assistant Director consults with the Director on a day to day basis regarding virtually all aspects of public library administration. In the absence of the Director, the Assistant Director assumes his duties and is responsible for the overall operation of the Public Library System. Attends and records minutes of meetings of the Library Board. Submits annual and special reports. Attends Librarians conferences and regular and special meetings of the Administrative Council and heads of departments to discuss library operations, services policies, procedures, problems, etc. Assists the Director and Chief of Branch Services, Chief of Central Services and Chief of Technical Services in developing new services and procedures.

Assists the Director in the administration of the Public Library System. Suggests revision of existing Library rules and drafts new rules. Recommends changes in public service. Presents and explains library policies to the staff. Makes visits to departments of Central Library to discuss and assist with operational problems. Serves as the Library representative on the board of the Friends of the Library.

Assistant Director is responsible for the operation of the Central Circulation Department and sees that its functions are carried out efficiently. Confers with and advises heads of Loan Section and System Overdues regarding policies, regulations and procedures. Personally handles more difficult questions involving the public.

Is responsible for the continuous program of forms analysis and control. Approves and processes all library publications through her office and controls development of the more significant publications such as book catalogs. Develops and keeps current a manual of procedures of all library operations.

Receives questionnaires from other libraries and outside organizations and routes to concerned department for reply. Explains the work and organization of the Public Library to visitors. Keeps abreast of new developments in the field of library science. Addresses groups on library subjects. Is an active and contributing member of the American Library Association, the Southwestern Library Association, and the State Library Association. Serves as a member of the Administrative Council.

Performs other duties as assigned.

QUALIFICATIONS

Master's degree in library science with 5 years' administrative and supervisory experience.

Special Classifications

Library O

POSITION TITLE: Coordinator of Adult Services. DEPARTMENT: Administrative Services. DIVISION: Administrative Services. TITLE OF IMMEDIATE SUPERVISOR: Asst. Executive Director.

PURPOSE OF WORK

Under the general supervision of the Assistant Executive Director of Administrative Services, plans and coordinates the educational, informational and cultural adult services programs for the library system with special emphasis on adult basic education, continuing education and service to special clientele such as the aged.

MINIMUM QUALIFICATIONS

1. Graduate degree from an ALA accredited school, with 3 years of experience in adult services or reader's advisory service.
2. Good ability to communicate.
3. Ability to develop effective working relationships with Main Library and branch personnel serving the adult user.
4. Extensive knowledge of literature and audiovisual resources.
5. Demonstrated ability to develop innovative and creative programming.
6. Possession of a valid drivers license and ready access to suitable transportation or a personal vehicle appropriate for use in the transaction of Library business and performance of job related duties (approved mileage reimbursed at prescribed rate).

TYPICAL DUTIES

1. Organizes and plans comprehensive adult services programs in concert with the administrative and professional staff.
2. Promotes and publicizes adult activities and resources in concert with the Director of Communications.
3. Coordinates the selection of book and other audiovisual resources for adult and special categories of adult clientele with the appropriate division and branch staff.
4. Evaluates the collections of the divisions and branches to determine weaknesses and strengths; recommends corrective action where appropriate.
5. Evaluates educational needs among the staff involved with service to adults and provides appropriate staff development.
6. Establishes a good working relationship betwen the Library and schools, colleges and other educational, cultural and recreational agencies in the county to complement and supplement their programs.
7. Serves as the chief consultant and specialist to the Library's administrative and professional staff in the field of adult services.
8. Devotes special attention to the needs of the disadvantaged and exceptional adults, adult basic education, continuing education, and the aged, and develops special programs to aid these clientele.
9. Regularly reports to the Administration on adult services.
10. Performs other duties as assigned.

POSITION TITLE: Coordinator of Children's and Young Adult Services. DEPARTMENT: Administrative Services. DIVISION: Administrative Services. TITLE OF IMMEDIATE SUPERVISOR: Asst. Executive Director.

PURPOSE OF WORK

Under the general supervision of the Assistant Executive Director of the Library, initiates and implements educational, informational, and cultural activities for young people in concert with the children's staff at Main and the branches.

MINIMUM QUALIFICATIONS

1. Graduate degree from an ALA accredited school, with 3–5 years of experience in children's and/or young adult services.
2. Good ability to communicate.
3. Ability to develop effective working relationships with Main Library and branch personnel.
4. Extensive knowledge of children's and young adult literature and audiovisual resources.
5. Demonstrated ability to develop innovative and creative programming.
6. Possession of a valid drivers license and ready access to suitable transportation or a personal vehicle appropriate for use in the transaction of Library business and performance of job related duties (approved mileage reimbursed at prescribed rate).

TYPICAL DUTIES

1. Organizes and plans comprehensive children's and young adult service programs in concert with the administrative and professional staff.
2. Promotes and publicizes children's and young adult activities and resources in concert with the Director of Communications.
3. Coordinates the selection of book and other audiovisual resources for children and young adults with the appropriate division and branch staff.
4. Evaluates the collections of the divisions and branches to determine weaknesses and strengths; recommends corrective action where appropriate.
5. Evaluates educational needs among the staff involved with service to children and young people and provides appropriate staff development.
6. Establishes a good working relationship between the library and the schools and other youth organizations in the county to complement and supplement their programs.
7. Serves as the chief consultant and specialist to the Library's administrative and professional staff in the field of children's and young adult services and resources.
8. Devotes special attention to the needs of the disadvantaged and exceptional children and young adults and recommends extended programs to aid this clientele.

9. Regularly reports to the Administration on children's and young adult services.

10. Performs other duties as assigned.

POSITION TITLE: Coordinator of Volunteer Services. DEPARTMENT: Administrative Services. DIVISION: Administrative Services. TITLE OF IMMEDIATE SUPERVISOR: Asst. Executive Director.

PURPOSE OF WORK

Under the general supervision of the Assistant Executive Director of the Library, promotes and coordinates volunteer activities and services for the library system.

MINIMUM QUALIFICAITONS

1. Graduate degree in an appropriate discipline, with 3–5 years of related experience or combination of specialized training or experience.

2. Good ability to communicate.

3. Ability to establish rapport between volunteer participants and library personnel.

4. Strong commitment to the volunteer concept.

5. Flexible with respect to work schedule.

6. Possession of a valid drivers license and ready access to suitable transportation or a personal vehicle appropriate for use in the transaction of Library business and performance of job related duties (approved mileage reimbursed at prescribed rate).

TYPICAL DUTIES

1. Organizes and coordinates the volunteer services program for the Library system in concert with the other administrative personnel.

2. Recruits, orients, and allocates volunteers to supplement library personnel throughout the system.

3. Works closely with department, division, and branch heads to define volunteer needs, refine basic orientation and training, and establish priorities in the allocation of volunteers.

4. Interviews and counsels all volunteers after referral from the Personnel Department to evaluate individual interests and skills in order to insure that maximum benefits are derived by both the volunteer and the library in the assignment.

5. Provides counseling, evaluation, reassignment (if necessary), and the appropriate recognition.

6. Prepares regular reports on volunteer service and activities to the Administration.

7. Promotes and publicizes volunteer service in concert with the Director of Communications.

8. Establishes working relationships with other volunteer service agencies in the County.

9. Performs other duties as assigned.

Library S

OPERATING TITLE: Librarian for Materials Selection

SUMMARY OF DUTIES: Assists the Head, Acquisitions Division in the selection activities of the Library; assists and advises the public service staff in developing the Library's collections.

DUTIES IN DETAIL:

1. Maintains awareness of current publishing trends through scanning publishers' catalogs and selected review and trade media, meeting with publishers' representatives, and monitoring regular order cycles.

2. Aids individual selectors through a variety of activities, such as identifying useful selection tools and bibliographies of recommended materials in various subjects, routing publishers' flyers and catalogs, requesting review copies, evaluating approval plans, and instructing clerical staff in the checking of bibliographies against library holdings.

3. Participates in studies and analyses of library materials needs of citizens.

4. Participates in consultation with other professional library staff in the preparation of Library collection development policy statements and guidelines for administrative consideration and approval.

5. Works with two standing staff committees, adult materials and youth materials, in implementing above duties.

6. Responds as appropriate in line with library policy to patron complaints about collection, including requests to have materials removed from the shelves.

7. Performs other duties as assigned.

REPORTS TO: Head, Acquisitions Division

Library Y

POSITION: Coordinator, Materials Management

RESPONSIBILITIES:

Under the general direction of the Chief, Public Services Support, is responsible for the materials selection and collections of the system.

EXAMPLES OF TYPICAL TASKS:

Makes recommendations regarding acquisition of all materials. Advises branch librarians and branch staff concerning the maintenance of collections. Makes budget recommendations regarding individual branch allotment and centralized allotments for all materials. Expends basic funds in establishing materials collections for new agencies. Works closely with the Chief, Public Services Support in developing collection management projects. Supervises Materials Selection and Interlibrary Loan Departments. Participates as a member of the Administrative Council. Keeps in touch with library developments by attending conferences, professional meetings and by reading professional literature.

QUALIFICATIONS

Completion of an MLS degree in an ALA accredited school and at least 6 years' suitable public library experience on a supervisory level. Comprehensive knowledge of materials interests and a wide general reading background. Thorough knowledge of library organization, policy, procedure, aims and service. Understanding of community relationships. Ability to write and speak clearly, concisely and effectively. Ability to relate work to that of other units. Ability to plan, instruct, lead and stimulate. Ability to anticipate needs of the system. Initiative.

Structural Classifications

Library D

COORDINATOR OF RESOURCES

Nature of Work: This is professional library work in planning, developing and coordinating the resources of the library system; general supervision is received from the Associate Director. In collaboration with the Chief of Public Services, coordinates information services to adults in the Central Library, in all branches and on the bookmobiles. The Coordinator of Resources also works with the Coordinator of Children's Services and the techncial processes division to assure complete coordination of library collection. In addition, this person is responsible for coordinating all collections of other libraries in the community and regions.

Reviews bibliographic, publishing and other professional publications, relating to library resources. Participates in the selection of books and other materials for the adult collection. Surveys area library resources to insure comprehensive and balanced coverage of subject fields within the City-County Library System and advises on the proper direction of collection development.

Studies research data on physical format of materials; investigates improvements in paper stock, binding and other new publication techniques and in non-book formats such as micro-film, recordings and magnetic tapes, stays abreast of trends in machine applications to information retrieval and bibliographic control. Advises staff on uses of various media formats and methods of handling information.

Maintains an awareness of the community's information needs. Refers such needs to the appropriate department or division. If exact information needs cannot be fulfilled, discusses with supervisor, whether such service should be added. Prepares reading lists and bibliographies, coordinates the flow of new gift materials, exchanges and weeding of collection throughout the system.

Plans and conducts staff training programs for information service to adults.

Knowledges, Abilities, and Skills: Wide knowledge of modern library service to adults.

Considerable skill in coordinating service in all areas and ability to work with groups of adults.

Thorough knowledge of general literature and book trade and other communications media.

Requires imagination, initiative, resourcefulness, good judgment, tact.

Desirable Experience and Training: Considerable experience in progressively responsible professional library work, including supervisory responsibility and experience in work with adults; and graduation from an accredited college or university, and attainment of a graduate degree from an accredited school of library science.

Library N

ADULT MATERIALS SELECTION SPECIALIST

PURPOSE OF THIS POSITION

Under the direction of the Director of Collection and Program Development, the Adult Materials Selection Specialist supervises the Adult Materials Selection Unit and coordinates the selection of adult library materials for the Public Library.

SPECIFIC EXAMPLES OF THE RESPONSIBILITIES OF THIS POSITION:

Supervises the preparation and distribution of materials selection lists by the staff of the Adult Materials Selection Unit.

Develops special bibliographies and selection lists designed to upgrade the level of library collections in the agencies of the Public Library and the affiliates.

Working in conjunction with Central Library Subject Division Heads,

Branch District Chiefs and affiliates, develops programs to improve the selection and use of library collections in the Public Library and the Library System.

In conjunction with the Head of the Acquisitions Unit and other appropriate Technical Services staff develops procedures for selecting and ordering library materials and prepares instructions to explain these procedures.

Interprets the Library's Selection Policy to the staff and patrons of the Public Library and the Library System.

Serves as a consultant to agencies of the Public Library and affiliates on matters of collection development and the selection of library materials for adult patrons.

Supervises the acceptance, evaluation, and distribution of gifts of books and other materials to the library.

Serves on committees and task forces working in the area of collection development and selection, including committees involved in the selection and evaluation of materials.

To represent the Public Library and the Library System to publishers' representatives and booksellers and before professional groups dealing with materials selection.

To be knowledgeable about the full range of library materials available to adult patrons and call trends or changes in these materials to the attention of the appropriate library staff.

QUALIFICATIONS AND REQUIREMENTS OF THIS POSITION:

Graduate degree in Library Science from an ALA accredited institution. Experience in library adult service work. Familiarity with library materials, publishing trends, the nature of information sources, and trends in literature and the use of literature. Supervisory ability. The ability to communicate well and tactfully. Planning capability.

DIRECTOR OF LIBRARY COLLECTION
AND PROGRAM DEVELOPMENT

PURPOSE OF THIS POSITION:

The Director of Library Collection and Program Development, reporting to the Deputy Commissioner for the Library System, is responsible for the coordination and direction of those persons on the Library staff given responsibility for program and collection development in the areas of children's services, young adult services, adult services, senior citizens' services, special programs to the Spanish-speaking and other ethnic groups determined to have unique needs in the community. He/she is also responsible for the overall improvement of the collections and the educational, cultural and informational programs of the Public Library.

SPECIFIC EXAMPLES OF WORK RESPONSIBILITIES:

Directs the daily activities of the Coordinator of Children's Services,

Coordinator of Young Adult Services, Coordinator of Adult Services, Coordinator of Senior Citizens' Services and the Coordinator of Services to the Spanish-speaking as well as other coordinators in his/her department.

Evaluates the collections of the Public Library and Library System for deficiencies in developing the annual materials budget in concert with the Assistant Commissioner for the Central Library/Cultural Center and the Assistant Commissioner for Extension Services.

Coordinates the work of the department staff in the development of programs which cross age and ethnic boundaries.

Insures that programs which are developed by the coordinators have sufficient portability to be used systemwide.

Stimulates program concepts and insures that they are relevant to the Library's long-range plan of service.

Develops special project proposals aimed at improving services to specific age classifications in the system.

Develops training programs to insure that the professional staff of the Library System grow in their familiarity with the literature of their respective fields and attain growth in programming skills.

Performs other duties as assigned by the Deputy Commissioner for the Library System.

QUALIFICATIONS AND REQUIREMENTS OF THE POSITION:

Graduate degree in Library Science from an ALA accredited institution. Five years of progressively more responsible experience in library service, the last two years of which shall have been as a coordinator in at least one area of library service, such as children's services, adult services, or young adult services. Ability to plan, coordinate and communicate well. Ability to work at a high administrative level as liaison with other community organizations and other departments of the Public Library and Library System. Sound knowledge of professional literature and the techniques of collection development.

COORDINATOR OF INTERLIBRARY COOPERATION

I. *Purpose*

The purpose of this position is to serve as a consultant and advisor for all special, academic and school libraries (i.e. affiliates) located within the geographic confines of the Public Library System. The person in this position shall work with the affiliates to develop interlibrary cooperation, and shall assist in educating the affiliates in the fullest utilization of the System and the State Information Network for their book and informational needs. This person shall create and maintain good professional and working relationships between the Public Library System and the affiliates.

II. *Responsibilities and Authority*

Under the direction of the Assistant Chief Librarian for The Central Library, the Coordinator of Interlibrary Cooperation performs duties with a wide degree of latitude and independence of action, exercising judgement and utilizing a background of experience in program/grant management, the functions of interlibrary loan, consultation and library service in special, academic and/or school libraries.

The Coordinator of Interlibrary Cooperation is responsible for and has the authority to accomplish the duties set forth below:

A. Further develop and strengthen the relationships between the present affiliate members and the System headquarters.

B. Establish and maintain communication with all potential affiliates and encourage their membership in the network.

C. Identify problems which hinder effective interlibrary cooperation between the System headquarters and the affiliates and strive to solve or alleviate such problems.

D. Develop plans and programs for increased interlibrary cooperation among the Public Library System members.

E. Conduct at least one major workshop annually for affiliate members. This workshop's purpose is to provide information and education on interlibrary cooperation as it relates to the Public Library System and the State Network.

F. Work cooperatively with Interlibrary Loan Center of the General Information Services Divison of the Central Library.

G. Be responsible for proper allocation of funds provided for the Interlibrary Cooperation Project.

H. Supervise, train and evaluate the support staff provided for this program.

I. Develop means of measuring and evaluating the effectiveness of the Project on a continuing basis.

J. Perform other duties as required in order to successfully fulfill the purpose of this position.

III. *Relationships*

A. Assistant Chief Librarian — Central Library

The Coordinator of Interlibrary Cooperation is accountable to this Assistant Chief Librarian for the fulfillment of the function, responsibilities and authority of this position, and for the proper interpretation of all elements of this position.

B. General Information Services Division Chief

The Coordinator of Interlibrary Cooperation shall maintain communication with this Divison Chief, who as supervisor of the Interlibrary Loan Center, is responsible for ILL Center's successful operation.

C. Interlibrary Loan Center Head

The Coordinator of Interlibrary Cooperation shall be in continual communication with the Interlibrary Loan Center Head so that the activities of these two positions are in agreement with the established policies of the system and the Library and Information Network.

D. Others

The Coordinator of Interlibrary Cooperation shall be active in professional library organizations, national, state and especially local, and shall maintain a continuing awareness of developments in the profession.

IV. *Qualifications*

The Coordinator of Interlibrary Cooperation must be a professional Librarian experienced in program/grant management, interlibrary cooperation, programming and planning. The Coordinator should be knowledgeable of the particular service requirements of various types of libraries, especially public and special libraries.

Library U

CIRCULATION MANAGER

DESCRIPTION OF WORK

General Statement of Duties: Performs professional, supervisory and administrative work in directing the circulation system activities of the General Library.

Supervision Received: Works under the direction of the Assistant City Librarian/Director of Public Services.

Supervision Exercised: Exercises supervision over data processing, clerical and shelving personnel.

EXAMPLES OF DUTIES: (Any one position may not include all of the duties listed nor do the listed examples include all tasks which may be found in positions of this class.)

Maintains organizational control of the Central Circulation Desk, Circulation Control, and Shelving Unit. Directs departmental staff selection, training, and evaluation; directs preparation of forms such as library cards, overdue and hold notices, invoices for delinquent library materials, and reports and documents for Library administration; originates considerations for circulation-shelving planning, policy, and procedural revision; formulates departmental goals and objectives and budget requests; handles complaints regarding delinquent materials.

Directs implementation, operation, and evaluation of on-line circulation system; maintains operational control of central processing unit, peripheral equipment, and input and output devices; controls password access to system functions; directs system-wide user training; maintains tape library.

Coordinates system-wide circulation training and evaluation services; provides instructional tours to staff attending clerical, new librarian, and advanced professional seminars; designs and conducts circulation and registration training programs; evaluates and recommends changes for Section Four (4) of the Staff Policy Manual; prepares monthly and annual reports and statistical reports for Library administration.

Performs related work as required.

QUALIFICATIONS FOR APPOINTMENT

Knowledges, Skills, and Abilities: Extensive knowledge of large public library circulation systems. Considerable knowledge of the principles of library science, management and organization, and data processing. Considerable knowledge of the operation of electronic computers, peripheral and auxiliary equipment as they relate to library circulation systems. Working knowledge of the methodology for conducting investigations and developing problem-solving techniques. Working knowledge of modern office methods, controls, practices, procedures, and equipment. Ability to exercise independent judgment. Ability to understand and interpret statistical data. Ability to analyze data-processing documentation and direct departmental work effort of a large group of office personnel based on that information. Ability to establish and maintain effective working relationships with employees, department and division heads, service directors, governmental agency heads, officials, and the general public.

Education: Graduation from a university or college with a Baccalaureate degree in any subject area.

Experience: Three years of experience in inventory control or data processing operation including two years in a supervisory capacity.

Alternative to the Minimum Education and Experience Requirements: Graduation from a college or university with a Masters degree in management or data processing and one year of experience in a supervisory position in a data processing or circulation management capacity.

SUBJECT DEPARTMENT MANAGER

DESCRIPTION OF WORK

General Statement of Duties: Performs professional, supervisory, and administrative work in the direction of a Central Library Department.

Supervision Received: Works under the general direction of the Central Library Administrator.

Supervision Exercised: Supervises professional, clerical, and other support staff.

EXAMPLES OF DUTIES: (Any one position may not include all of the duties listed nor do the listed examples include all of the tasks which may be found in this class.)

Develops and recommends goals and objectives for the operation of the department in conjunction with the overall Library goals and objectives. Plans action to meet the goals and objectives, evaluates progress, and makes necessary adjustments as conditions change.

Interprets Library policy for staff and Library users. Establishes departmental policy and procedure that support overall Library policy and procedure, and that satisfy Departmental needs.

Directs, coordinates, and participates in the daily operations of the department and supervises staff in the execution of Departmental responsibilities; schedules staff.

Requisitions, interviews, and recommends professional and support staff; evaluates all Department staff members, and recommends appropriate personnel actions.

Determines staff training requirements and consults with appropriate staff to establish programs to meet those needs.

Plans, directs, and records the Department's contribution to the central Library's ongoing community analysis and studies.

Prepares, justifies, and submits Departmental budget requests that relate to goals and objectives suggested by community analysis.

Prepares and submits required reports and surveys, such as annual reports, statements of goals and objectives, Job Inventory Breakdowns, skills inventories and statistics.

Responsible for development and maintenance of departmental materials collection, and ensures that materials purchased do not exceed the prescribed materials budget.

Directs and participates in outreach activities that inform the public of the services and materials the Library system is able to provide, coordinates programming within the Department.

In coordination with the Volunteer Services Administrator, recruits, trains, and supervises volunteers in the Department.

Performs related work as required.

QUALIFICATIONS FOR APPOINTMENT

Knowledges, Skills, and Abilities. Thorough knowledge of the methods of administration of a library department or facility. Thorough knowledge of the principles, practices, and organization of library activities and collection maintenance. Ability to train, motivate, and supervise employees. Ability to develop, coordinate, and direct library activities. Ability to analyze community needs and resources and adapt library programs to meet them. Ability to plan and adhere to goals, objectives, and budgets. Ability to coordinate, analyze, and utilize reports and records. Ability to communicate effectively both orally and in writing. Ability to establish and maintain working relationships with other employees and the public.

Education: Graduation from an American Library Association accredited college or university with a Master of Library Science degree.

Experience: Four years of professional or paraprofessional librarian work, two of which must be in a supervisory capacity.

No alternatives or substitutions to education or experience.

SUBJECT DEPARTMENT SPECIALIST

DESCRIPTION OF WORK

General Statement of Duties: Performs complex reader guidance and reference service in a highly specialized subject area.

Supervision Received: Works under the general supervision of the Subject Department Manager.

Supervision Exercised: None. (May be required to supervise the department in the absence of the Subject Department Manager.)

EXAMPLES OF DUTIES: (Any one position may not include all of the duties listed nor do the listed examples include all tasks which may be found in positions of this class.)

Responsible for the review, selection, and weeding of materials within the area of expertise. May also assist in the selection of materials in other areas of the department. Develops the department's collection within the specialty area. Develops displays to encourage use of specialty materials.

Performs extensive community relations work specifically within the specialty area. Promotes acceptance and use of the facilities including activities such as speaking to, or participating in, functions with professional groups, community organizations, and related agencies. Plans and develops programming to present the specialty area or subject material to staff, community groups, professional groups, and related agencies. Coordinates and participates in activities associated with implementation of programs. Conducts tours within the department.

Provides in-depth reference and reader guidance to all levels of library patrons with emphasis in their specialty. Serves as the in-house "expert" in the subject area.

Trains other staff members in the materials and proper delivery of services which pertain to the specialty area.

Gathers, evaluates, and reports information for community analysis, especially as related to the specialty area, as directed by the Subject Department Manager.

Assists the Subject Department Manager in the formulation of department goals, objectives, and budget requests.

Prepares bibliographies, pathfinders, subject guides, and related information within their specialty service.

Maintains current awareness of professional literature and participates in appropriate professional activities.

Performs related work as required.

QUALIFICATIONS FOR APPOINTMENT

Knowledges, Skills, and Abilities: Extensive knowledge of reader guidance, reference, community outreach, and programming. Thorough knowledge of a specialized subject area which includes a thorough knowledge of the literature of that field. Some knowledge of preparing goals and objectives. Skill in utilizing resources and techniques pertaining to the specialty. Skill in analyzing the communities at which the collection is directed. Ability to develop and maintain the subject area collection. Ability to communicate effectively, both orally and in writing. Ability to train staff in the area of specialization. Ability to establish and maintain working relationships with other employees and the public.

Education: Graduation from an American Library Association accredited college or university with a Master of Library Science degree. Baccalaureate degree must be in the specified subject area.

Experience: Two years of professional or paraprofessional reference work in the specified subject area in a library.

Alternatives to the Minimum Education and Experience Requirements: Graduation from college or university with a Masters degree in the specified subject area and four years of professional or paraprofessional work in the subject area, or graduation from a college or university with a Baccalaureate degree in the specified subject area and five years of professional or paraprofessional experience in the subject area.

COORDINATOR COLLECTION DEVELOPMENT

DESCRIPTION OF WORK

General Statement of Duties: Performs professional and administrative work as a general consultant in the selection, acquisition, organization, maintenance, preservation, use and justification of the various materials in the collections of the Library.

Supervision Received: Reports directly to the Assistant City Librarian/Director of Public Services on all matters.

Supervision Exercised: Exercises supervision over Material Selection Officer and clerical staff.

EXAMPLES OF DUTIES: (Any one position may not include all of the duties listed, nor do the listed examples include all tasks which may be found in positions of this class.)

Coordinates development of research collections with parallel collections in other state libraries and with supportive materials in the adult service agencies in the Central Library.

Maintains communications with local and out-of-state rare book dealers and with private collectors of materials which could be added to the Library's holdings.

Studies preservation techniques and applies the best of them to the Library's irreplaceable holdings.

Assists in the development of research capacities of Public Service Departments through recommendations for and/or purchases of out-of-print and rare, unusual and expensive materials.

Assists Technical Services with information necessary to solve special cataloging problems.

Coordinates with professional groups in the subject areas of research collections by attending their meetings, conferences, etc.

Coordinates with the Library Commission and the Library Foundation on endowments and related matters. Recommends how gift and endowment funds can be best used.

Is a permanent member of the Materials Review Committee and the City Librarian's Advisory Committee.

Formulates and recommends annual budget requirements and distributes the materials budget to the Central Library and to branches.

Participates in the purchase of rare books, manuscripts, large microform sets, G.K. Hall Catalogs and private libraries.

Participates in monitoring the special binding fund and the preparation of materials for hard binding and professional restoration (collating, arranging completion of missing or mutilated pages, determining type of binder or binding, writing special instructions, receiving, invoicing, etc.).

QUALIFICATIONS FOR APPOINTMENT

Knowledges, Skills, and Abilities: Extensive knowledge of general collection development for a library. Extensive knowledge of the development, organization and use of rare book and manuscript collections and the maintenance and preservation of such collections. Some knowledge of French, German and Spanish. Ability to formulate a materials budget for a large library.

Education: Graduation from an American Library Association accredited college or university with a Master of Library Science degree.

Experience: Five years of experience in progressively complex library collection development, two of which must have been spent in the administration of a research or rare books collection.

No alternatives or substitution to education or experience.

INTERLIBRARY LOAN SUPERVISOR

DESCRIPTION OF WORK

General Statement of Duties: Performs professional and supervisory library work directing an Interlibrary Loan Unit.

Supervision Received: Works under the direction of the Central Library Administrator.

Supervision Exercised: Supervises paraprofessional and clerical staff.

EXAMPLES OF DUTIES: (Any one position may not include all of the duties listed nor do the listed examples include all tasks which may be found in positions of this class.)

Directs, coordinates and participates in the daily operations of the Interlibrary Loan Unit, including supervision, training, and scheduling of staff.

Develops and recommends to the Central Library Administrator, long and short-range goals and objectives for the unit in conjunction with overall goals and objectives of the Library.

Compiles and interprets statistical data reflecting Unit activity.

In cooperation with the Central Library Administrator, interviews and selects staff. Prepares and conducts employee performance evaluations.

Answers reference questions or contacts appropriate staff members to obtain answers to questions received by mail or courier.

Utilizes a computer terminal to determine material availability in other libraries and requests materials not available at the Library. Conversely searches the Library collection for materials requested by other libraries and provides materials that are available. Prepares billing and receives payment for materials on loan. Prepares, justifies, and submits budget requests for the Unit, that relate to the overall goals and objectives of the Library.

Performs related work as required.

QUALIFICATIONS FOR APPOINTMENT

Knowledges, Skills, and Abilities: Considerable knowledge of library philosophies, policies, procedures, and organization of library activities. Working knowledge of computerized systems in library applications. Working knowledge of supervisory and training principles. Ability to develop, coordinate, and direct library activities. Ability to plan and adhere to goals and objectives and budgets. Ability to coordinate, analyze, and utilize reports and records. Ability to communicate effectively both orally and in writing. Ability to establish and maintain working relationships with other employees and the public. Ability to train, motivate, and supervise employees.

Education: Graduation from an American Library Association accredited college or university with a Master of Library Science degree.

Experience: One year of experience in general professional or paraprofessional work in a library.

Alternatives to the Minimum Education and Experience Requirements: Graduation from a college or university with a Masters degree in any subject area and two years of experience in general professional or paraprofessional library work or graduation from a college or university with a Baccalaureate degree in any subject area and three years of experience in general professional or paraprofessional library work.

Library V

Business, Science & Technology Dept.
Librarian IV: Department Head

Qualifications: Master's degree in library science with undergraduate degree in subject field plus three years of professional experience.

The Department Head is responsible to the Chief of the Central Library for the following activities:

1. Overall operation of the Business, Science & Technology Dept. including public service, collection development, and support systems in accordance with library goals.
2. Applying knowledge of the library field and professional judgement to guide the development of department services and functions.
3. Staff selection, training, and evaluation, and for making recommendations for promotions, transfers, dismissals, and other personnel actions.
4. Encouraging staff development and education through in-service training and orientation programs, access to academic and professional workshops and seminars, professional conferences, and staff meetings concerning the library's policies, procedures, and programs.
5. Advises the Chief of the Central Library of services, personnel development, activities, projects, problems, etc. of the department through frequent consultations, informal discussions, and memoranda.
6. Preparation of monthly and annual reports, budget requests, bibliographies, tours, and other library related programs.
7. Represent the department and the library at public functions, professional meetings, etc.
8. Supervise and coordinate the work of the First Assistant, Collection Development Assistant, Government Documents Librarian, and Support Services Supervisor.
9. Cooperate with other members of the BST and Library staff in performing any duty essential to the achievement of efficient library operation.

Business, Science & Technology Dept.
Librarian III: First Assistant

Qualifications: Master's degree in library science plus two years of professional experience.

The First Assistant is responsible to the Department Head for the following activities:

1. Effective provision of reference service of a consistent, high quality.
2. Selection, training, and evaluation of the reference staff.
3. Supervision and scheduling of the reference staff.
4. Maintenance of reference records and statistics.
5. Development of orientation programs for the reference staff.
6. Encouragement of staff development by being aware of current developments in the field, workshops, and programs that staff members would be interested in attending.
7. Coordinating and scheduling tours and programs that the department is responsible for, as well as exchange programs with branches and/or other departments.
8. Supervision and monitoring of online services.
9. Perform reference work, serving as an example and a resource person for other staff members.
10. Collection development: may have an assigned ordering area. Also responsible for having extensive knowledge of department collections and contributing to their development.
11. Working with the Collection Development Assistant and the Support Services Supervisor to coordinate departmental operations and to assure the smooth functioning of the entire department.
12. Responsible for the overall operation of the department in the absence of the Department Head.
13. Serve as liaison with other public service departments and branches.
14. Represent the department in the absence of the Department Head.
15. Evaluate department policies, procedures, and systems, and recommend changes for their improvement.
16. Active participation in professional associations, meetings, and conferences.
17. Advise the Department Head of any factors affecting reference service or the reference staff.
18. Cooperate with other BST staff members in performing any duty essential to efficient library operation.

Business, Science & Technology Dept.
Librarian III: Collection Development Assistant

Qualifications: Master's degree in library science plus two years of professional experience.

The Collection Development Assistant is responsible to the Department Head for the following activities:

1. Coordinate and supervise collection development in BST Dept.

2. Recommend the organization and assignment of ordering areas for reference librarians.

3. Recommend allocation of city, state, and federal funds.

4. Schedule submission of orders throughout fiscal year.

5. Select materials from routed media.

6. Evaluate reference, circulating, stack, A/V, and periodicals collections and recommend directions for their development based on patron needs.

7. Conduct orientation program for new ordering librarians to introduce them to collection development and ordering routines.

8. Review orders submitted by librarians.

9. Evaluate gifts offered to the department.

10. Spend department gift monies.

11. Serve as liaison with COMS office.

12. Serve as liaison with Gifts & Serials, Acquisitions, Materials Processing, and Catalog Depts. to expedite collection development.

13. Serve as senior reference librarian.

14. Supervise department operation in the absence of Department Head and First Assistant.

15. Work with the First Assistant and Support Services Supervisor to coordinate department operations and to assure the smooth functioning of the entire department.

16. Cooperate with other members of the BST staff in performing any duty essential to efficient library operation.

Business, Science & Technology Dept.
Librarian III: Government Documents Librarian

Qualifications: Master's degree in library science plus two years of professional experience.

The Government Documents Librarian is responsible to the Department Head for the following activities:

1. Management and supervision of the government documents collection in accordance with GPO guidelines.

2 .Supervision of technical processing of government documents.

3. Training and supervision of personnel to process and maintain collection.

4. Preparation of biennial reports to GPO and monthly reports for the Library.

5. Serve as liaison with Government Printing Office.

6. Evaluation of new items for selection.

7. Review of items currently selected and weeding of collection.

8. Classification of documents not cataloged by GPO.

9. Development of systems and procedures to improve organization of collection and accessibility of documents.

10. Reference work with documents, serving as a resource person for other staff members, knowledgeable and well-informed of current developments.

11. Introduce new librarians in BST to government documents.

12. Continuing education — inform staff of new developments in documents, new tools, new publications, in-service training programs.

13. Foster public awareness of documents at the Library.

14. Provide reference service in BST as assigned.

15. Cooperate with other members of the BST staff in performing any duty essential to efficient library operation.

Business, Science & Technology Dept.
Librarian II: Reference

Qualifications: Master's degree in library science.

The Reference Librarian II is responsible to the First Assistant and the Collection Development Assistant for the following activities:

1. Reference

   a. Provide reference service and information to patrons in person, by telephone, and by mail.
   b. Furnish information on library activities, facilities, policies, and services.
   c. Develop knowledge of department and library collections and community resources, including sufficient familiarity with department resources to use them effectively to locate information and to assist patrons in their use.

2. Collection Development

   a. Evaluate and select materials for circulating, reference, a/v, and periodicals collections in an assigned subject area.
   b. Become familiar with patron use of the collection, in order to evaluate and anticipate patron needs.
   c. Become a reference and collection development expert in assigned subject field, knowledgeable about the collection and its use, new developments and publications in the field.
   d. Conduct reference orientation for new staff members in assigned ordering area.
   e. Assist in weeding and withdrawal of materials from department collections.
   f. Contribute to overall development of department collections by offering suggestions and recommendations to Collection Development Assistant.

3. Conduct library and department tours.

4. Prepare bibliographies and user guides.

5. Recommend systems and procedures to improve the organization and use of materials in the department and to improve department collections and services.

6. Participate in special programs and projects as assigned.

7. Participate in professional associations, attend meetings and conferences, and maintain knowledge of current developments in the library field.

8. Cooperate with other members of the BST staff in performing any duty essential to the achievement of efficient library operation.

Business, Science & Technology Dept.
Librarian I: Support Services Supervisor

Qualifications: Bachelor's degree and one year of professional experience.

The Support Services Supervisor is responsible to the Department Head for the following activities:

1. Organizing and maintaining BST standing order and continuation procedures and files.

2. Supervising the work of the BST Stack Supervisor.

3. Supervising the work of the BST Directory Service Supervisor.

4. Supervising all other staff assigned to Support Services for the following work:

    a. Check-in and maintenance of all BST periodicals, serials, and business services including current issues and backfiles located on the second floor.

    b. Check-in, filing, and maintenance of BST microform services (ASI, VSMF, 10K, Proxy, SRI, etc.).

    c. Discard, bindery, book preparation procedures.

    d. Reserves.

    e. Check-in of new books.

    f. Maintenance of on order files.

    g. Mail delivery.

    h. Special check-outs.

    i. Reporting missing periodicals.

    j. Vertical File maintenance.

    k. Annual reports collection maintenance.

    l. Photo-copying.

    m. Time sheets for all part time employees.

    n. Ordering and receiving supplies for department.

    o. Notifying appropriate people for building maintenance, telephone repair, etc.

    p. Interviewing, hiring, training, evaluating Support Services staff.

5. Work at Information Desk as assigned.

6. Cooperate with other members of the BST staff in performing any duty essential to the achievement of efficient library operation.

Business, Science & Technology Dept.
Librarian I: Reference

Qualifications: Bachelor's degree plus one year of professional experience.

The Reference Librarian I is responsible to the First Assistant and the Collection Development Assistant for the following activities:

1. Reference

   a. Provide reference service and information to patrons in person, by telephone, and by mail.
   b. Furnish information on library activities, facilities, policies, and services.
   c. Develop knowledge of department and library collections and community resources, including sufficient familiarity with department resources to use them effectively to locate information and to assist patrons in their use.

2. Collection Development

   a. May be assigned development and maintenance of vertical and ready reference files.
   b. May be assigned to evaluate and select materials for circulating, reference, a/v, and periodicals collections in an assigned subject area, depending on strong subject expertise.
   c. Become familiar with patron use of the collection, in order to evaluate and anticipate patron needs.
   d. Become a reference and collection development expert in assigned subject field, knowledgeable about the collection and its use, new developments and publications in the field.
   e. Conduct reference orientation for new staff members in assigned ordering area.
   f. Assist in weeding and withdrawal of materials from department collections.
   g. Contribute to overall development of department collections by offering suggestions and recommendations to Collection Development Assistant.

3. Conduct library and department tours.
4. Prepare bibliographies and user guides.
5. Recommend systems and procedures to improve the organization and use of materials in the department and to improve department collections and services.

6. Participate in special programs and projects as assigned.

7. Maintain knowledge of current developments in the library field, participate in professional associations, attend meetings and conferences.

8. Cooperate with other members of the BST staff in performing any duty essential to the achievement of efficient library operation.

Business, Science & Technology Dept.
Librarian I: Government Documents

Qualifications: Bachelor's degree plus one year of professional experience.

1. Assist Government Documents Librarian in special searches and projects as assigned.

2. Search for class numbers of non-depository documents.

3. Search for class numbers of unclassed archival documents.

4. Assist Government Documents Librarian in selection of newly received material for display to reference staff.

5. Maintain periodicals, serials, and annual check-in file and any other shelf-listing as may be required.

6. Maintain item file, including recording class corrections and changes and filing new item cards.

7. Assist Government Documents Librarian in withdrawing superseded and obsolete documents from collection.

8. Type correspondence and make telephone contacts as directed by Government Documents Librarian.

9. Prepare material for bindery and type bindery slips.

10. Assist with duties of Government Documents Library Assistant I as assigned.

11. Assist at Information Desk as assigned.

12. Cooperate wtih other members of the BST staff in performing any duty essential to efficient library operation.

Business, Science & Technology Dept.
Librarian I: Support Services

Qualifications: Bachelor's degree and one year of professional experience.

The Support Services Librarian I is responsible to the Support Services Supervisor for the following activities:

1. Reserves

   a. Verify reserves accepted at reference desks.
   b. Assist pages in filling reserves by checking branches, sorting room, and popular library.
   c. Notify patrons as reserves are filled.

d. Notify patrons regarding unfilled reserves.

e. Maintain reserve records and statistics.

2. Special Checkouts

a. Maintain special checkout records, clearing records as materials are returned.

b. Contact patrons regarding overdue special checkout materials.

c. Maintain special checkout statistics.

3. Assist at Directory Services as assigned.

4. Assist at Information Desk as assigned.

5. May assist at reference desk as assigned, depending on background and experience of employee.

6. Cooperate with other members of the BST staff in performing any duty essential to the achievement of efficient library operation.

Business, Science & Technology Dept.
Library Assistant III: Stack Supervisor

Qualifications: High school diploma or equivalent plus two years of library or related experience. College attendance may be substituted for work experience.

The Stack Supervisor is responsible to the Support Services Supervisor for the following activities:

1. Assuring that all books and resources are shelved quickly and correctly.

2. Maintaining a neat and orderly collection through a daily inspection.

3. Insuring that shelf-reading throughout the collection is done on a continuous basis.

4. Pulling books that need to be mended or repaired.

5. Training and supervising pages in shelving methods and in maintaining a neat and orderly collection.

6. Planning, organizing, coordinating, and measuring work activities of pages.

7. Interviewing and hiring pages with the Support Services Supervisor.

8. Evaluating work of paging staff with the Support Services Supervisor.

9. Preparing time sheets for paging staff.

10. Maintaining BST A/V equipment, including doing minor repairs, requesting repair service when necessary, and keeping machines supplied and filled with toner and paper, light bulbs, etc.

11. Collecting photocopying monies and turning in to Business Office, leaving supply of change at reference desks.

12. Cooperating with other members of the BST staff in performing any duty essential to the achievement of efficient library operation.

Business, Science & Technology Dept.
Library Assistant II: Directory Service Supervisor

Qualifications: High school diploma or equivalent plus one year of library or related experience. College attendance may be substituted for work experience.

The Directory Service Supervisor is responsible to the Support Services Supervisor for the following activities:

    1. Overall operation of Directory Service.
    2. Scheduling of Directory Service staff, including reporting sick time, etc.
    3. Interviewing and hiring Directory Service staff with the Support Services Supervisor.
    4. Training and development of Directory Service staff.
    5. Evaluation of Directory Service staff with the Support Services Supervisor.
    6. Carrying out service policies of Directory Service.
    7. Development of Directory Service collection.
    8. Maintenance of index records of directories in collection.
    9. Addition and withdrawal of telephone books, city directories, and Phonefiche.
    10. Shelving and maintenance of an orderly collection.
    11. Recording monthly statistics for Directory Service.
    12. File and maintain looseleaf and updated services received in department.
    13. Cooperate with other members of the BST staff in performing any duty essential to the achievement of efficient library operation.

Business, Science & Technology Dept.
Library Assistant II: Support Services

Qualifications: High school diploma or equivalent plus one year of library or related experience. College attendance may be substituted for work experience.

The Support Services Library Assistant II is responsible to the Support Services Supervisor for the following activities:

    1. Check-in and maintenance of BST periodicals, serials, and business services.
    2. Update and correct BST check-in records on a continuous basis.
    3. Report missing periodicals.
    4. Reshelve and keep in order all periodicals, serials, and business services on the second floor.
    5. Distribute BST mail.
    6. Assist at Directory Service as assigned.
    7. Cooperate with other members of the BST staff in performing any duty essential to the achievement of efficient library operation.

Business, Science & Technology Dept.
Library Assistant II: Government Documents

Qualifications: High school diploma plus one year of library or related experience. College attendance may be substituted for work experience.

The Government Documents Library Assistant II is responsible to the Government Documents Librarian for the following activities:

1. Retrieve documents for delivery to the public service departments.
2. Check-in, sort, and shelve new documents, distributing to the appropriate departments as necessary. This includes documents received in microfiche as well as hard copy.
3. Shelve "used" documents.
4. Maintain documents in the Business, Science & Technology Dept. on the second floor, including topographical maps and patent and trademark materials.
5. Perform shelf reading and shifting when needed.
6. Pick up mail from the Sorting Room.
7. Record statistics of documents received and checked in.
8. File claims for missing items.
9. Cooperate with other members of the BST staff in performing any duty essential to efficient library operation.

Business, Science & Technology Dept.
Library Assistant I: Support Services

Qualifications: High school diploma or equivalent.

The Support Services Library Assistant I is responsible to the Directory Service Supervisor for the following activities:

1. Answer questions by telephone and by mail related to city directories and telephone directories.
2. Assist patrons in person using directory collection.
3. Reshelve telephone books, city directories, and keep in order.
4. Check-in new telephone books, city directories, and Phonefiche.
5. Maintain index file of directories in collection.
6. Weed collection of superseded directories, discarding or sending to Local History Dept. as appropriate.
7. Keep monthly statistics on telephone and mail questions, directories added and withdrawn.
8. Pickup and deliver department mail.
9. Cooperate with other BST staff members in performing any duty essential to the achievement of efficient library operation.

III
Structures and Meanings
of Public Librarianship

According to Hall,

> the process of professionalization probably is based on much more than what the occupation does in trying to professionalize itself. A key, but often neglected, element of the whole process would appear to be public (community) acceptance of the occupation as a profession.... Although it is not clear exactly what leads to such public acceptance, it is probably some combination of performance and public relations.[1]

That people form opinions about their social institutions is self-evident. But that people likewise adopt a social position with respect to their formal organizations such as business enterprises, professions, and libraries has only recently been examined carefully. Researchers have learned that formal organizations are much more than simply the product of the division of labor. They exert a powerful effect on the way we perceive the world around us; they receive loyal affiliation from us as participants; and they carry within them the prevailing interpretations of reality. In short, formal organizations carry social meanings. This chapter will attempt to draw together the data from the previous chapters and make explicit the social meanings of the public library that previously have been only assumed.

Organizational Culture

The theory of organizational culture transfers to the study of formal organizations the anthropological concept of culture. Culture may be simply defined as the shared, learned behavior of a group of individuals. It consists of symbols, meanings, beliefs, values, and behaviors, and is passed from one generation to another through a variety of methods such as formal instruction, social sanction, modeling, generalization, and others.

Thus we can regard *organizational* culture as the shared behaviors and beliefs maintained by an organization's members during their participation in the organization. Organization theorists perceive the formal organization as a small society with its own distinctive and powerful socialization patterns. Obviously, involvement in a formal organization constitutes a set of activities that occupy a significant amount of the time, thought, and social behavior of its employees. It is not surprising, therefore, that the employees would react to the formal organization somewhat as they would react to a culture. Ouchi says:

> The organizational culture consists of a set of symbols, ceremonies, and myths that communicate the underlying values and beliefs of that organization to its employees. These rituals put flesh on what would otherwise be sparse and abstract ideas, bringing them to life in a way that has meaning and impact for a new employee.[2]

Speaking of the development of the study of organizational culture, Ouchi and Wilkins observe:

> Perhaps it is through culture, rather than formal structure, that large firms can be bent to the will of their masters and rendered predictable, "rational."
> It was a curious turnabout, to say the least, in which the study of informal organization as the opponent or organizational rationality was thus transformed into the study of organizational culture as the basis for organizational rationality.[3]

In other words, there lies beneath the informal organization, which once was suspected of working against the rationality of the formal organization, a pattern of shared beliefs and behaviors — a culture — which supplied the rationale for the formal organization itself.

Little has been written about organizational culture in libraries. Yet the documentation presented in the previous chapters demonstrated empirically that there are two types of culture in any public library. First is the pattern of behaviors and assumptions that are specific to a particular library. Usually these are in the form of procedures and policies that contribute to the continuous operation of the library as a bureaucracy. They maintain the library as a formal organization. These may be called the organizational prerogatives. They may be more or less arbitrary; they may be imposed by an outside agency, usually the library's parent organization; they almost certainly receive primary attention in the day-to-day operation of the library; and they are the domain of the library's administrators.

These prerogatives determine, for instance, what sort of subject departmentation a library will use, as well as staffing patterns, budget allocations, and so forth. They establish the particular job classifications to be used in the library and divide the labor of library service among them. As previous chapters have shown, these prerogatives may vary significantly from one library to another. They are the most visible characteristics of a library's organizational culture. Yet they exist only to facilitate the second type of cultural force at work in the library.

This second culture may be called the professional imperatives. These behaviors and beliefs are general to all libraries and in fact distinguish a public library from all other formal organizations. The behaviors must be performed and the beliefs adhered to if the organization is to be recognized by individuals as a public library. Less visible, perhaps, than the organizational prerogatives, the imperatives are nevertheless the basis of librarianship. They appear in some recognizable form in all public libraries.

On the behavioral level, these imperatives appear in the form of a circulating collection, precise classification, collection development, reference interviewing, and, of course, service to the general public as opposed to some special audience. The library staff performs the tasks necessary to provide these characteristic services expected by the public and the staff alike. The public library has grown into its role as the provider of these services because society had the need for such an institution. Consequently, those needs became the guiding principles of the public library. As will be discussed below, these needs may be called structures.

The imperatives, as might be expected, also exist on the level of belief. On this level, these imperatives are embodied in the professional ethics of librarianship. First, librarianship is service-oriented. It shares this quality with all professions. Second, librarianship denounces censorship and endeavors to protect against it. Librarianship assumes that if people are presented with sufficient and unencumbered information, they will make good decisions. Third, librarianship stipulates that access to the information be basically free of charge. Fines, fee-based data base searching, and taxes notwithstanding, the services of librarianship are extended by its practitioners with no profit-making in mind.

These are the fundamental beliefs and behaviors, the customs as it were, of a public library's organizational culture. They are made up of behaviors and beliefs of two types, and determine the broad range of services the public library will provide, although they also allow for considerable diversity in the way these services are organized and delivered by a specific library.

Structures

Culture, be it of a society at large or a formal organization, is ordered by structures which underlie its characteristics. In cultural anthropology, structures are principles of association according to which social institutions are organized. As a result, an understanding of the nature of a culture and its primary organizing motifs may be grasped through a study of its structures.

Piaget observes:

> We may say that a structure is a system of transformations. Inasmuch as it is a system and not a mere collection of elements and their properties, these transformations involve laws: the structure is preserved or enriched by the interplay of its transformation laws.[4]

Piaget is referring to the "transformational aspect of perception." That is, for humans there are internalized "laws of organization by which the sensory given is formed" into compatibilities and incompatibilities with existing systems of meaning.[5] Levi-Strauss uses the transformational nature of structures to interpret myth:

> Mythology confronts the student with a situation which at first sight appears contradictory. On the one hand it would seem that in the course of a myth anything is likely to happen. There is no logic, no continuity. Any character can be attributed to any subject; every conceivable relation can be found. With myth, everything becomes possible. But on the other hand, this apparent arbitrariness is belied by the astounding similarity between myths collected in widely different regions. Therefore the problem: If the content of a myth is contingent, how are we going to explain the fact that myths throughout the world are so similar?[6]

Levi-Strauss attempts to interpret the underlying, or structural, meaning of myth by comparing the variant versions of a myth. Comparison of the variations will accomplish two things. First, the incidental elements will disappear or be replaced by other insignificant features. Second, the myth's subliminal message will remain, often transformed into different but equivalent terms.

This book has presented numerous organizational configurations to demonstrate that despite the variations that exist among individual institutions, public library organization is bound to certain functional constants such as circulation, subject departmentation, precise classification, and others. These constants are actually the underlying structures of public librarianship that, in addition to permitting the operation of the library as an organization, determine the parameters within which a library will be organized. They lie beneath the diversity of public library organizational configurations portrayed in the charts and job descriptions of this book. They are the beliefs which initiate the unchanging professional imperatives, which in turn permit the formulation of the institutional prerogatives.

To say that precise classification, subject departmentation, a circulating inventory, public service, and exhaustive cataloging are characteristically present in public libraries is hardly novel. But their presence as structures is hardly investigated either. We have not before discovered, in empirical terms, how the institutionalization of the particular structures underlying these characteristics is accomplished, and what social meanings they may convey.

Structures are not normally perceivable. They reside in the subconscious of individual members of a culture, and are manifest in the underlying correspondence between many types of institutions at once. Piaget observes that "only when there is some sort of dis-adaptation does the individual become aware of structures, and then this awareness is always quite dim and partial."[7] By mapping these correspondences when they become dimly observable as the institution in question struggles to adapt to a changing environment, one can trace a structure as it becomes apparent across a variety of homomorphic institutions. Piaget says:

> Once an area of knowledge has been reduced to a self-regulating system or "structure," the feeling that one has at last come upon its innermost source of movement is hardly avoidable.[8]

The public library is clearly in a state of disadaptation, to use Piaget's term. This is evident in the sweeping reorganization projects underway in many large libraries, the rush to automate library processes, the severe cutbacks plaguing many libraries, and the appearance of new services, new marketing methods, new strategies, and new goals.

As such, the moment is appropriate to study the organization of the public library to find the structures that give it meaning and continued vitality. As the traditional backgrounds shift within the organizational configurations, the meaning becomes visible in relief.

Symbols and Meanings

The organization and structure of any social institution is a system of symbols. It is the same with the public library. The public library's organization itself communicates information to its users and employees apart from the information carried by any of the books in its collections.

The messages symbolically communicated by the library's organization and structure to its users include order and rationality. The formal organization itself is a product of rationality; it bespeaks rationality in the division of labor as a means to achieve desired goals. As a formal organization, the library is a rational attempt to coordinate the activities of many individuals in order to achieve objectives that are beyond the scope of any single individual.

The library goes even further in its symbolism of rational thinking because its "products" are books, themselves a very rational packaging of information. The library in fact mimics a book. It is divided into subject departments analogous to chapters; it relies on precise cataloging and a catalog to make information retrievable the way an index functions in a book; and, like a book, it offers to enlighten or otherwise change the status of the individual who partakes of its resources.

Because there appears to be a predetermined place in the library for all knowledge, even that which may not yet be discovered, the library also connotes finiteness of knowledge, the knowability of the universe, and the ability of society to accommodate all knowledge. Although the layperson may be unfamiliar with classification schemes, their expandability and their limitations with respect to accommodating new knowledge, library users often assume the library to be a repository of all information, as any reference librarian can attest.

That the library, by virtue of its organization, symbolizes these things is evident in part from the uniform reactions of people who come to use the library. Whether or not they eventually find what they need, they come with the attitude that the library holds, or at least can hold, the answers to all questions. In addition, the library forms a link with the past. Unlike museums, which most people see as repositories of curiosities, historical artifacts, or aesthetic objects, the library is assumed to form a chain of human understanding and knowledge from the distant past to the present and even into the future.

We know also that libraries constitute a system of symbols because, as this book has shown, they are all virtually the same. Certain features may be arranged differently, some may be more automated than others, and some may be highly specialized in their holdings and services. But the structures contained in the organizational patterns are characteristics, unchanging, and unmistakable.

For librarians, the public library symbolizes additional messages. Subject departmentation, especially if it is as extreme as shown in the charts of some of the large libraries, suggests organizational complexity, which can be frustrating to the staff as they attempt to work across departmental lines. It can also diminish a sense of personal efficacy among the staff if they feel the organization is too complex for them to have any effect on its direction. Subject departmentation, however, is also an opportunity to develop additional expertise, as discussed earlier. As such, it can contribute to enhanced professional status.

On another level, subject departmentation suggests a few characteristics about the nature of knowledge itself, which is the librarian's special commodity. First, subject departmentation makes knowledge appear fluid, easily compartmentalized, and constantly growing. It can be obtained, organized, and dispensed as needed to answer the needs of library users. These perceptions address the belief that is quite general in our modern, rational society that knowledge is the panacea for all personal and societal ills. It also corresponds to the ethical consideration of professional librarianship that with enough freely accessible information society stands its best chance of successful self-direction.

Second, because subject departmentation separates fields of knowledge into categories more or less commonly accepted as natural, it symbolizes incompatibilities within the body of assembled knowledge. Despite the assumption that knowledge can solve any type of problem, our society perceives oppositions within that knowledge which must be maintained in the arrangement of a library if it is to be an orderly reflection of reality, and especially of human learning.

Actually, the notion of oppositions in the body of learning is a peculiarity of the western analytical approach to reality. Many other cultures have no such perception, and consider reality to be much more unified and consistent. Yet the fact remains that libraries reflect a cultural orientation that itself becomes a structure and an organizational principle of the public library as a social institution.

In the public library, then, a sense of opposition is connoted by organizational complexity, subject departmentation, and underdeveloped professionalism. They give their meaning to the public library for librarians as well as users. But the library also performs collection development and acquisition. These activities give hope that the oppositions between fields of knowledge may eventually be resolved by expansion of knowledge within each of those discrete fields. This offsets the somewhat negative implications of oppositions within learning, and balances the public library's almost mythic mission of being the gateway to all knowledge.

The tension between opposition and resolution, subject departmentation and collection development, interpersonal reference skills and organizational exigencies are, in Piaget's words, the innermost source of movement in the public library. These are some of the meanings of the structures of librarianship in the minds of its users and employees. At times the meanings are more explicit than at others, but usually they are below the conscious level, giving the library a subliminal meaning to individual users and staff. But explicit or subliminal, the meanings help define the role of the public library as an institution and place it in society.

This book has discussed only the public library. In light of the breadth of knowledge available and the different types of agencies and publics to be served, it would seem that libraries conceivably could be very different from each other based on their holdings profile and their patronage. And indeed, librarians know that libraries are remarkably different for these reasons. Academic, public, and special libraries differ widely by type and by individual institution. But they differ within a very definable institutional range, as previous chapters have shown.

When we think of libraries as institutions, as do nonprofessionals most of the time and most professionals at least subconsciously, we see past the differences between libraries. We see, as it were, symbolically that libraries have to do with the containment and arrangement of all knowledge. Admittedly, many other types of organization share this commitment, to a degree. As organizations they, too, communicate a search for and application of knowledge and at least imply that knowledge is finite, cumulative, and obtainable. But due to the organization and structure of the library, its symbolic communication of these messages is far more explicit, and is the basis for the organizational arrangement itself, much more so than, say, hospitals, courts, congresses, or even universities.

Library organization, then, involves much more than simply drawing lines of authority or inventing new departments, functions, and services. Library organization proceeds within a strongly felt, even if vague and unvoiced, set of values and corresponding symbols. Contrary to Bradshaw's remarks which appeared at the beginning of Chapter 1, a library's organization is hardly "only a hatrack." It is instead an articulation of a professional philosophy and a cultural orientation, and is a structured, meaningful, and even symbolic social institution.

Conclusions

In the simplest of terms, library organization is determined by the way we organize knowledge. The practice of librarianship, however, in terms of mediating the collection, is not. Instead it is determined by the interpersonal transactions that may result from the few basic relationships that are possible between the librarian, the library user, and the library collection, as discussed in Chapter 2.

Thus, there is a double structure operating in public libraries — one for the formal organization and another for professional duties — as is the case for other professions. (As discussed in Chapter 2, reference interviewing and other interpersonal relations structure a librarian's time and activities as effectively as the library's organization).

These two structures conflict, and the nature of public libraries is determined by this conflict. It is a tension that underlies most library reorganizations. Whenever library managers struggle with budget shortfalls, staffing cutbacks, modernization, or any of the political imbroglios that beset them with increasing frequency, they are actually weighing the perpetuation of the existing library organization against the professional services it provides, and deciding which will be sacrificed for the sake of the other.

The topics discussed here suggest a number of recommendations for public libraries and for the profession in general. First, the goal of every library organization should be to allow users and librarians to get together with enough time to complete a thorough consultation, with a collection suitably developed to meet the user's needs and support the librarian's expert search strategies.

Second, a more collegial method of organizing library departments would minimize the organizational formality and undoubtedly enhance the professionalism of librarianship. Perhaps library departments should be organized more like college and univeristy departments, with rank based on expertise and accomplishments instead of administrative and supervisory responsibility. This would require a different basis for compensating librarians, but the equality might make the profession more attractive to prospective librarians. And over time, the stature of librarianship as a profession would probably rise in the estimation of the public as well.

Third, the profession should define clearly what functions and tasks are the domain of librarians and train library school students to perform those duties with exceptional skill. Furthermore, the profession should prepare itself to relegate to nonprofessionals, paraprofessionals, and non–library experts those tasks that clearly fall outside the complement of a librarian's duties and conflict with the librarian's professionally established responsibilities. This will minimize the organizational-professional conflict.

As discussed in the previous chapter, the core of librarianship is the building and mediating of a collection, not necessarily the management of a formal organization. While it may be true that as semi-professionals librarians are more apt as administrators than other full-fledged professionals, the increased sophistication of available information and the systems used to store and retrieve it will certainly require greater professionalization of librarians. As they increase their level of professionalism, they may lose the administrative edge previously enjoyed. In such a case, the profession of librarianship will face the alternatives of organizing the library as a law firm is organized, that is, with professionals in the administrative position that attend to the organizational formalities of the institution, or as hospitals, which leave the nonprofessional chores to nonprofessionals. It is a decision the professional will have to make.

These changes would have an enormous effect on the role of the public library in society, and alter its image, values, and meanings as a social institution. But public libraries have been aimless in our rapidly changing society. They have been buffeted by technological developments in the information industry, political impotence in the operations of local government, and crippling economic reversals. A positive assertion by public librarians to redefine and take control of their profession in the present turmoil would stabilize the institution and establish a new and more meaningful role for the public library.

Through these changes, moreover, the functions that are essential to the practice of public librarianship would be narrowed and strengthened, thus forming a base from which to provide better and more valuable service to the public.

Notes

Introduction: Modern Society and the Formal Organization

1. Robert Presthus, *The Organizational Society* (New York: Knopf, 1962).

2. William H. Whyte, *The Organization Man* (New York: Simon and Schuster, 1956).

3. Alex Inkeles and David H. Smith, *Becoming Modern: Individual Change in Six Developing Countries* (Cambridge MA: Harvard University Press, 1974). See especially chapters 11–13.

4. Robert Grandford Wright, *The Nature of Organizations* (Encino CA: Dickenson, 1977), p. 7.

5. Wright, p. 7.

6. Wright, p. 6.

7. Amatai Etzioni, *Modern Organizations* (Englewood Cliffs NJ: Prentice-Hall, 1964), p. 3.

8. Richard H. Hall, *Organizations: Structure and Process* (Englewood Cliffs NJ: Prentice-Hall, 1972), p. 9.

9. John Kenneth Galbraith, *The New Industrial State* (Boston MA: Harvard University Press, 1968), p. 130.

10. Chester I. Barnard, *The Function of the Executive* (Cambridge MA: Harvard University Press, 1968), p. 73.

11. Barnard, p. 240.

12. Galbraith, p. 130.

13. Etzioni, p. 3.

14. Etzioni, p. 1.

15. Jacques Ellul, *The Technological Society,* trans. by John Wilkinson (New York: Knopf, 1964), p. xxv.

16. Whyte, p. 13.

17. Jacques Barzun, *Science: The Glorious Entertainment* (New York: Harper & Row, 1964), p. 282.

18. Barzun, p. 283.

19. See T.D. Webb, *Reorganization in the Public Library* (Phoenix AZ: Oryx, 1985).

I. The Public Library as a Formal Organization

1. Malcolm Getz, *Public Libraries: An Economic View* (Baltimore MD: Johns Hopkins University Press, 1980), pp. 172–173.

2. Peter Drucker, "Managing the Public Service Institution," *College & Research Libraries* 37 (January 1976): 5.

3. Lowell Martin, "The Late Great Public Library — RIP," *ALA Yearbook, 1981* (Chicago: American Library Association, 1981), p. 4.

4. Michael K. Buckland, *Library Service in Theory and Context* (New York: Pergamon, 1983), pp. 135–136.

5. Kenneth G. Peterson, "Trends in Library Organization," in *Emerging Trends in Library Organization,* ed. by Sul H. Lee (Ann Arbor MI: Pierian, 1978), p. 1.

6. Laurence J. Kipp, "Scientific Management in Research Libraries," *Library Trends* 2 (Jan 1954): 390–400.

7. Beverly P. Lynch, "Libraries as Bureaucracies," in *Strategies for Library Administration,* ed. by Charles R. McClure and Alan R. Samuels (Littleton CO: Libraries Unlimited, 1982), p. 44.

8. Amatai Etzioni, *Modern Organizations* (Englewood Cliffs NJ: Prentice-Hall, 1964), p. 17–19.

9. See T.D. Webb, *Reorganization in the Public Library* (Phoenix AZ: Oryx, 1985).

10. Robert D. Stueart and John Taylor Eastlick, *Library Management,* 2nd ed. (Littleton CO: Libraries Unlimited, 1981), pp. 58–61.

11. Keyes D. Metcalf, "Departmental Organization in Libraries," in *Current Issues in Library Administration,* ed. by Carleton B. Joeckel (Chicago: University of Chicago Press, 1939), pp. 90–110.

12. See Webb, 1985.

13. Stueart and Eastlick, p. 60.

14. J.P. Wilkinson, "Subject Divisionalism: A Diagnostic Analysis," in *Advances in Library Administration and Organization: A Research Annual,* ed. by Gerard B. McCabe and Bernard Kreissman (Greenwich CT: JAI, 1983), p. 32.

15. Wilkinson, p. 32.

16. There have been numerous articles on generalism as practiced at Baltimore County Public Library. See, for instance, E[thel] L. H[eins], "Children's Librarians: An Endangered Species," *Hornbook* 57 (October 1981): 502–503; Cornelia Ives, "One County's View of Library Service Without Age-Level Specialists," *American Libraries* 11 (April 1980): 205–206; Margaret Mary Kimmel, "Baltimore County Public Library," *Top of the News* 37 (Spring 1981): 297–301; Margaret Meacham, "The Generalist Concept," *Library Journal* 107 (April 15, 1982): 779–781. Nora Rawlinson, "Give 'Em What They Want," *Library Journal* 106 (15 November 1981): 2188–2190.

17. Stueart and Eastlick, p. 60.

18. Etzioni, pp. 24–25.

19. Buckland, p. 135.

II. Professionalism in Public Librarianship

1. See Amatai Etzioni, *Modern Organizations* (Englewood Cliffs NJ: Prentice-Hall, 1964), pp. 75–93; Richard H. Hall, "Professionalization and Bureaucratization," *American Sociological Review* 33 (1968): 92–104; N. Toren, *Social Work: The Case of a Semi-Profession* (Beverly Hills CA: Sage, 1972), p. 42.

2. Etzioni, p. 78.

3. Richard H. Hall, *Organizations: Structures and Process* (Englewood Cliffs NJ: Prentice-Hall, 1972), p. 122.

4. Hall, *Organizations,* p. 122.

5. Hall, *Organizations,* p. 121.

6. Etzioni, p. 79.

7. Beverly P. Lynch, "Libraries as Bureaucracies," in *Strategies for Library Administration: Concepts and Approaches,* ed. by Charles R. McClure and Alan R. Samuels (Littleton CO: Libraries Unlimited, 1982), p. 45.

8. Jerald Hage, "An Axiomatic Theory of Organizations," *Administrative Science Quarterly* 10 (December 1965): 295.

9. Hall, *Organizations,* p. 190.

10. Hall, *Organizations,* p. 121.

11. Etzioni, p. 87.

12. Hall, *Organizations,* pp. 143–145.

13. Miriam A. Drake, "The Management of Libraries as Professional Organizations," *Special Libraries* 68 (May/June 1977): 181–186.

14. Robert S. Taylor, "Question Negotiation and Information Seeking in Libraries," *College & Research Libraries* 29 (May 1968): 182.

15. Taylor, p. 183.

16. Taylor, p. 183.

17. Marcia J. Bates, "What Is a Reference Book? A Theoretical and Empirical Analysis," *RQ* 26 (Fall 1986): 44.

18. J.P. Wilkinson, "Subject Divisionalism: A Diagnostic Analysis," in *Advances in Library Administration and Organization: A Research Annual,* Vol. 2, ed. by Gerard B. McCabe and Bernard Kreissman (Greenwich CT: JAI, 1983), p. 32.

19. Robert B. Pursell, "Job Evaluation and Pay Plans: Engineering, Technical, and Professional Personnel," in *Handbook of Human Resources Administration,* 2nd ed., ed. by Joseph J. Famularo (New York: McGraw-Hill, 1986), pp. /30-2/–/30-3/.

20. Lynch, p. 47.

21. Lynch, p. 47.

22. G. Edward Evans, *Management Techniques for Librarians,* 2nd ed. (New York: Academic, 1983), p. 48.

III. Structures and Meanings of Public Librarianship

1. Richard H. Hall, *Occupations and the Social Structure* (Englewood Cliffs NJ: Prentice-Hall, 1969), p. 90.

2. William Ouchi, *Theory Z: How American Business Can Meet the Japanese Challenge* (Reading MA: Addison-Wesley, 1981), pp. 41–42.

3. William G. Ouchi and Alan L. Wilkins, "Organizational Culture," in *Annual Review of Sociology, Vol. 11, 1985,* ed. by Ralph H. Turner and James F. Short, Jr. (Palo Alto CA: Annual Reviews, 1985), p. 469.

4. Jean Piaget, *Structuralism,* trans. by Chaninah Maschler (New York, Harper & Row, 1971), p. 5.

5. Piaget, p. 11.

6. Claude Levi-Strauss, *Structural Anthropology,* trans. by Claire Jacobson and Brooke Grundfest Schoepf (Garden City NY: Doubleday, 1967), p. 204.

7. Piaget, p. 99.

8. Piaget, p. 14.

Bibliography

Barnard, Chester I. *The Function of the Executive.* Cambridge MA: Harvard University Press, 1968.

Barzun, Jacques. *Science: The Glorious Entertainment.* New York: Harper & Row, 1964.

Bates, Marcia J. "What Is a Reference Book? A Theoretical and Empirical Analysis." *RQ* 26 (Fall 1986): 37–57.

Buckland, Michael K. *Library Service in Theory and Context.* New York: Pergamon, 1983.

Drake, Miriam A. "The Management of Libraries as Professional Organizations." *Special Libraries* 68 (May/June 1977): 181–186.

Drucker, Peter F. "Managing the Public Service Institution." *College & Research Libraries* 37 (January 1976): 4–14.

Ellul, Jacques. *The Technological Society.* Trans. by John Wilkinson. New York: Knopf, 1964.

Etzioni, Amatai. *Modern Organizations.* Englewood Cliffs NJ: Prentice-Hall, 1964.

Evans, G. Edward. *Management Techniques for Libraries,* 2nd ed. New York: Academic, 1983.

Galbraith, John Kenneth. *The New Industrial State.* Boston MA: Harvard University Press, 1968.

Getz, Malcolm. *Public Libraries: An Economic View.* Baltimore MD: Johns Hopkins University Press, 1980.

Hage, Jerald. "An Axiomatic Theory of Organizations." *Administrative Sciences Quarterly* 10 (December 1965): 289–320.

Hall, Richard H. *Occupations and the Social Structure.* Englewood Cliffs NJ: Prentice-Hall, 1969.

_____. *Organizations: Structure and Process.* Englewood Cliffs NJ: Prentice-Hall, 1972.

_____. "Professionalization and Bureaucratization." *American Sociological Review* 33(1968): 92–104.

H[eins], E[thel] L. "Children's Librarians: An Endangered Species." *Hornbook* 57 (October 1981): 502–503.

Inkeles, Alex, and David H. Smith. *Becoming Modern: Individual Change in Six Developing Countries.* Cambridge MA: Harvard University Press, 1974.

Ives, Cornelia. "One County's View of Library Service Without Age-Level Specialists." *American Libraries* 11 (April 1980): 205–206.

Kimmel, Margaret Mary. "Baltimore County Public Library." *Top of the News* **37** (Spring 1981): 297–301.

Kipp, Laurence J. "Scientific Management in Research Libraries." *Library Trends* **2** (January 1954): 390–400.

Levi–Strauss, Claude. *Structural Anthropology.* Trans. by Claire Jacobson and Brooke Grundfest Schoepf. Garden City NY: Doubleday, 1967.

Lynch, Beverly P. "Libraries as Bureaucracies." In *Strategies for Library Administration.* Ed. by Charles R. McClure and Alan R. Samuels. Littleton CO: Libraries Unlimited, 1982.

Martin, Lowell A. "The Late Great Public Library — RIP" *ALA Yearbook, 1981.* Chicago: American Library Association, 1981.

Meacham, Margaret. "The Generalist Concept." *Library Journal* **107** (April 15, 1982): 779–781.

Metcalf, Keyes D. "Departmental Organization in Libraries." In *Current Issues in Library Administration.* Ed. by Carleton B. Joeckel. Chicago: University of Chicago Press, 1939.

Ouchi, William. *Theory Z: How American Business Can Meet the Japanese Challenge.* Reading MA: Addison-Wesley, 1981.

————, and Alan Wilkins. "Organizational Culture." In *Annual Review of Sociology, Vol. 11, 1985.* Ed. by Ralph H. Turner and James F. Short, Jr. Palo Alto CA: Annual Reviews, 1985.

Peterson, Kenneth G. "Trends in Library Organization." In *Emerging Trends in Library Organization.* Ed. by Sul H. Lee. Ann Arbor MI: Pierian, 1978.

Piaget, Jean. *Structuralism.* Trans. by Chaninah Maschler. New York: Harper & Row, 1971.

Presthus, Robert. *The Organizational Society.* New York: Knopf, 1962.

Pursell, Robert B. "Job Evaluation and Pay Plans: Engineering, Technical, and Professional Personnel." In *Handbook of Human Resources Administration,* 2nd ed. Ed. by Joseph J. Famularo. New York: McGraw-Hill, 1986.

Rawlinson, Nora. "Give 'Em What They Want." *Library Journal* **106** (November 15, 1981): 2188–2190.

Stueart, Robert D., and John Taylor Eastlick. *Library Management,* 2nd ed. Littleton CO: Libraries Unlimited, 1981.

Taylor, Robert S. "Question Negotiation and Information Seeking in Libraries." *College & Research Libraries* **29** (May 1968): 178–194.

Toren, N. *Social Work: The Case of a Semi-Profession.* Beverly Hills CA: Sage, 1972.

Webb, T.D. *Reorganization in the Public Library.* Phoenix AZ: Oryx, 1985.

Whyte, William H. *The Organization Man.* New York: Simon and Schuster, 1956.

Wilkinson, J.P. "Subject Divisionalism: A Diagnostic Analysis." In *Advances in Library Administration and Organization: A Research Annual.* Ed. by Gerard B. McCabe and Bernard Kreissman. Greenwich CT: JAI, 1983.

Wright, Robert Grandford. *The Nature of Organizations.* Encino CA: Dickenson, 1977.

Index to Job Descriptions

Subject Index

administrators 94, 97
American Library Association 11

Barnard, Chester I. 2, 229, 233
Barzun, Jacques 5, 6, 229, 233
Bates, Marcia J. 99, 231, 233
Bradshaw, Lillian 8, 9
Buckland, Michael K. 9, 20–21, 230, 233
bureaucracy: defined 16; in libraries 16, 91, 98, 102

cataloging and classification 14, 19, 20, 93, 96, 219, 221, 222
censorship 219
change and flexibility in libraries 12, 13, 19; influences on 6, 8–9, 10
children's services 15–16
circulation and circulating collections 14, 19, 20, 96, 219, 221
classical school of organization theory see scientific school of organization theory
classification, library see cataloging and classification
clerical positions 92, 96
collection development 95–96, 219, 224, 225
collection mediation 98, 100, 225, 226
community analysis 11
comparative analysis 4, 7, 10
conflict, organizational see goals, organizational and individual: conflict
conflict theory 4
culture 217, 223–224; defined 217, 220; in libraries 218, 220; organizational 218–220

departmentation 11, 12–19, 96; clientele 13, 15, 18; form of resource 13, 17; functional 13, 18; mixing 17, 18; subject 16, 18, 19–20, 96, 219, 221, 223 (see also subject departmentation and library professionalism); territory 13, 15
division of labor 11, 19, 92, 93, 97, 222; see also departmentation
Drake, Miriam A. 98, 231, 233
Drucker, Peter F. 8, 230, 233

Eastlick, John Taylor 12, 16, 17, 230, 234
Ellul, Jacques 5, 6, 229, 233
ethics of librarianship 219, 223; see also professionalism; philosophy of librarianship
Etzioni, Amatai 2, 4–5, 17–18, 90–91, 94, 229, 230, 231, 233
Evans, G. Edward 231, 233
extension services 15

flexibility see change and flexibility
formal organization 1, 3, 6, 11, 19, 20, 99, 217–218, 219; defined 1–3; in modern society 1
formalization 92–96, 102, 226

Galbraith, John Kenneth 2–3, 229, 233
generalism 16, 230
Getz, Malcolm 8, 230, 233
goals: library 225–226; organizational and individual 3, 11, 20, 222; conflict 6, 17, 91, 93–94, 95, 97, 102, 223, 226

Hage, Jerald 231, 233
Hall, Richard H. 2, 91, 94, 217, 229, 231, 233